Fur Trade and Exploration

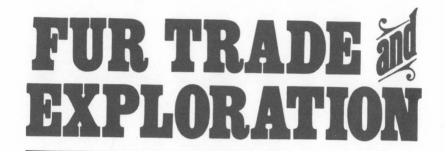

FUR TRADE and EXPLORATION

OPENING THE FAR NORTHWEST
1821–1852

BY

THEODORE J. KARAMANSKI

UNIVERSITY OF
BRITISH COLUMBIA PRESS
VANCOUVER

Library of Congress Cataloging in Publication Data

Karamanski, Theodore J., 1953–
  Fur trade and exploration.

  Bibliography: p.
  Includes index.
  1. Fur trade—Northwest, Pacific—History—19th century. 2. Northwest, Pacific—Discovery and Exploration. I. Title.
HD9944.U46A193   1983   380.1′456753′09795   82-40453

34, 126

University of British Columbia Press edition for sale only in Canada
(International Standard Book Number 0-7748-0144-1)

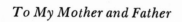

To My Mother and Father

Contents

Illustrations

Maps

Preface

IT SOMETIMES SEEMS that the discovery and exploration of North America has had more historians than actual explorers. Since the beginnings of historical writing in the United States and Canada, scholars and laymen alike have devoted volumes to these themes. From Washington Irving to William Goetzmann the fur trade, in particular, has received the attention of historians of exploration. Still, although the field of fur-trade exploration has been much worked, it has its share of unknown elements. The most important terrae incognitae in fur-trade historiography have been in the Far Northwest, a region that included the interior of northern British Columbia, the western Northwest Territories, the Yukon, and eastern Alaska. It is the purpose of this book to discuss the role of the fur trade in the exploration of that region and thus to fill a gap in fur-trade historiography.

Between 1821 and 1870 the Hudson's Bay Company ruled much of Canada as an independent power. The British government was content with the situation and for practical purposes served merely as a broker for the company in the area of international diplomacy. John S. Galbraith, in *The Hudson's Bay Company as an Imperial Factor, 1821–1869*, examines closely the company's continent-spanning operations and the commercial and diplomatic problems that arose where its districts bordered on foreign territories.[1] Territorial expansion played a large role in the company's relations with foreign rivals, because, according to Galbraith, the company engaged in expansion in order to crush potential and existing competitors and thus insulate its operations from possible encroachment.[2]

Such a negative motivation for exploration certainly determined the company's policy toward what is now the northwestern United States. Alexander Ross, Peter Skene Ogden, and John Work were dispatched with bands of trappers to sweep clean of furs the eastern borders of the company's Columbia District. The company felt that, if there were no furs in the region, it would not have to worry about competition from American fur traders, such as those of the Rocky Mountain and American fur companies.[3] A similar negative motivation may be ascribed to the first phase of the Hudson's Bay Company's explorations in the Far Northwest. Between 1824 and 1839 the company was exploring toward the Pacific Slope in order to intercept the furs that were being traded to the Americans and Russians along the Northwest Coast.

The desire to outflank or preempt competition was not, however, the sole motive behind the explorations in the Far Northwest. The explorations there had their roots in the history of the fur trade. Since the early commercial explorations of Samuel de Champlain, Pierre Esprit Radisson, and Médard Chouart des Groseilliers the expansion of the fur trade and the exploration of the continent had progressed as one. The regions of the greatest undeveloped fur potential were always beyond the frontiers of geographic knowledge. This was not because the fur traders had a finely developed geographic sense (though some did; David Thompson, for example) , but because the nature of fur-trade operations thrust the traders onto the frontier.

The fur trade, as it was practiced from the discovery of the continent until the early twentieth century, was an extractive industry. Fur traders were not concerned with developing the total resources of a region. They had a specific object in view —furs—and did all they could to get as many pelts as possible. When the furs of a frontier area had been significantly reduced in quantity and quality, the traders again moved westward. Such a process is common to all extractive industries. The mining frontier, particularly placer gold mining, followed a similar pattern, as did the oil industry until recently.

The fur trade's expansion was complicated by its dependence on the Indians, who were in most cases the trader's source of furs. The Indians were not merely trappers but also merchants of sorts. Utilizing prehistoric and protohistoric intertribal commercial contacts, they acted as middlemen between the fur traders and tribes not yet in contact with white men. Such a situation became more and more common as the hunting grounds of the Indian middlemen became exhausted from overtrapping. Trade then became their main source of furs. The white fur traders thus found themselves out of touch with the trappers and forced to pay a middleman's tariff on the furs. Since expansion was the only way to reestablish contact with the trappers, it was an integral part of the fur business, and the fur trade played a leading role in the exploration of the continent. This formula determined the Hudson's Bay Company's exploration of the Far Northwest.

A third factor impelling the fur traders to undertake the early exploration of the region was the expanding geographic perception of North America. In the mid-nineteenth century the largest tract of unknown territory on the continent lay in the Far Northwest. Such concepts as the Northwest Passage and the Great River of the West, which determined so much of the exploration of North America, also influenced the exploration of this region. Captain James Cook, Peter Pond, and Sir Alexander Mackenzie all had broached the possibility of a great river valley west of the northern Rocky Mountains. The Hudson's Bay Company had fallen heir to America's last great geographic puzzle.

Thus the Hudson's Bay Company's explorations sprang from three separate but entangled roots: (1) the need to outstrip international competitors, (2) the natural expansion of the fur trade as an extractive industry, and (3) the expanding geographic picture of North America. These incentives were all at various times the company's rationale for exploration.

The importance of exploration in the history of the Canadian fur trade after 1821 is underappreciated. The period from 1821 to 1850 is often seen as one of retrenchment for the Hudson's Bay Company. Internally the company was striving to establish a regimen of monopoly, while economically and diplomatically it struggled with American interests over the Oregon Territory. The nature of these policies is brought into sharper focus when events in the Far Northwest are considered. The company policies of economy and conservation were tied to a program that included exploration and expansion along the undeveloped frontiers of British North America, of which the most important was the Far Northwest. The process of exploring frontier areas and expanding trading operations into the new lands became an important feature of Hudson's Bay Company operations in the nineteenth century.

The man who conceived and directed this strategy was Sir George Simpson. Simpson was the overseas governor of the Hudson's Bay Company, which had its home office in London, during most of the crucial period between 1821 and 1860. Because of his viceroylike power over western British America, Simpson was nicknamed "the Little Emperor" by his foes. He has rightly been considered one of the commanding figures in both the nineteenth-century fur trade and the imperial administration. Yet his direction of the exploration of the Far Northwest was hesitant and inconsistent. He spurred the company to expand and explore, while at the same time he held back the funding and the personnel necessary to do the job. The exploration of the Far Northwest reveals his limitations as a manager. These were to a large extent imposed by economy and geography: he did not control the finances of the company, and he could not manage personally operations that were half a continent away. Yet his limitations as a person and as an administrator were important factors in the Hudson's Bay Company's eventual failure to expand into the upper Yukon Country.

The explorations discussed here were unspectacular. There was no single journey that could rival Lewis and Clark's voyage, or Sir Alexander Mackenzie's crossing of the continent. Nor did these explorations produce an important map maker, such as David Thompson, or a scientific explorer, such as Alexander von Humboldt. Instead, these explorations were conducted for commercial purposes by men whose principal duty was to commerce. Most of the Hudson's Bay Company's explorers were ordinary men who, because of accidents of placement or past displays of energy and competence, were pressed into service as explorers. Although they have not won the fame of other explorers, they shouldered their share of the hazards of an explorer's life. That they achieved no spectacular results reflects not on their abilities but on the company's uncertain direction of their efforts.

This book is not an economic history of the fur trade in the Far Northwest, though the economic background of events is at times considered. Nor is it a diplomatic history, though the rivalry between the Russians and British over the Far Northwest is discussed. It is instead the story of the explorers and their explorations of a remote and distant part of the continent. Their attitudes, actions, and adventures are the principal concerns of the book.

The Setting

When one is discussing geographic exploration, the physical context of the events is of paramount importance. Two great rivers dominate the Far Northwest: the Mackenzie and the Yukon. Besides the Mackenzie River proper, five other major rivers are in the Mackenzie basin: the Peace, the Athabasca, the Slave, the Liard, and the Peel. Of these the Peace, the Liard, and the Peel were of particular importance in the exploration of the region. They pierced the continent-spanning Rocky Mountain system and thus were potential routes through the mountains. They also provided access to other water routes. The Peace River, through its southern branch, the Parsnip River, led to Summit Lake and the portage to the Fraser River. The Peace's northern branch, the Finlay River, was a difficult but direct route to Thutade Lake, the ultimate source of the Mackenzie River, and to an overland route to the Stikine River. The Liard River provided the most direct access to the heart of the Far Northwest, and through its tributaries, the Frances and Dease rivers, its provided access to the Stikine and Pelly rivers, respectively. The Peel River,

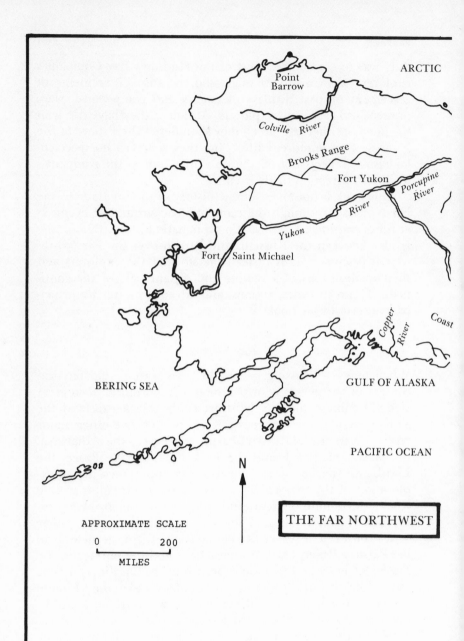

ARCTIC

Point
Barrow

Colville River

Brooks Range

Fort Yukon

Porcupine River

River

Yukon

Fort Saint Michael

Copper River

Coast

BERING SEA

GULF OF ALASKA

PACIFIC OCEAN

N

APPROXIMATE SCALE

0   200

MILES

THE FAR NORTHWEST

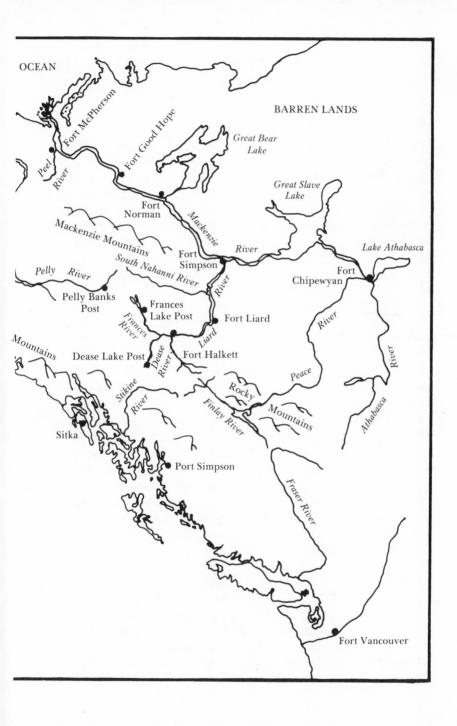

OCEAN

BARREN LANDS

Fort McPherson

Fort Good Hope

Great Bear
Lake

Peel
River

Great Slave
Lake

Fort
Norman

Lake Athabasca

Mackenzie Mountains

Mackenzie

River

South Nahanni River

Fort
Simpson

Fort
Chipewyan

Pelly   River

River

Pelly Banks
Post

Frances
Lake Post

Fort Liard

River

Frances
River

Liard

River

Mountains

Dease Lake Post

Fort Halkett

Dease
River

Peace

River

Athabasca

Stikine

River

Rocky

Finlay River

Mountains

Sitka

Port Simpson

Fraser River

Fort Vancouver

which is farther north than the Peace and the Liard, provided
via the Rat River portage access to the Porcupine River and
the Yukon River valley.

The Yukon is the fourth largest river in North America.
Like the Mackenzie River it boasts many major tributaries.
The exploration of the Far Northwest was centered around
the areas where two of those tributaries, the Pelly and Porcupine rivers, reach toward the westernmost fingers of the Mackenzie basin. The union of the Mackenzie and Yukon waters
is prevented by a series of mountain ranges that have determined the history and geography of the region. The Mackenzie Mountains, stretching for six hundred miles on a northwest, south-west axis between the Mackenzie River delta and
the Liard River, are the major obstacle separating the two
great river valleys. The main range of the Rocky Mountains
bisects the region from the southeast, reaching as far north as
the Liard River. North of the Liard the Rockies are represented by a series of ranges, among which are the Selwyn, the
Ogilvie, and the Richardson mountains. Those ranges, in addition to the Mackenzie Mountains, constitute the last divide,
the final section of the Rocky Mountain system to be breached
by the fur trade.

West of the Rocky Mountains and its subordinate ranges is
the rugged cordillera region. The cordillera is the birthplace
of both the Mackenzie and the Yukon rivers, as well as the
smaller but historically significant Stikine River. From its
sources in a series of large lakes in northern British Columbia
the Yukon makes a great northwesterly arc before discharging
its waters into the Bering Sea. The Stikine takes a more direct
path to the Pacific Ocean, through the Coast Mountains. The
Coast Mountains, the Saint Elias Mountains, and the Alaska
Range separate the cordillera region from the Northwest
Coast and from the western boundary of the Far Northwest.

The terrain of this region is among the most rugged in the
world. The rivers are for the most part glacial streams. Their
currents are swift; the rapids and falls frequent and violent.
Save for the barren peaks and the area along the Arctic Coast
north of the tree line, the region is thickly timbered with for-

ests of spruce, tamarack, and hardwoods. Lowlands and valleys are choked with brush and stretches of muskeg. Travel through the region is difficult. Even today few roads scar its face; few towns mark the map.

Acknowledgments

This book was conceived in the summer of 1974 while I was visiting Fort Simpson, a small settlement in the Northwest Territories. As I looked down at the junction of the Liard and Mackenzie rivers, I wondered what life was like for the fur traders who founded such a remote settlement. In satisfying that curiosity I have had the advice and assistance of many people. Over the past few years Robert McCluggage of the Department of History, Loyola University, has been a valuable source of experience and support. His patience and encouragement guided this study in its evolution from a seminar paper, to a dissertation, to publication. My colleagues James L. Penick and Franklin Walker in the Loyola University history department have also provided valuable assistance.

Ethnohistorical data concerning the Indians of the Far Northwest were generously given by Catharine McClellan in the University of Wisconsin and James Vanstone, Curator of North American Archaeology and Ethnology in the Field Museum of Natural History.

I owe an intellectual debt to R. M. Patterson, whose books and articles on adventure and travel in western Canada were extremely helpful and spurred me to undertake my own travels in the region. I was also influenced by John S. Galbraith's *The Hudson's Bay Company as an Imperial Factor, 1821–1869.*

I would like to thank Shirlee Anne Smith, Archivist of the Hudson's Bay Company, Winnipeg, Manitoba; her former assistant Garron Wells; and the rest of the staff. Without their knowledgable assistance this work would not have been possible. In the same vein I would like to thank the staff of the Public Archives of Canada, Ottawa. The staffs of the Newberry Library, Chicago; the Northwestern University Library,

Evanston, Illinois; Cudahy Library, Loyola University of Chicago; and the Morris Library, Southern Illinois University, Carbondale, must also be thanked.

The fieldwork phase of the project, conducted by canoe in nothern Canada, was eased through the assistance of understanding companions: David J. Keene on the South Nahanni and Liard rivers and James Hunter and Jeffrey Konyar on the Frances and Dease rivers.

Loyola University Graduate School facilitated my research through a fellowship for the 1978–79 academic year. Paul Brankin and Anie Sergis assisted in the preparation of the supporting maps. Maydean Worley prepared the final typewritten manuscript.

Finally, I must express a deep debt of gratitude to Glenn A. Peterson. His support throughout the project, both on the trail and in the preparation of the manuscript, was invaluable. Much that is worthwhile in this study is the result of Peterson's assistance.

Fur Trade and Exploration

CHAPTER 1

The Northwest in 1821

IN THE SUMMER OF 1821 two groups of wary men gathered at York Factory, the Hudson's Bay Company's great tidewater depot on the shores of Hudson's Bay. One group was sullen-eyed but "stalked about the buildings of the old dilapidated fort" with a "haughty air and independent step."[1] They were the Nor'Westers, the vanquished partners of the recently defunct North West Company. In over three decades of competition they had challenged and nearly conquered the Hudson's Bay Company.

In the end geography had brought the Nor'Westers down. The three thousand miles of canoe trails leading back to their Montreal headquarters had proved too fragile a bond to hold their continentwide trade empire together. The English, with a deep-water access at York Factory on Hudson's Bay, had a much more economical avenue to the interior. By 1820 this fundamental advantage, plus the vicious price wars that the English company was financially strong enough to endure, had put the North West Company in perilous straits. Anticipating destruction only one or two years distant, the partners of the North West Company had agreed that union, or absorption by the Hudson's Bay Company, was the only course.

By the end of February, 1821, the union had been accomplished, and during the following summer the first Nor'Westers began arriving at York Factory. They were bitter men, independent managers of their own businesses, who had been

Sir George Simpson. Reproduced from his Narrative of a Journey Round the World During the Years 1841 and 1842. *Courtesy of the Hudson's Bay Company.*

bought out by a larger concern. They were also proud men, and, though the accountants' ledgers may have shown them to be beaten, they had bullied, outmuscled, and outwitted the Hudson's Bay men up to the very end; on the frontier they were still masters. Most of all, they were wary and unsure of what their places would be in the new concern. Would they be scorned as junior partners, shunned from the promotion rolls, their names merely tolerated on a ledger until they retired, or died, in some distant corner of the continent? Or were they to be partners in fact as well as name, able to exercise their considerable skills of organization and leadership? And how was one to work with a Hudson's Bay Company bourgeois (as the man in charge of a fur trading post was called)? The Nor'Westers and the Hudson's Bay men had shot at one another on occasion and had played havoc with one another's rabbit snares and fishnets, trying to starve out the opposition. After the disappointments of the past year, and with uncertainties for the coming years, the Nor'Westers had reason to be wary.

Finally the dinner bell rang for the gala affair that the Hudson's Bay Company had arranged for the two groups of officers to get acquainted. The fur traders filed into the mess hall, but still remained in two completely separate groups. John Todd, a young Hudson's Bay clerk, described the scene:

Evidently uncertain how they would seat themselves at the table, I eyed them with close attention from a remote corner of the room, and to my mind the scene formed no bad representation of that incongruous animal seen by the King of Babylon in one of his dreams, one part iron, another of clay; though joined together [they] would not amalgamate, for the Nor'Westers in one compact body kept together and evidently had no inclination at first to mix with their old rivals in trade.[2]

The tense situation was saved by George Simpson, a thirty-four-year-old Scotsman whom Todd referred to as "that crafty fox." Simpson had only one year of practical experience in the fur trade, but that one year had been spent commanding the Hudson's Bay Company's operations in the Athabasca country, the very cockpit of the competition. There he had been involved in a bitter rivalry with the very best of the

Nor'Westers and had earned their respect as a man cut from the same cloth. Under the terms of the union Simpson was given command of the Northern Department, which included much of the Canadian West (not to mention a good chunk that was later to become part of the United States). Now, at the very beginning of this new era in the company's history, Simpson was faced with a problem that could have nipped the first buds of progress and prevented any further development. How did one take open enemies and mold them into a unified company? How did one join iron with clay?

George Simpson was up to the demands of the occasion. He stepped up to the Nor'Westers and, "with his usual tact and dexterity on such occasions, succeeded . . . somewhat in dispelling that reserve in which both parties had hitherto continued to envelope themselves." Because of Simpson's "stratagems in bows and smiles" and his good-natured, open attitude toward all, the natural confidence of self-made men emerged, and the good-natured camaraderie of the forest replaced the animosities of the past. "Their previously stiffened features began to relax a little; they gradually but slowly mingled together, and a few of the better disposed, throwing themselves unreservedly in the midst of the opposite party, mutually shook each other by the hand."[3]

Of course, there were a few alarms before all was good cheer. For example, someone had foolishly (or maliciously) seated Nor'Wester Allan MacDonell opposite his old Hudson's Bay Company foe from the Swan River District, Chief Factor Alexander Kennedy. Only a few months before, they had been dueling with swords. Now they stood literally growling at each other. Fortunately, their good-natured, and no doubt slightly amused, comrades separated the two without a renewal of violence, and with the length of the table between them their anger subsided.

Then out came the wine, puddings, and tarts that marked most fur-trade feasts. The main course was of moose, goose, partridges, and whatever else the fort hunters had been able to run down. As the wine and the meal mellowed their memories, the men's conversations turned to trapping and Indians and to far-off mountains and seldom-visited country, such as the Athabasca District, New Caledonia, Peace River, and the Barren Lands—the shoptalk of nineteenth-century fur barons. With the words from both sides of the table tumbling forth in thick Highland brogues and the mutual interests, ambitions, and experiences to be exchanged, the scrimmages and defeats of the previous years began to look less like Culloden and more like a family squabble. In the good cheer of that evening, and in the exciting and prosperous days that were to come, the unyielding iron and the supple clay were fused.

The union of March 26, 1821, successfully joined the Hudson's Bay Company's capital and superior geographic location with the methods and spirit of the North West Company. Thus the two greatest commercial concerns on the continent, each boasting an impressive tradition of adventurous capitalism, were joined. As their bitterness subsided, many of the Nor'Westers would see that they had been more than well received into the Hudson's Bay Company. Former Nor'Westers commanded the richest and most extensive fur-trade districts, New Caledonia, Columbia, Athabasca, and Mackenzie River. Of the twenty-five chief factors—the generals of the fur trade—eighteen were former Nor'Westers.[4]

The Hudson's Bay Company had been founded in 1670 by King Charles II of England. According to its charter the company was to have full commercial, legal, and administrative control over the entire Hudson's Bay drainage. Even the determined attacks of New France's merchants and military men were unable to dislodge the great company. The Nor'Westers were the most serious foes that the Hudson's Bay Company ever faced.

The North West Company had been formed in 1779 by an aggressive group of Montreal merchants who wished to secure a monopoly of their own in the western fur trade.[5] Oblivious to difficulty and disdainful of distance, they spread their trade to the base of the Rockies and eventually across the mountains to the Pacific Ocean. When economics forced the amalgamation of the two companies, they held absolute sway over an area larger than western Europe.

News of the unification agreement was unwelcome to many in both of the companies. George Simpson himself was disap-

pointed; flushed with his success in the Athabasca, he saw no
reason to give quarter now that the enemy was on the run.[6]
Those Bay Company inland managers who had been more
skilled in bullying and brawling than in sound commercial
management were galled to find themselves replaced by Nor'-
Westers. John Clarke, of Astoria fame, wrote bitterly, "To the
joint efforts of Mr. Robertson & myself are the H B Coy in a
great measure indebted for the splendor & importance of their
rank in the great commercial world."[7] Neither Clarke nor
Colin Robertson was able to adapt to the changing needs of
the trade. Pensions, not pelts, were in their future.

Union was, however, a very necessary action. The competition not only had wrecked the North West Company but also
had severely affected the land. The final stages of the long rivalry had brought a proliferation of trading posts in nearly
every area of the Northwest. To keep overhead low, each of
these posts relied upon the fish and game of the countryside
to feed its staff. If provisions had to be shipped into the interior, the post would be too costly to maintain. Hence many
areas had become dangerously overhunted. The situation in
the Lac la Pluie District was typical: "The large game animals are the Rein Deer and Moose, but in such small numbers that natives cannot kill enough to supply themselves with
leather for their moccasins and snow shoes."[8] So dire was the
situation in that district that many bands were forced to reduce their trapping activities to devote more time to the quest
for game.

Fur returns also were declining. The intensive competition
had diminished the forests' fur-bearing populations. The formerly rich reserves of the Churchill River, the Red River,
and Rainy Lake (Lac la Pluie) were in critical condition.[9]
The "cry of no beaver" was even echoed in the Athabasca
District, for years the very heart of the industry.[10] It seemed
that the boom period of the fur frontier was at an end.

As if that were not enough, George Simpson, the Northern
Department governor, was faced with a dangerous overstaffing
problem. The union had rendered useless many trading posts
whose sole function had been to oppose rival traders. With all
of the Northwest under one flag the men who staffed those

posts were no longer needed. Furthermore, in the final stages
of competition each side had strained to keep its staff at full
strength and, in doing so, had often accepted men who were
less than competent. They were now superfluous. Simpson
would have to reassess the utility of every post and sift out the
incompetent and untrustworthy to make way for the energetic
and responsible.

These were difficult problems, and to them Simpson turned
his considerable administrative skills. With characteristic energy he launched a reorganization of the overtrapped districts,
moving posts out of barren territory and reducing the number of establishments in each district. The Indians were en-
couraged to follow the Hudson's Bay men to these new posts,
leaving the former hunting areas free to recover their diminished fur and game populations. This was the beginning of
the Hudson's Bay Company's attempts to put the fur trade on
a sustained-yield basis.

Less happily received were Governor Simpson's plans to reduce the excessive employment rolls. Betwen 1821 and 1825
the company's staff was cut more than 50 percent, and the
wages of those remaining in service were slashed from the
high levels of the competitive era.[11] "In short, the North-West
is now beginning to be ruled with an iron rod," said former
Nor'Wester Willard-Ferdinand Wentzel.[12] On the bright side
of the ledger, the company did arrange transport for those un-
fortunates and their families to the Red River of the North,
where homesteads (river lots) were made available to them.

The Indians were also affected by Governor Simpson's
economy measures. Union meant the end of price wars. Union meant the end of liquor regales. Union meant the beginning of monopoly control. Prices were gradually brought into
line with the reduced supply of trade goods, and the native
trapper had little voice or choice in the matter. The Company tried to wean the Indians to more conservation-minded
trapping habits. Underaged beaver were no longer accepted,
nor were summer beaver with their next-to-worthless hides.
In fact, in some districts, such as Nelson River, there was a
moratorium on beaver trapping, and only fox, marten, and
other lesser furs were accepted.[13]

The final and, for our concern, the most important of Governor Simpson's new policies was his decision to expand the company's frontiers. As an inducement to consummate the marriage of the Hudson's Bay Company and the North West Company, the British government presented as a dowry full monopolistic control over the whole of British North America west of Rupert's Land. This legitimatized the new company's operations in the Columbia, New Caledonia, Athabasca, and Mackenzie River regions. In the last two districts, New Caledonia and Mackenzie River, the possibilities for expansion of the trade were prime. Hence those districts became the scene of determined exploration. As Governor Simpson explained, "I have turned my attention very particularly to the affairs of McKenzies River generally, as there is a greater Field for the extension of trade there than in any other part of the Country."[14] Exploration was necessary to sustain the exhausted older districts as they recovered their fur-bearing populations, and exploration was necessary to show the British government that "no exertion is wanting on our part to secure to the mother country by discovery as much of this vast continent and trade there of as possible."[15]

In summary, Governor Simpson's ambitious program for putting the Hudson's Bay Company's affairs on solid footing consisted of conservation, economy, and exploration. Since exploration was necessarily but one plank of his platform, the other two must also be kept in view.

Early Exploration in the Far Northwest

When considering the early exploration of the Mackenzie, one must mention two men who never knew the great river's valley, Captain James Cook and Peter Pond. Cook, on his 1778 voyage into Arctic waters, had sailed the length of America's Northwest Coast. Unfortunately for the dreamers and schemers of the day the captain failed to discover the fabled Strait of Annian, the western opening of the hoped-for Northwest Passage. Furthermore, as Cook continued up the coast, he found that the continent of North America extended much farther west than most geographers thought it did and than most cartographers portrayed it. Thus he quashed the hopes of the many individuals expecting a sea route through the Americas. Nevertheless, his findings did encourage those who sought a fresh-water passage to the Pacific.

When cruising the coast of Alaska, Cook entered the large inlet that today bears his name. At first it appeared to be a deep-water strait; visions of the long-sought Strait of Annian and the strait of Juan de Fuca danced in the heads of many of the crew. As they proceeded east, a high range of mist-shrouded mountains sealed off the waterway, but the piles of driftwood, the silty fresh water, and an open channel on the north of the inlet seemed to indicate that the expedition had discovered the mouth of a large river. William Bligh (who was later to be the subject of the mutiny on the *Bounty*), ascended the supposed river a short way and found it deep and navigable. The saltwater voyagers failed, however, to grasp the importance of their discovery. A large river flowing from east to west and emptying into the Pacific might have proved to be a new avenue of commerce, a western Saint Lawrence, but it was not of interest to Cook, Bligh, and their mates because it was freshwater. They simply noted the location of the river and cast off. Had they explored the supposed river farther, they would have prevented much idle speculation and fruit-less searching. Just upstream, a matter of yards from where Bligh turned back, Cook's River, as it was called, became shallow and unnavigable; it was no great stream but merely the junction of mountain freshets. That, however, was not to be known for some time, and the apocryphal concept of Cook's River attracted future explorers.

It was not long before Cook's findings reached the various dreamers, adventurers, and fur traders who were probing westward, opening up the area to commerce and trying to sift out the geographic realities of the continent. The nonexistence of a saltwater Northwest Passage was no news to most of them, but the supposed discovery of a great western river was something to mark.

It was of special interest to Peter Pond, a Connecticut Yankee who at this time was employed by the North West Company. In the year of Cook's voyage he had established the first

fur-trade post in the Athabasca region, but his travels had
taken him even farther north—to Great Slave Lake. There he
had heard Indian reports of a large river flowing from the
west end of the lake. When he returned to Montreal in 1784,
he produced a map of his explorations. This chart, although
only mildly in error concerning the latitude of Great Slave
Lake, was grossly mistaken in portraying only a small unexplored territory between the lake and the Pacific Ocean. Pond
had, however, correctly plotted the course of the river draining great Slave Lake: it turned north and emptied into the
Arctic Ocean.

A year later Pond was back in the Northwest, continuing
his geographic inquiries and his pioneer commerce. As he did
so, his perception of the region began to change. Undoubtedly having read the journals of Cook's expedition, he began
to work Cook's discoveries into his picture of northwestern
America. Furthermore, he seems to have traveled some distance down the river that flows from Great Slave Lake known
today as the Mackenzie River. He found that it did not initially flow north but continued west. Could this be the beginning of the river that Cook thought he had discovered on the
Pacific? Cook had located the mouth of his river roughly sev-
enty miles north of the sixtieth parallel. Pond's source was on
almost exactly the same latitude. Since Pond misconstrued the
longitude and was trusting that the river held its westward
course, it seemed to him that the river must be the freshwater
Northwest Passage.[16]

Peter Pond never had a chance to act on his theories. He
was exiled from the Northwest forever in 1788, after John
Ross, a rival trader, was accidentally killed in a scuffle with
Pond's men. That was the second time that Pond's name had
been linked with a competitor's death, and the consensus
among fur traders was that two such accidents were enough.
Nevertheless, before he left, Pond had laid the groundwork
for further expansion of the trade in the region. In addition
to the Athabasca establishments Pond had supervised the
founding of Fort Resolution at the mouth of the Slave River
on Great Slave Lake and Fort Providence on the north shore
of the lake. More important, he had laid out, in his letters,

journals, and maps, a perceptive interpretation of Indian reports and maritime discoveries.

The man who fell heir to Pond's work was a twenty-five-year-old Scot, named Alexander Mackenzie, who at this time was also in the service of the North West Company. With the same rare mixture of inquisitiveness and energy that Peter Pond had, Mackenzie set out in the spring of 1789 to track down the truth about this promising freshwater passage. On Monday, June 29, twenty-six days after leaving Fort Chipewyan, Mackenzie entered the river that he had heard of for so long. Its course was, indeed, westward, and, as each day passed, the Scotsman's spirits probably rose in expectation. By the first of July, Mackenzie had passed "the river of the Mountain" (the Liard River), and on the south he could see the rising ground of distant mountains. As long as the river continued west, and those mountains remained on the south, the passage would be clear. On the next day, however, Mackenzie recorded, "We perceived a very high mountain ahead, which appeared on our nearer approach, to be rather a cluster of mountains, stretching as far as our view could reach."[17] The river still flowed westward, but the Scotsman could not hide his apprehension.

On the next day the river turned north, and for a week the great stream held substantially to this course. As each day passed, Mackenzie's gloom grew, until on July 10 he admitted defeat: "From hence it was evident that these waters emptied themselves into the Hyperborean Sea."[18] The great freshwater passage was not to be. The dream of a great Northwest trade empire based on the far Pacific was quashed, at least temporarily. Nonetheless, Alexander Mackenzie's determination and indomitable curiosity remained unshaken, though he called the waterway which bears his name a river of "Disappointment." He had entered upon its exploration, and he would not be stopped until he had reached its mouth.

As Mackenzie bore north, his attention was constantly turned to the west, to those distant, uplifted shadows, the mountains that separated him from his goal. The mountains had deflected his river to the desolate north. Their imposing and foreboding presence was to a man of Mackenzie's bent an agonizing question mark, a mystery to be solved. On the far side of the mountains might lie the blue waters of the Pacific, or the valley of a river as yet unnamed, or streams alive with beaver and meadows lush and luxuriant with flowers and game. Whatever was there, Mackenzie had to know. At every opportunity he questioned the Indians whom he met. On his return voyage he learned from their reports of a great river flowing west that was many times the size of the Mackenzie. The Indians reported that white men had built a fort at this river's mouth. To the Scotsman this could mean only one thing: the river on the west was Cook's River, and the white outpost was a Russian settlement. Excited by the news, Mackenzie began to make overtures to set out at once in search of the river. Fortunately neither the Indians nor the members of the exploration party were ambitious or foolhardy enough to join him (it was late in the season), and he abandoned the thought.

On July 15, 1789, Mackenzie's party camped on Whale Island in the great Mackenzie delta, where they erected a memorial, on which, Mackenzie recorded, "I engraved the latitude of the place, my own name, the number of persons which I had with me and the time we remained there."[19]

The great voyage had, like Cook's, helped to dispel the notion of the Northwest Passage. If the passage had existed, Mackenzie would have passed it on his trek northward. Also like Cook, Mackenzie had raised the prospect of a river on the west. Instead of answering the major geographical question of the Northwest, he merely postponed it. Pond's theories and the supposed Cook's River had excited the interest of the British government, which had gone so far as to authorize an expedition to trace Cook's River from its source to the sea. The discouraging reports of Mackenzie's voyage cut short that expedition and quickly deflated public interest in the issue. The search for the great westward-flowing river would have to wait until the fur frontier had assimilated the huge area that Mackenzie had just explored. It was enough that the Mackenzie River had been discovered, and its vast territory opened up to the North West Company.

Early Fur Trade of the Mackenzie Valley

At first the partners of the North West Company were less than enthusiastic about Mackenzie's discoveries—an attitude that eventually would drive Alexander Mackenzie out of their ranks and into opposition. Not until 1796 was an attempt made to take advantage of the Mackenzie River as an avenue of fur-trade expansion. In that year Duncan Livingston, a North West Company clerk, founded a post on the Mackenzie not far from its outlet from Great Slave Lake. After three years of trade there, Livingston attempted to descend the Mackenzie to its mouth. Instead of retracing Alexander Mackenzie's great voyage, however, he met with disaster: about two hundred miles from his goal he and his party encountered Eskimos, whose deadly arrows left only one survivor. That unfortunate, James Sutherland, was reportedly taken to the river, weighted with a large stone, and thrown into the water, where he drowned.[20]

No doubt shaken, but still undaunted, the Nor'Westers returned to the Mackenzie the following year. Clerk John Thompson, after abandoning Livingston's post, founded Rocky Mountain Fort across from the mouth of the North Nahanni River and Great Bear Lake Fort on the shores of that freshwater sea.

In the next four years there was a proliferation of trading posts in the Mackenzie region. A group of wintering partners rebelled from the main body of the North West Company and formed the XY Company (later Sir Alexander Mackenzie and Company). This new concern quickly followed the Nor'Westers into the Mackenzie valley. During the rivalry an opposition establishment was erected by XY-Company men at Great Bear Lake. Also dating from this period were Fort Alexander, near the Willow Lake River; Fort George, near Great Slave Lake; Fort Castor, below the Keele River; Fort Norman, south of the Great Bear River's mouth; Fort Good Hope, near the Hare Indian River; and Fort of the Forks, at the junction of the Liard and Mackenzie rivers, as well as other less significant establishments.[21]

A reconciliation of the two warring concerns occurred in 1805, and the new North West Company consolidated its hold on the Mackenzie valley by abandoning all the upper posts except Fort Norman, Fort Good Hope, and "Forks" Fort. In the same year the fur trade made its first advances up the Liard River westward toward the Mackenzie Mountains. Fort Liard was established where the Petitot River joins the Liard. Sometime between 1805 and 1807, Fort Nelson was built where the Fort Nelson River joins the Liard.[22]

The founding of Fort Nelson and Fort Liard indicated that the Nor'Westers recognized the Liard River as the best avenue for expanding the trade. For practical purposes the only possible direction for expansion was up the Liard. The way northward, as we have seen, was blocked by the Eskimos (the traders were not eager to suffer Livingston's fate). East of the Mackenzie valley were the Barren Lands, a thousand miles of rocks and lakes where lichens, caribou moss, and occasional stunted spruces were the only vegetation. That area was hardly inviting country for beaver hunters. Besides, the furs from the region were drawn off by the Hudson's Bay Company's Fort Churchill. Rival fur traders were pushing up from the south. On the west the Mackenzie Mountains formed a wall flanking the Mackenzie River and blocking its progress westward. The Liard was the only passage through that wall.

The Nor'Westers knew little of the country into which they proposed to expand their enterprises. We know it today as rough, undulating terrain dissected by the Rocky Mountains. To the geographers of that time the concept of the continent-long mountain chain was not yet in focus. There appeared to be no reason why the fur traders could not expect to find an open and commercially feasible route around or through the Mackenzie Range. The Liard River itself was a mystery. The traders had traveled the first 250 miles or so regularly, but nothing broke the obscurity of the Liard's upper stretches but the flickering lights of legends and Indian reports. The mysterious land was supposed to be inhabited by strange creatures, such as a great beast that was "about the size and bulk of an elk, with short legs, a long neck, and has two great horns like a stag, under which two small ones sprout out"[23] (probably a woodland caribou). Venomous springs were reported, whose bubbling clear cold waters quenched not the adventurer's thirst but attacked his nerves, bringing on a "slow fever" and a peaceful, composed death.[24] The mountain tribes were the Nahannis, the "Dahoteenas," and the "Nombahoteenais." They were as yet unknown to white men; like swiftly moving shadows, they stayed out of sight in the high country, living on the flesh of the caribou and mountain sheep and making war on one another.[25]

The upper shores of the Liard River thus were ready for some enterprising adventurer to explore their wonders. Already the Liard was providing the best pelts in the entire Mackenzie District. But, surprisingly, the Nor'Westers did not follow up their fine beginning on the river. This was not because of a lack of adventurous spirits but because the North West Company's enterprises in the Mackenzie valley were checked by unforeseen reverses.

In the winter of 1812–13, Fort Nelson was destroyed. Its walls had marked the North West Company's deepest penetration of the Liard valley. A mixture of distress, starvation, and despair among the local Tsattine (or Beaver) Indians and the "morose" and "inconsiderate" nature of the post trader, Alexander Henry, probably incited the unfortunate affair.[26] Although fur-trade sources provide few details of the massacre, Indian tradition has preserved the event.

It had been a difficult winter. No doubt there were many empty bellies in the vicinity of Fort Nelson that year. Alexander Henry was upset by the fur returns that he was receiving because they were considerably less than those of previous years. The Indians, unsuccessful in trapping furs, were short of ammunition, which was a necessity if they were to keep their families fed. In their distress they adopted a desperate plan. They sent a runner to Fort Nelson to inform Henry that one of the bands had made a successful hunt and they had much meat. Henry and a couple of *engagés* set off for the hunting camp to trade for provisions. Since this was the routine by which the Nor'Westers' posts were usually supplied, Henry suspected nothing. The Indians waited in ambush along the trail, and, as the fur traders passed, they sprang to

the attack, killing Henry and his men. Triumphant, they then
descended on Fort Nelson, killing Henry's wife and children
and plundering the post.[27]

The massacre shook the entire district. It was a blow to the
traders' strongest prop in support of their empire, their elevated and respected position among the native peoples. One
trader considered the situation so serious that, "unless some
strong measures are applied soon to recover in some degree
our former respectability, matters must soon come to an end
in this Department."[28]

Food supplies also proved to be a problem for the Mackenzie River posts. Because the fur traders depended upon the
country for most of their food, they were vulnerable to the
fluctuations of wild game. In the winter of 1810–11, the usually abundant rabbits, an important food source in the Mackenzie District, became critically scarce. To make matters
worse, the moose seemed also to have disappeared. Hardest
hit was Fort of the Forks. There Willard-Ferdinand Wentzel,
a Norwegian-born fur trader, suffered a winter of unrelenting
hardship. As his own strength wasted away, he watched his
comrades die one by one. When spring came, he and his family were still eating only every three days. Unfortunately for
the company, one of Wentzel's main foodstuffs was beaver
skins; "upward of three hundred" were eaten.[29]

The failure of local food resources meant that more supplies had to be shipped into the Mackenzie River area. The
corollary was, of course, an increase in overhead for the North
West Company. At the same time that the company was hit
by the Indian problems, the provisions crisis, and the increased costs, fur returns from the entire Northwest declined.
The dependable supply of high-quality pelts from the Athabasca District had been the rock upon which the company was
based. Yet even the Athabasca began to suffer the effects of
overtrapping.[30] The harassments and retraints brought on by
the War of 1812 added to these problems.

These developments culminated in 1815 in the adoption
by the North West Company of a new economy program to
reduce expenses on the Arctic slope. After a review of the
Mackenzie District's operations, it was decided that its high

overhead rendered the district "incapable of defraying the expenses." During the summer of 1815 the fur traders were ordered to abandon all their forts along the Mackenzie and Liard rivers. This greatly angered the Indians of the region. For nearly a generation they had had access to fur posts in the Mackenzie valley, and they were not pleased to have to travel all the way to Great Slave Lake or Fort Chipewyan for the trade goods on which they had grown to depend. According to one trader, the evacuation of the region was done "with great hazard of our lives."[31] The Indians, having gotten wind of the move, "had formed the design of destroying us on our way out."[32] There was no violence, however, and the retreat went smoothly. Twenty-six years after Alexander Mackenzie's journey the great river valley was again the little-explored domain of the red man.

The North West Company maintained its trade contacts along the Mackenzie River by sending a trade canoe to descend the river the next year. Willard-Ferdinand Wentzel carried out the operation in 1816. The Indians greeted him with "extravagant demonstrations of joy": "They danced and cryed by turns, rushing up to their knees in the water to pull my canoe ashore, begging at the same time that the whites would return to their lands and promising their utmost endeavors to render our situation with them as comfortable as possible."[33] Wentzel reported to the company the Indians' desire to have the Mackenzie River trade reopened.

In 1817 the wintering partners heeded Wentzel's information and sent Charles Grant with a limited supply of trade goods to reestablish the company's presence on the Mackenzie River.[34] Rather than reoccupy any of the Nor'Westers' former forts, Grant chose to construct a new fort. Building at a site about three hundred miles down the Mackenzie River, Grant named the establishment Fort Alexander.[35] Between 1818 and 1820 the North West Company again enlarged its presence in the Mackenzie valley, reestablishing many of its former posts in an attempt to keep the Hudson's Bay Company out of the region. But at this time the North West Company was well on the way to extinction. The stage had been set for the merger of iron and clay in 1821.

The First Franklin Expedition

In the summer of 1820 the Mackenzie District was again the scene of exploration. The British government, whose interest in exploration had been deferred by the Napoleonic Wars, emerged from the conflict eager to maintain the island nation's leadership in polar exploration. In 1818 the Admiralty dispatched John Ross and William Edward Parry on another attempt to discover the Northwest Passage. A year later, Parry led a second naval expedition on the same mission, achieving a good deal of success but stopping short of the passage. At the same time the British Arctic Land Expedition was making its way through Rupert's Land. This expedition, commanded by Lieutenant John Franklin of the Royal Navy, was under orders to journey to the coast of the Arctic Ocean and there make a survey of North America's northern shoreline. After wintering at Cumberland House in Saskatchewan, the expedition proceeded to Great Slave Lake.

Wentzel served as the expedition's liaison with the Indians of the Barren Lands north of Great Slave Lake. He also helped in the construction of Fort Enterprise, the expedition's winter quarters, near the headwaters of the Coppermine River.

On June 4, 1821, Franklin's exploring party set out for the Arctic Coast. After hard travel they reached salt water and began surveying the top of the continent, which had been seen only once before by white men. In open birchbark canoes the twenty explorers pushed up the rocky coast, risking heavy rolling seas. More than once they only narrowly missed disaster during the dangerous traverses of exposed water. They eventually mapped approximately 675 miles of coastline before turning back on August 17 with their canoes damaged and their supplies exhausted.

The expedition's return march overland across the Barren Lands was an epic of human suffering. Hunger was an ever-present numbness in their stomachs, and starvation gradually settled in among their ranks. As the brief Arctic autumn began, their march was slowed by ankle-deep snow and ice. The ice was not yet strong enough to support a man but thick enough to lure him out onto it before breaking beneath him and plunging him into the frigid water. A major part of the explorers' diet became tripe-de-roche, a lichen, which they scraped from bare rock and, when lucky, cooked over a fire made from a few willow-bush twigs. When they were fortunate enough to shoot a musk-ox, the explorers fell upon it like wolves, wasting nothing; "the contents of its stomach were devoured upon the spot."[36]

The three months of trials on the return march brought out the worst in some of the men. On more than one occasion food was stolen from the expedition's stores or from a weakened member of the party. Eventually one of the party's voyageurs, Michel Terohaute, an Iroquois Indian, was accused of cannibalism. Before being shot himself, Michel slew Midshipman Robert Hood, one of the expedition's most valued officers.[37]

When the explorers finally reached their winter quarters at Fort Enterprise, they faced further difficulties. The fort, instead of being well stocked with the provisions that they had assumed Wentzel would have waiting for them, was in fact abandoned. Franklin and his men were reduced to rooting about in the year-old garbage dump for any nourishing scraps. Midshipman George Back volunteered to set out in search of the Indian hunters who were supposed to be supplying the fort with meat. Fortunately Back was successful, and with help from the Indians, Franklin and the remaining members of the expedition were saved from starvation.

The Franklin expedition traveled, all told, 5,550 miles, conducting the first survey of the top of the continent and making important scientific observations and collections.[38] Half of the exploring party perished from hunger or exposure. The expedition's activities, concentrated along the Arctic Coast and in the Barren Lands, were not immediately significant in unlocking the major geographic mysteries of the Northwestern American interior. Still, the expedition was important to the Hudson's Bay Company because it demonstrated the British government's commitment to exploration.

One factor that spurred the government was the fear of Russian activities in the North Pacific Ocean. Britain was not going to allow the sacrifices of her mariners, from Martin Frobisher to Captain Cook, to be exploited by Russian explorers profiting from England's pioneering. Also, the Hudson's Bay Company could be hurt by Russian advances into the Northwest. By exploration the company could show its solidarity with British imperial aims and forestall a foreign competitor as well.[39]

CHAPTER 2

The Diplomatic Horizon

THE NORTH AMERICAN fur trade, from the discovery of the continent through the nineteenth century, was intimately involved with international rivalries. Where there were profits to be made on the frontier, the fur traders energetically entered the fray regardless of boundaries or the lack of them. The fur trade in the Far Northwest, at the very edge of the continent, was no exception to this pattern. By the second decade of the nineteenth century a complex, tripartite rivalry had sprung up among the traders of Russia, Great Britain, and the United States.

The Russian American Fur Company

The story of Russia's imperialist drive into northwest America is long and complex. It began with the daring and colorful conquest of Siberia. An epic endeavor, seldom celebrated, it was launched through the efforts of almost mythical figures such as Ivan the Terrible, Boris Godunov, and Ermak, a bold, turbulent frontiersman who broke the Tartars' hold on the trans-Ural region. With the door forced open, the Cossack fur hunters, or *promyshlenniks*, fanned out across northern Eurasia, pushing up new rivers, crossing mountains and marshes, wrestling fortunes in ermine and sable from the *Taiga*. By 1639 the *promyshlenniks*, Russia's equivalents of the *coureurs de bois*, had reached the Pacific Ocean.[1]

The sea proved to be only a temporary obstacle to the Cossacks. By the beginning of the eighteenth century they had exchanged their skin boats and canoes for rudely rigged sailing vessels. Risking the frigid waters of the Okhotsk Sea, they extended the fur frontier to the Kamchatka Peninsula. In 1725, Peter the Great, "to find glory for the state and science," dispatched Vitus Bering to survey the Kamchatka coast and seek a land bridge to North America. Bering, a Danish navigator, was destined to lead two expeditions eastward toward Alaska. He proved that the continents were not joined and on his second voyage gained a glimpse of the Alaskan Peninsula. The second expedition's return voyage was beset by shipwreck and scurvy, to which Bering and thirty of his men eventually succumbed. Those who survived the ill-fated voyage returned with tales of rich fur lands on the east.

A stampede followed the news as the *promyshlenniks* threw themselves into the Alaskan trade. Based on Russia's Pacific Coast, the traders used the Aleutian Islands as stepping-stones to the mainland. As one *promyshlennik* described it, "The sea was like a river"; and along its banks vast profits in sea otter awaited the men bold enough to claim them.[2]

One such man was Gregor Shelekhov. Unscrupulous and ambitious, Shelekhov founded the first permanent Russian settlement in America at Kodiak Island in 1784. It was an unimpressive collection of log huts with small patches of pastureland and an experimental farm plot nearby.[3] Nevertheless, it was the basis for the Russian American Fur Company, which was chartered in 1799. Czar Paul I granted the company mercantile and administrative control of Russia's ill-defined American territories.[4]

Those territories grew swiftly under the guidance of Aleksandr Baranov, the overseas governor of the company. Washington Irving described him as "a rough, rugged, hospitable, hard-drinking old Russian; somewhat of a soldier, somewhat of a trader; above all, a boon companion of the old roystering school, with a strong cross of the bear."[5] His initiative spurred the Russian American Company to remove its American headquarters from Kodiak Island to Sitka, or, as the Russians called it, New Archangel. This strategic move extended Rus-

Sitka. Illustration by Frederick Whymper in his Travel and Adventure in the Territory of Alaska *(1868).*

sian influence into the Alexander Archipelago, an area rich
in furs—six hundred miles closer to British North America.
That was just the beginning for Baranov, who in 1812 supervised the extension of Russian America into northern California with the construction of Fort Ross. Even the Hawaiian
Islands for a brief while seemed destined to become part of
the czar's Pacific empire.[6]

Expansion was not without its costs. The Tlingit Indians
of the Sitka region were a proud and powerful lot, and they
were not at all pleased with the growing Russian presence in
their homeland. In 1802 they attacked Sitka, overran the fort's
palisades, and scattered or killed the entire garrison. It took
Baranov two years to recoup the company's strength and make
a successful counterattack.[7] Still, in 1818, when Baranov was
replaced as governor, the Russian American Company could
boast of twenty-four trading posts scattered along the Alaska
coast and a trade worth seven million rubles.[8]

In spite of those profits the company's directors were troubled. Alaska's waters were becoming crowded with foreign
competition. The once-abundant sea otters, which had gathered in large numbers in the bays around Sitka, were swiftly
diminishing. The Russian American Company's trade was being attacked by interlopers who threatened to ruin all that
Baranov had built.

The Russian–Anglo-American Trade Rivalry

Principal among the Russian American Fur Company's rivals
were American maritime merchants. The Americans were
drawn to the Northwest Coast by Captain James Cook's journals, which were published in 1784. Shippers and traders, particularly the ambitious New Englanders, paid close attention
to Captain James King's account of the small fortunes that
Chinese merchants had offered for sea-otter furs.[9] In 1787 a
group of merchants organized the first American effort to
enter the Pacific Northwest trade, the voyage of the bark
Columbia. Captains Robert Gray and John Kendrick failed
to reap large profits from the voyage, but the knowledge that
they acquired was the basis for the prosperity that New En-

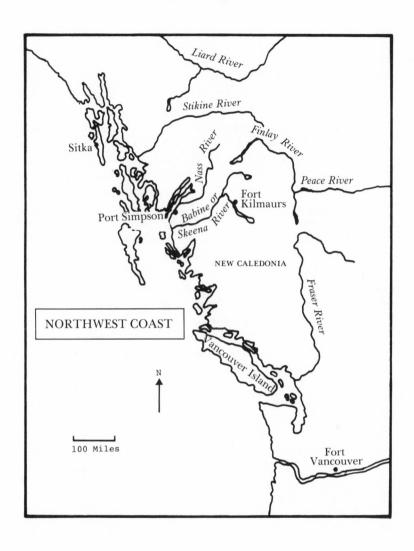

NORTHWEST COAST

Liard River

Stikine River

Sitka

Nass River

Finlay River

Peace River

Port Simpson

Babine or Skeena River

Fort Kilmaurs

NEW CALEDONIA

Fraser River

Vancouver Island

N

100 Miles

Fort Vancouver

gland skippers were to enjoy from the northwest trade in the future.[10]

The British seamen, although they had discovered the maritime trade, met little success in their attempts to exploit it. Paramount among their problems were the ancient charters of the British East India Company and the British South Seas Company, which together barred much of the Pacific to the private entrepreneur. Those who paid the exorbitant license fees levied by the monopolies found themselves underpriced by the scores of Yankee traders who descended upon the coast. With the dawning of the Great Age of American Sail the British merchants were forced into a secondary role.[11]

That, however, was not enough for one American merchant. John Jacob Astor, a German immigrant with ambition and a genius for commerce on a continental scale, aspired to monopolize for himself the trade of the Northwest Coast. By 1812, Astor's Pacific Fur Company had a permanent base on the Columbia River and a number of inland posts and had dispatched a trading vessel up the coast. Astoria represented a farsighted attempt to dominate the trade's inland sources of furs as well as the maritime region. Unfortunately for Astor, the first shoots of progress were nipped by the commencement of the war with Great Britain in 1812.[12]

The War of 1812 signaled the return of the British into serious contention for the trade in the Northwest. The North West Company had reached the Pacific Ocean on three separate occasions with the probes of Alexander Mackenzie in 1793, Simon Fraser in 1808, and David Thompson in 1811. Yet the company had no trading posts on the tidewater. When war broke out with the United States, however, the North West Company, through Edward ("Bear") Ellice, its liaison with the British government, was able to gain the support of the Royal Navy to expel Astor's Americans from the Columbia River valley.[13]

The Nor'Westers enjoyed a good trade along the Columbia River, but did not play a large role in the maritime trade. The company made half-hearted efforts to circumvent the

East India Company's monopoly through an arrangement with the Boston firm of T. H. Perkins,[14] but in the main it directed its furs overland to its Montreal headquarters rather than to the uncertain conditions of the China trade. The Nor'Westers' energies were invested in building up the trade of the interior not only along the Columbia but also in New Caledonia.

Nevertheless, the Russian American Company's principal concern was the maritime trade of the Yankee merchants, whose trading practices were troublesome to the Russians.[15] The trading of the American ships was unrestrained. For the Russians, who not only traded for furs but also trapped them on their own and had permanent establishments on the coast, it was of paramount importance that the warlike coastal Indians be held in check. The Americans were mere birds of passage; they shared no such concern and freely traded firearms, ammunition, knives, and liquor to the Indians. This not only hurt the Russians' trade but also cost them dearly in blood. In 1805 the Russians discovered that the very Tlingit Indians who had slain several *promyshlenniks* and sacked Sitka three years before had been rearmed "by the Bostonians with the best guns and pistols, and even have falconets."[16] The Russians blamed the Americans for the Indians' killing and mutilation of two hundred Aleutian hunters and over one hundred *promyshlenniks*.[17]

With such vigor and in such large numbers did the Americans enter the northwest trade that the sea otter, the principal object of their efforts, was dangerously overhunted. Yet neither the American seamen, the Russian traders, nor the coastal Indians wished to decrease their trade. As a result, by the second decade of the nineteenth century coastal commerce had begun to rely more and more upon mainland furs, such as beaver. Most of those furs came from the interior of British North America, particularly the New Caledonia area. The coastal Indians acted as middlemen rather than trappers. The decline in furs along the coast intensified the competition and made the Russians more unwilling to accept their American rivals. It was becoming clear that there were not enough furs for all.

The American merchants profited from the Russians' distress when they augmented their fur returns by trading with the Russian American Company's Alaska settlements. Originally, this was a mutually accommodating commerce. The Yankee shipmasters often had surplus goods and welcomed the chance to turn them into a profit. The Russian settlements chronically suffered shortages of supplies, particularly foodstuffs. Their settlements in northern California were supposed to alleviate the problem, but they were plagued by innumerable problems and never became a paying proposition.[18] The American ships rounded off their northwest trade by calling at Sitka and exchanging bread, rice, and molasses for otter and beaver furs.[19]

Supplies were just the opening wedge of the growing American influence in Russian America. Soon Yankee skippers were transporting Russian furs to Chinese markets, and American artisans and craftsmen were finding work in the Russian settlements. Benedict Kramer, Jr., an American businessman in Saint Petersburg, sat on the Russian American Company's board of directors. An example of some of the strange cultural by-products of close contact with the Americans came in 1809, when a revolutionary society was formed in Russian America. With the help of their fellow republicans—the Americans— the nine conspirators planned to assassinate Baranov, pirate a ship, and sail to Easter Island, where they would establish a model republic. This harebrained scheme came to nothing, as the dismayed revolutionaries found the Yankees more interested in sea-otter pelts than politics.[20]

Beginning in 1810, the Russians became increasingly alarmed by American influence in the Northwest. Russian naval officers, visiting Alaskan waters for the first time, were repelled by the presence of "North American hucksters" in the czar's territory.[21] When Aleksandr Baranov was ungratefully dismissed from control of the colonies in 1818, the era of *promyshlennik* and adventurous-capitalist control of the Russian American Company was over. The company became the responsibility of Imperial Navy officers. These maritime martinets were not disposed to view the presence of the American traders realistically as a necessary evil; instead, they ordered a ban on trade with the Yankee vessels. The Americans, however, clandestinely continued their commerce.

The Ukases of 1821

The year 1821 was a pivotal year in the escalation of the northwest trade rivalry. On September 16, Czar Alexander I issued an imperial ukase, or decree, claiming for Russia nearly the entire Northwest Coast of North America. Henceforth the territory "from Behring straits to 51° northern latitude" was off limits to British and American merchants, and their pursuit of "commerce, whaling, and fishery, and all other industry" was to cease.[22] To enforce this decree, the czar also claimed that the waters surrounding the American territories for one hundred miles were Russian territory. He dispatched three Russian warships to the region to remind anyone who chose to forget the fact. A second ukase followed nine days later. The Russian American Company's charter was renewed, and its authority was extended to the newly claimed territory.

The czar's ukases, promulgated at the Russian American Company's insistence, sought to redress the Russian merchants' grievances against the Americans. The Yankee liquor and gun trade with the coastal Indians, as well as the trade with Russia's settlements, would be ended by making the coastal waters Russian territory. At the same time the Americans would be barred from the trade of inland furs by the czar's claim to control of the mainland north of 51° latitude. The naval officers and the board of directors of the Russian American Company were delighted; they congratulated themselves that with one bold stroke the Yankee traders had been put in their place.

Unfortunately, in their desire to secure a monopoly of the northwest trade, the Russians had made a very serious blunder. By claiming the "shores of northwestern America," Russia had run against the interests of the British fur traders in New Caledonia.[23] The British trade had only recently been reorganized by the merger of the North West Company with the Hudson's Bay Company, which was now a gigantic, monolithic business concern. George Simpson, at the helm of the English company's inland operations, was planning expansion into the very area that the czar's ukase claimed. Russia had committed the serious diplomatic blunder of opening up a two-front international dispute.

The Russian position was made even more uncomfortable because the United States Secretary of State, John Quincy Adams, was an old Russian hand, having served as the American minister in Saint Petersburg from 1809 to 1812. Because of his distinguished parentage, he had been reared, so to speak, in the midst of continental diplomacy.[24] As a New Englander he was acutely aware of the value of the maritime fur trade.

Count Karl Nesselrode, the Russian foreign minister, was quick to assure the British government that the ukase of September 16 was not directed against them. He told Sir Charles Bagot, the British minister in Saint Petersburg, that "the object of the measure was to prevent the 'commerce interlope' of the Citizens of the United States."[25] George Canning, the British foreign secretary, knew that to ignore the ukase would be to give tacit recognition to Russia's territorial pretensions in the Northwest. At John Quincy Adams's suggestion the British and American governments collaborated in pressing their protests against the ukase.[26]

The British interests in the Northwest were, of course, the interests of the Hudson's Bay Company. Canning based Britain's case upon what the company had decided were its objectives. Initially, those were rather grandiose. John Henry Pelly, the company's London governor, claimed that his traders had been the only ones to occupy the territory from the mouth of the Fraser River to latitude 60° north. Thus the entire mainland would be considered British territory.[27] Although what Pelly claimed was strictly true, it was misleading. His traders did occupy sections of the interior between the mouth of the Fraser and the sixtieth parallel, but there was no Hudson's Bay Company post nearer to the coast than Fort Kilmaurs at Babine Lake. That post, established after the Russian ukase, was still over one hundred miles from the nearest ocean inlet.

The British had a valid claim to the interior, but not to the coast.

The Duke of Wellington presented Great Britain's claims to the Russians at the Congress of Verona in November, 1822. The czar's negotiators complained of the misrepresentation involved in Britain's case, but little more occurred at Verona relating to the Northwest.[28] Even so the Russians were shaken. The extreme pretensions of the Hudson's Bay Company showed the Russians that they were in danger of losing the very territory that the ukase was intended to secure. The news followed that the United States and Great Britain would jointly pursue their negotiations. Only then, in the spring and summer of 1823, did the czar's government realize how imprudent the ukase had been.

The most logical course for Count Nesselrode was to try to fragment the opposition by reaching an independent settlement with one of the parties. Great Britain and Russia were facing each other over a score of international questions, not the least of which were the Spanish and Greek revolutions. In negotiations between the two governments the northwest coast often had to take second place to more pressing European concerns. Furthermore the dispute with Britain was a territorial matter and promised to be a very involved question.

Thus the Russian government was drawn into negotiations with the United States. Nesselrode was now playing a game that he could not win. The inadvisability of the ukase was now apparent to all. Russian American settlements were suffering severe distress as a result of the ban on American supply ships. The foodstuffs dispatched from Baltic Russia were always too little, too late, and too costly. Matvei Muraviëv, the new governor of Russian America, pleaded with his government to lift the ban and allow the Yankees back into Sitka.[29] One of the principal reasons for the ukase had already been rendered meaningless.

John Quincy Adams drove a hard bargain. The Russian-American Convention of 1824 was a complete surrender of all the ukase's claims. Both parties agreed to the $54°40'$ north latitude as a boundary between their spheres of influence, but the Americans were allowed the right to trade with both the

Indians and the Russian settlements north of that line. The convention, which was to last for ten years, gave the Americans irrevocable trade privileges in waters where they had had no rights at all before the ukase. Russian policy had been completely reversed.[30]

The American treaty, although distasteful, strengthened Russia's hand with Great Britain. With his flank protected, Nesselrode was prepared to back up the Russian American Company's claim to control of the Northwest Coast. For over a year, however, negotiations remained deadlocked, with Russia's determination to back her fur traders matched by Canning's support of the Hudson's Bay Company.[31]

Meanwhile, on the frontier Governor Simpson was maneuvering for position. It was against the background of the long drawn-out territorial negotiations that he ordered the Hudson's Bay Company's first exploratory surveys of the Far Northwest. The company hoped to legitimize its claims to the territory west of its establishments and at the same time "keep the Russians at a distance."[32] To do this, Simpson needed information concerning the trade patterns of the interior. He suspected that the land along the northwest coast was not valuable fur territory. The furs that the coastal Indians had were either sea-otter furs or furs bartered from inland tribes.[33] If Simpson's suspicions were correct, the company merely had to control the trade of the interior Indians; for commercial purposes it would be immaterial whether Russia controlled the coastline.

The Hudson's Bay Company's explorers were not the only ones roused by the Russian ukase. Sir John Barrow, secretary of the Admiralty and the guiding hand behind English Arctic exploration, feared the ukase's challenge to freedom of the seas. In November, 1823, his protegé John Franklin volunteered to lead a second expedition to the Polar Sea. Franklin believed that the "objects to be attained are important at once to the Naval character and the Commercial interests of Great Britain."[34] He proposed to push westward from the mouth of the Mackenzie River, exploring the top of the continent. If all had gone as planned, Franklin would have succeeded both in extending the frontiers of science and in "the preservation

Boats ascending the Mackenzie River. Illustration in Franklin, Narrative of a Second Journey to the Shores of the Polar Sea.

of that Country, which is most rich in Animals, from the encroachment of Russia and preventing the Establishment of another and at some Period perhaps a hostile Power on any part of the Northern Continent of America."[35] The Hudson's Bay Company eagerly fell in with these plans and offered its considerable assistance. The Admiralty was also excited and escalated the effort by dispatching Captain William E. Parry to find a navigable Northwest Passage. Captain Frederick W. Beechey was sent to the Bering Sea to rendezvous with Franklin or Parry if they succeeded in making the passage.

Nor were the Russians inactive in exploration. In 1818, increasingly alarmed by English Arctic exploration, they had begun a modest program of survey and expansion centered on the mainland of western Alaska, a vast *terra incognita.* In 1821 and 1822, V. S. Kromchenko and A. K. Etolin, Imperial Navy officers in the service of the Russian American Company, surveyed the coastline of the region. Inexplicably they failed

to discover the mouth of the Yukon River, but they did bring
back valuable details concerning Alaska's second longest river,
the Kuskokwim.[36] This knowledge was the basis of future fur-
trade expansion as the Kuskokwim became one of the most
important trade centers in Russian America. Thus both Russia and Great Britain, while engaged in controversy over the
northwest coast, made moves to secure additional room for
expansion away from the disputed area.

In the negotiations with the Russians, George Canning had
a critical advantage over his opposite number, Count Nesselrode. The Russian government had already given away much
of what it had hoped to gain by the ukase in their treaty with
the United States. Nesselrode was now trying to hang onto the
last remaining fiber of the ukase's claims, Russian control of
the North American coastline from $51°$ latitude, or at least
$54°40'$, to the Bering Sea. Unless this territory was secured,
the Russian American Company would perish. Canning, on
the other hand, was representing the extreme pretensions of
the Hudson's Bay Company.[37] The Hudson's Bay Company
would have liked to control the entire northwest coast, but
its principal aims were (1) to keep the mouth of the Fraser
River open and have access to the coast for expansion as far
north as the fifty-fifth parallel, (2) to retain the right of passage through Russian territory by way of any rivers flowing
from New Caledonia to the Pacific, and (3) to protect from
competition the Mackenzie River District, the Company's
treasure vault.[38] Thus Canning and the Hudson's Bay Company had considerable room for negotiation between what
they claimed and what they would settle for.

The Anglo-Russian Convention of 1825 reveals how skill-
fully Canning used this flexibility. He acted out the role of a
moderate man trying to bring agreement between the un-
moving Hudson's Bay Company and the entrenched Russian
American Company. His Machiavellian performance completely duped Russia's chief negotiator, Count Lieven, who
confided to Count Nesselrode, "I must confess that Canning
has exerted himself very faithfully to satisfy us completely,
but he has to struggle against a violent opposition on the part
of the companies interested."[39] Hence, when Canning offered

Ascending the Great Bear River, 1825. Illustration in Franklin, Narrative of a Second Journey to the Shores of the Polar Sea.

the Russians the control of the northwest coastline, it appeared to them to be a major concession. The Russians, almost out of good faith, agreed to his provision that the English would have the right to pass through the Russian zone via any rivers emptying into the Pacific.[40]

On paper it appeared that Count Nesselrode had secured for the Russian American Company all that it had hoped to gain from the English. The Russians would control a strip of land from the ocean to "the nearest chain of Mountains not exceeding a few leagues of the coast."[41] This strip of land, or *lisière*, would be the boundary between Russian and British America from 54°40′ north to the point 141° west longitude, and from there north to the Arctic Sea. In fact, Nesselrode gave the game away when he allowed the Hudson's Bay Company free passage through the *lisière*. It was an invitation to the English to outflank the Russian trading posts and intercept the furs as they came down to the coast.

Both the Russian-American Convention of 1824 and the

Anglo-Russian Convention of 1825 were stunning blows to the Russian American Company. All that the company had hoped to gain had been reversed, all its worst fears realized. How such an unfortunate train of events had befallen them must have been the subject of much discussion among the company's directors. The answer is obvious: the liaison between the Russian American Company and the imperial government had been poor. Nesselrode could not have been too pleased with the company's timing in appealing for the ukases. Russia was mired in a morass of post-Napoleonic diplomatic problems, and it is unlikely that Nesselrode would have welcomed another, especially in an area peripheral to Russia's vital interests. John Middleton, the American minister in Saint Petersburg, advised John Quincy Adams that the ukase "appears to have been signed by the Emperor without sufficient examination, and may be fairly considered as having been surreptitiously obtained."[42]

Once they obtained the ukase, the Russian American Company's directors did not make adequate provisions to supply their settlements. Within a year they were begging the czar to allow the Yankee ships back into Sitka. This imprudent policy of drawing the imperial government into dangerous diplomatic waters and then withdrawing did not endear the company to the czar. Furthermore, an investigation into the company's employee practices and its treatment of Indians and of Russian clergy revealed extensive abuse. Alexander I, a humanitarian and sometime liberal, was disgusted.[43] The Russian American Company was not even consulted during the final negotiations with Great Britain. Since the commercial and diplomatic arms of the empire were estranged, the diplomatic reverse was inevitable.

CHAPTER 3

Preliminary Westward Explorations

CHIEF TRADER Alexander Roderick McLeod was a worried man in the fall and winter of 1822. As the gentleman in charge of the Mackenzie District he felt that his destiny and the fortunes of the district were intertwined. Of late he had seen signs that did not bode well for the district.

First of all, news arrived that Willard-Ferdinand Wentzel was to be recalled. Wentzel was a clerk in the district and had recently served on the Franklin Expedition. Although his "jovial" disposition and happy talent with a fiddle had won him friends among his fellow traders, his "sarcastic turn of mind" and indiscreet ways often left him unappreciated in high places.[1] Nonetheless, of all the fur traders in the entire Northwest few could claim Wentzel's degree of expertise in affairs in the Mackenzie District. He had spent over twenty years in the Far North. Only the year before, he had supervised the relocation of the Fort of the Forks. The old site under the shadow of the Gros Cap at the Liard's mouth was abandoned, and construction of a new post was begun on an island a short distance up the Mackenzie.[2] If the district was to grow, men of Wentzel's talents were going to be needed. His sudden recall would certainly give Chief Trader McLeod pause.

Also plaguing McLeod was another action by Governor Simpson. Following Simpson's tour of the Athabasca District during the previous summer, the governor had traveled north to Great Slave Lake. McLeod had expected the governor to continue north and visit the new district headquarters at the Mackenzie River Forks. When McLeod heard that the governor instead had turned about and was returning to Fort Chipewyan, he was left speculating about the possible reasons why Simpson might avoid the district. Perhaps as part of his new economy programs Simpson would withdraw the fur traders from the Mackenzie District just as the North West Company had done in 1815.

At the base of McLeod's concern was uncertainty about what the recently completed amalgamation would bring. An old Nor'Wester like the chief trader would naturally be suspicious of what this "gentleman," George Simpson, planned to do. Was Wentzel to be merely the first of many Nor'Westers to be fired from the district's rolls? Perhaps in his agitation McLeod looked back on his own role in the North West Company's Athabasca Campaign—that violent yet unsuccessful attempt to drive the Hudson's Bay Company from the valuable Far North. Were the sins of the past really buried? To ease these doubts, McLeod resolved to address a letter directly to the governor, who was wintering at Fort Chipewyan, on Lake Athabasca.

Simpson responded promptly, and his letter of January 2, 1823, alleviated McLeod's uncertainties. Not only did Simpson accept McLeod's judgment that Wentzel should stay in the district, confessing, "I find we have been giving the prooning hook too much latitude," but also he reassured McLeod that it had been only the want of a guide to the lower Mackenzie that had prevented him from visiting the Forks during the past summer.[3] As for curtailing the Mackenzie District operations, Simpson chided McLeod that he could not have been more wrong: "The Trade of Mackenzie's River is so valuable and important and holds out such prospects of extension to advantage that instead of wishing to curtail its means as you seem to apprehend the Council is desirous of rendering its every support and assistence, that may be considered necessary."[4]

After easing McLeod's mind, Simpson proceeded to instruct

timbered topography where the beaver hunting had been abundant and signs of the creature gradually disappeared. The riverbed narrowed, and the current quickened; progress was slow. Mountainous country made tracking upstream doubly difficult. On July 18 the interpreter, the Indians, the entire crew with one voice called for going back.

McPherson agreed. He had fulfilled his instructions, which had been vague. The Beaver River was becoming difficult, and it seemed that they might be near the end of the navigable part of it. Furthermore, they had found no Nahanni Indians; the encampments that they did stumble on were so old that even the scaffolds were barren and weathered. The Nahannis had long ago deserted this area in fear of the Fort Liard Indians. The best beaver country that they had visited lay behind them. McPherson decided to divide the party, half to return to Fort Liard, half to trap for beaver. The downstream trip was surprisingly quick: by July 22, McPherson was back at Fort Liard.

The accomplishments of the voyage were few. The expedition had ascended the Beaver River only about one hundred miles. They had encountered no new tribes. Indeed, McPherson had made no concerted effort to make contact with the Nahannis. He had lit no signal fires, as McLeod had done. Some of McPherson's problems were of his own making. He seems to have picked a poor group of traveling companions; they were improvident, out of shape, and unambitious. McPherson was evidently unable to discipline them. To complain of fatigue after less than a week of travel was very unusual; the Indians seem to have known that they could have their way with him. McPherson may have been a good Indian trader, but he was not a leader of men.

On the plus side of the ledger, new beaver country had been opened. McPherson was correct in perceiving the Beaver River as "a long time a treasure" for both the Indians and the company. Furthermore, the frontiers of the Mackenzie District had been broadened "to the westward." McPherson completed his journal and compiled a map of the Liard area, incorporating his explorations with those of the Indian hunters whom he had dispatched the summer before. He sent the report to the district headquarters, giving the impression that he had accomplished more than he actually had. If Murdock McPherson did not know how to lead men, he did know how to deal with his superiors.[51]

The explorations of McLeod and McPherson were the first steps of the Hudson's Bay Company's exploration of the Far Northwest. The expeditions were not impressive endeavors in their design, in what they were intended to accomplish, or in their execution. The South Nahanni and Beaver Rivers did not become routes to the interior, and their exploration did not directly aid the search for the rich fur country that the company hoped to find west of the Mackenzie Mountains.

Nevertheless, the efforts of John McLeod and Murdock Mc-Pherson laid the groundwork for future explorations that were more fruitful. Although the South Nahanni and Beaver rivers were not the main hunting grounds of the Nahanni Indians, the company did learn that most of these Indians were to be found farther up the Liard River. In this way the explorations of 1823 and 1824 pointed the direction for the future expansion of the fur trade.

The British also discovered that the tribes west of the mountains were in contact with white traders on the Pacific Coast. This meant that the Hudson's Bay Company was nearing one of the sources of the Russian American Company's trade. The Hudson's Bay Company was not in a position to take advantage of that information. Indeed, the most important revelation of these early explorations was the difficulty of penetrating the interior. Exploration up the Liard River would be a prolonged endeavor, whose rewards were as yet many years in the future.

him in the specifics of his policy of expansion. He first described his plans for the New Caledonia District:

With Mr^{er}s [Edward] Smith and [Peter Warren] Dease I have
had a great deal of conversation on this topic.[5] . . . the later has
undertaken a very interesting and I hope important expedition
next summer [in] the country laying to the West of the Mountains, through which by Indian reports there is a water communication running parallel with the Mackenzie River [that] is quite
unknown to us, altho supposed to be rich in Fur bearing animals.[6]

Once again rumors were reported of a western river resembling Cook's River. Smith and Dease's expedition would proceed up the Peace River to a place where the river divides
into its two main feeders, the Parsnip and the Finlay rivers.
From there the expedition was to travel "due west across the
Mountain and along the skirts of it or as the water communications to the North West may serve as far as the season per-
mits with safety, and when across it so as to fall upon the
headwaters of the River au Liard, or some of the streams leading into Mackenzie's River."[7]

After describing these plans, Simpson turned his attention
to affairs in McLeod's own district. For many years the fur
traders had heard reports of Indian tribes dwelling in the
mountains west of the Liard and Mackenzie rivers. One of
these tribes was known to the Slave Indians of the Mackenzie
as the Nahannis. The mountain retreats of the Nahannis were
reported to be rich in beaver. Simpson wanted these natives
to be lured down from the mountains and induced to bring
their furs to trade at Fort Liard. Dispatches from Fort Norman, one of the lower posts, also mentioned a distant tribe,
called the Dahotys, whose hunting grounds extended to the
Russian settlements on the coast. Therefore Simpson suggested to McLeod, "It is desirable that our discoveries and
intercourse with those distant tribes should be prosecuted,"[8]
adding, "I trust you will set every engine to work consistent
with your means."[9]

McLeod was relieved and pleased with the company's plans
for expanding the trade. The plans were truly in keeping with

what George Simpson called the "ancient spirit of the Nor'-West." Imbued with that spirit himself, the chief trader immediately began preparations to follow through with the governor's wishes. At that time he was about forty years old and a "stout strong active man; a good pedestrian." He set out in the middle of the subarctic winter, accompanied by a group of Indian trappers, and headed southwest up the frozen Liard.[10] After a 110-mile march the party arrived at the junction of the Liard River and the South Nahanni, a large river that tumbled through the mountain sanctuaries of the Nahanni Indians. McLeod led his party up the South Nahanni and into the Mackenzie Mountains.

The details of McLeod's winter journey have been lost. We do know, however, that although he passed through rich beaver country, the journey was a failure. He met no Nahannis, an unfortunate consequence of bringing Fort Liard (Slave) Indians on the trip; the Nahanni Indians remained in their lairs, wary of a party containing their enemies. McLeod retraced his steps in disappointment. On the sixth of March he arrived back at Mackenzie River Forks, but not before he had "suffered considerably from privation—for the natives who accompanied him were no animal hunters."[11]

McLeod's unsuccessful endeavor did not deter the company's desire to open commercial relations with the Nahanni Indians. In April, 1823, the chief trader wrote to Simpson about his failure, but he reassured Simpson that he was not giving up the fight by announcing that he had "appointed Mr. John McLeod to command a party . . . on a voyage of discovery to the westward."[12]

John M. McLeod (no relation to A. R. McLeod) was twenty-nine years old when he reached Mackenzie Forks. Born in 1794 in Lochs, Scotland, he had left his homeland like many another young Scotsman with the hope of finding better prospects in Canada.[13] He joined the North West Company in 1816 and saw service on the Churchill River. John McLeod appears to have been the trader named McLeod who, while stationed at Ile-à-la-Crosse, sacrificed his own supplies to aid the Franklin Expedition. He further helped the explorers by dispatching a canoe to relieve their overloaded outfit.[14]

McLeod had recently spent an interesting winter as Governor Simpson's traveling companion on the long journey from York Factory to Fort Chipewyan. During the arduous days on the trail and around the evening fire McLeod came to know the governor. He learned of Simpson's plans for the Northwest and his dream of pushing the frontier to the shores of the western sea. Simpson, for his part, was favorably impressed with what he saw of McLeod under the revealing conditions on the trail. He described him to A. R. McLeod as "a young gentleman of much promise . . . and I am mistaken if he does not turn out to be a valuable acquisition on your staff."[15] Indeed, it seems that John McLeod may have been Simpson's personal choice to lead the western explorations. In any event, he left the governor early in the spring of 1823 and arrived at Mackenzie River Forks (which was beginning to be known as Fort Simpson) before the ice went out.

From his journals and letters only a cursory outline emerges of John McLeod the man. He was not a man of reflection; in times of despair he would not muse on the fickleness of fate but would strive to alleviate reversals. In that respect he was not like his successor, Robert Campbell, who would turn to Providence for consolation and guidance. John McLeod would as soon be left to his own devices as drag the Almighty into the affair. He would later explain to missionaries, "There is no Sabbath in this country."[16] On the trail McLeod was boss; griping or sullen and mumbled complaints were likely to be treated with a dose of "corporal chastisement." On his 1831 voyage, when he noted "some discontent in the bosoms of some part of our crew," he prescribed just that "medicine." Yet he was wise enough not to embark again the next day in the rain, keeping the men "snug to our encampment" to rest and revive their spirits.[17] This same firm yet flexible disposition marked his dealings with the Indians, with whom a man with an unyielding nature could never successfully trade. McLeod used his firmness to keep relations with the Indians on an even keel; he was respected but not overly aloof. His success can be seen in his impressive trade returns and a record devoid of violent confrontations. McLeod further endeared himself to the Indians by his skill as a woodsman and by his proven abilities as a crack shot and a successful hunter; these qualities were, by necessity, valued highly in the Athabascan Indian culture. Post journals also show him to have been active, more comfortable outdoors maintaining a fort than indoors checking inventories or account books.

Later in his life, while leading Hudson's Bay brigades to the Rocky Mountain Rendezvous, McLeod revealed another side of his personality. Returning from the 1836 rendezvous, McLeod agreed to escort the Whitman Mission party to Walla Walla, Washington. Narcissa, bride of the missionary Dr. Marcus Whitman, had already become the belle of the mountains at the rendezvous. She had won the rough frontiersmen's hearts with her kindness, smiles, and plucky attitude toward the adversities of the trail. John McLeod was attracted to her also. He had her tent ready and waiting as she rode into camp. When Narcissa grew weary of pemmican for breakfast, lunch, and supper, he would hunt up some ducks or grouse or perhaps bring in a mess of fine mountain trout. Around the evening fire he spun tales of his lifetime of wilderness travel. Nevertheless, although he was especially fond of Narcissa Whitman, his conduct was ever exemplary, and his relationship to her was that of a "gentleman to a lady."[18]

The story of McLeod's tenure in the Columbia District, while showing us a very human side of the man, also presents a wrinkle that should be smoothed out. On the return trip from that same 1836 rendezvous William Gray, a young American with the mission party, took sick and could not keep up with the fast-moving Hudson's Bay party. Whatever the illness, it was not serious. After struggling to keep up, the young man could not go on and wanted to rest by the side of a mountain stream. As Gray tells it, "A word from McLeod would have stopped the caravan." When the word did not come, Gray surmised, "My impression of this transaction has always been that McLeod wished to get rid of this young American."[19]

The record should be made clear. At the time when he decided that he "could not keep up," Gray was miles behind the caravan and even farther from McLeod, who was probably at its head. He was in the care of a physician, Marcus Whitman,

Portaging Around a Waterfall. Illustration in Franklin, Narrative of a Journey to the Shores of the Polar Sea in the Years 1819, 20, 21, and 22.

and obviously was not at death's door, for he caught up with the caravan before the end of the day. Gray was not McLeod's responsibility; the caravan was. Narcissa related that Gray eventually made it to camp with the aid of an Indian, probably sent back by McLeod. In reporting the incident, Gray himself neglected to mention the Indian. He was bitter, envious of many, spiteful toward all. He hated mountain men, hated the Whitmans, and hated gentlemen. John McLeod was part mountain man, a friend of the Whitmans, and every bit a gentleman, especially with Narcissa. In all the records I have researched, this incident is the only black mark against John McLeod. If one considers the source of the accusation, it is probably to McLeod's credit that Gray was his enemy.[20]

John McLeod began his first exploration for the company on June 5, 1823. His party consisted of two Canadian voyageurs, a half-blood interpreter, and seven Indian hunters. The expedition was later joined by several other Indians who were recruited en route. Their goal was to ascend the South

Nahanni River (which enters the Liard River just over a hundred miles upstream from Fort Simpson) and establish commercial contacts with the Indians who lived along its banks.[21]

The headwaters of the South Nahanni River reach far westward, almost to the very crest of the Mackenzie Mountains. It is one of the largest tributaries of the Liard River. Unfortunately, the South Nahanni's course through the mountains to the Liard is scarred by frequent rapids and unpassable cataracts—of which the most impressive, Virginia Falls, is actually higher than Niagara. While it is one of the most beautiful rivers in North America, the canyons and hard-driving current of the South Nahanni made the task of pushing west extremely difficult for John McLeod and his voyageurs.

After spending two days trying to push their North canoe upstream, the explorers decided to abandon river travel and proceed overland. Their line of march took them over various kinds of terrain, from swamp lowlands with thick vegetation to the barren, tundralike mountain ridges.

Eventually McLeod made contact with a Nahanni band, who numbered fourteen in all. The Indians were led by a man known as White Eyes, who was "a tall strong and robust built man," according to McLeod, with a beard that reminded him of "an old Roman sage." According to the Fort Simpson Journal, McLeod gave the chief and his band many "wonderful" gifts to whet their appetites and make them regular customers in the future. The gifts included such marvels as mirrors, kettles, axes, knives, fire steel, and vermilion.[22] The Nahannis' friendly reception, however, should properly be credited to two Indians whom McLeod had sent out to scout a few days before. These men had met the Nahannis and no doubt assured them of the Hudson's Bay Company's peaceful intentions.

McLeod was unable to receive much geographic information from White Eyes and his band, but after a second night of singing and dancing he made arrangements to rendezvous with them the following year. Before starting for home, he also "sent five young Indians to the upper part of the Nahanny [sic] River with instructions to make pine canoes and

go downstream, and await my arrival where we left our canoe."[23] After a hot and uncomfortable march the McLeod
party reached Mattson Creek, where the canoe was found in
fine shape. After regumming it, the expedition set out for
Fort Simpson, which they reached on July 10.[24]

When McLeod reached Fort Simpson that July, it was quite
a different place from the bustling establishment he had left
in June. The reason was that, since he had embarked, the
summer brigade had departed. About the middle of June each
year the chief trader of the district would travel down the
Mackenzie to the lower posts, Fort Norman and Fort Good
Hope, to inspect those establishments and to collect the annual fur returns. When he arrived back at Fort Simpson, he
supervised the loading of the Fort Simpson and Fort Liard
returns (which were brought downstream by canoe or boat)
and again embarked, this time for Fort Chipewyan and Portage la Loche. To help speed the brigade in its summer-long
race with fast-closing winter, Fort Simpson was stripped of
every available hand. Hence, the quiet, peaceful atmosphere
that McLeod found at the post.

After leaving Fort Simpson, the brigade headed east, up the
remaining two hundred miles of the Mackenzie and out across
the Great Slave Lake. At Fort Resolution the brigade abandoned lake travel and entered the Slave River. The most trying part of the journey was at Pelican Rapids, where the river
rips through a succession of chutes and falls and drops more
than one hundred feet in sixteen miles.[25] The Mackenzie brigade eventually left the Slave River and entered one of the
great river deltas in North America just northwest of Lake
Athabasca. There the Slave, Peace, and Athabasca rivers come
together, creating a mass of ponds, channels, and backwaters.
As the brigade emerged from the delta's swampy environs, it
arrived at Lake Athabasca and Fort Chipewyan.

At Fort Chipewyan the fur traders deposited the Mackenzie
District's furs and reloaded their boats with a year's supply of
trade goods. During the few days that the Mackenzie men remained at the fort, there was a small-scale reenactment of the
larger rendezvous that was held annually near Lake Winnipeg,

at Norway House or in the Rocky Mountains. There were contests of strength and daring and drinking and gambling; friendships were renewed and acquaintances made.

In 1826 the Mackenzie brigade's itinerary was modified. Governor Simpson, who studied the company's operations, always looking for a more efficient mode of business, eliminated Fort Chipewyan as the Mackenzie District's exchange point in favor of Portage la Loche.[26] This change added an additional two hundred miles to the Mackenzie brigade's summer odyssey, but it spared the voyageurs who were coming north from Norway House the ordeal of the long La Loche portage. That twelve and a half miles had long been the test of a voyageur's mettle. After Simpson's directive the voyageurs seldom had to hike the entire trail; instead, the men coming up the Churchill River packed the trade goods just over halfway across the portage to a point, known as Rendezvous Lake, where they met the Mackenzie brigade. Here the voyageurs exchanged burdens, a bale of furs for a load of trade goods. For the Mackenzie brigade it was the end of a summer-long battle mostly upstream; from Rendezvous Lake to Fort Good Hope it was downstream all the way.

In the summer of 1822, Chief Trader A. R. McLeod was the factor leading the Mackenzie brigade south. When, however, it came time for the boats to head north again, he was not in charge. Edward Smith, a chief factor, was the new master at Fort Simpson. Although some fur traders had accused McLeod of "preposterous and galling use of authority" in managing the district, Governor Simpson assured him that the change was not a reflection on his ability.[27] Chief Factor Smith had been given the position because the company felt that the Mackenzie District "is now so important and extended a charge that the presence of another commissioned gentleman is considered desirable."[28]

In the hierarchy of Rupert's Land the rank of chief factor was the honor most coveted. The select group was limited to twenty-five men, who were full shareholders in the Hudson's Bay Company, occupying a position similar to that of the "wintering partners" of the North West Company. Generally they were senior fur traders who were able, loyal, and long-

CHAPTER 4

Explorations in Northern New Caledonia

THE HUDSON'S BAY COMPANY directed a third probe west-ward in the summer of 1824. This time the expedition was not dispatched from the Mackenzie District. It began in that section of northern British Columbia where the Hudson's Bay Company's Peace River District bordered on the unknown reaches of New Caledonia.

Origin of the Finlay River Expedition

New Caledonia was the fur trader's name for a vast territory that is now the northern and central interior of British Columbia. It had been pioneered in the early nineteenth century by Simon Fraser, who had followed Alexander Mackenzie over the Rocky Mountains. Those Nor'Westers had pushed over five hundred miles up the Peace River to where that river divides into two branches. One branch, the Parsnip River, flows from the south to Summit Lake and the pass between the Peace River system and the Fraser River valley. Like the Mackenzie District, New Caledonia remained the sole domain of the North West Company until the union of 1821. Therefore the land had been spared the ruinous effects of competition and had become one of the Hudson's Bay Company's most valued treasures.

Because of New Caledonia's distant position west of the Rockies and its rough topography, its true extent was un-

known. Great Rivers, lakes, and mountain valleys rich with
fur-bearing animals might be hidden over the mountain
ranges. The unmapped geography of the region held infinite
promise. Particularly inviting was the northern branch of the
Peace River, the Finlay, which had been explored only a short
distance by John Finlay of the North West Company in 1797.
His report had not been sufficiently encouraging for the North
West Company to take further interest in the river. Occasionally bands of roving Iroquois trappers would move up the Finlay, but for practical purposes the fur trade ignored the area.
Governor Simpson changed that indifferent attitude. He saw
the Finlay as a possible avenue to the large river that he expected to find west of the northern Rocky Mountains.[1] After
all, the Peace's southern branch, the Parsnip River, led to the
Fraser River. Perhaps the northern branch, the Finlay, might
also lead to a major river valley.

In January, 1823, the governor assigned Peter Warren
Dease, another former Nor'Wester, to the job of exploring the
Finlay. He was to follow the river to its source in the mountains and then strike out overland until he found either the
great transmountain river described in Cook's and Mackenzie's reports or the sources of the Liard River. That was a tall
order. Peter Warren Dease does not appear to have been eager
to execute it. He produced several delays and excuses in 1823.
First he complained that he had received his orders too late
in the season to prepare properly. Then it was a problem of
inadequate transport upriver. As a result the expedition was
postponed until 1824. Whether Dease's tarrying was legitimate, or he just did not want the mission, is of no consequence. In disappointment Simpson wrote to his superiors in
London that the exploration of northern New Caledonia "has
occupied my attention for these two years but [I] could not
succeed in procuring anyone to undertake it."[2]

George Simpson wasted no time in replacing Dease with a
more active man, Samuel Black. Black was yet another Scot-
tish-born Nor'Wester. Baptized in May, 1770, as an illegiti-
mate child, Black grew to manhood in County Aberdeen. At
the age of twenty-two, having acquired a solid education, he
left his home for Canada.[3] Entering the North West Company

in 1804, he was dispatched to the Far Northwest, where he quickly showed a talent for bullying and harassing the rival traders of the Hudson's Bay Company. Aided by another young Nor'Wester, Peter Skene Ogden, who was a kindred spirit, Black so terrorized the clerks of the "Honorable Company" that they saw his tall, thin frame behind every misadventure. Like a true swashbuckler he went into every fray ready for anything, armed with dagger, sabre, and pistol—even his superiors granted that "Black is certainly a desperate character."[4] He was not just a mere brawler, however; he learned the fur business as well as any man, was a natural leader, and was fiercely loyal to the North West Company.

In 1820, when the North West Company's fortunes were fast shrinking, Black's fiery reputation still burned bright. During his first year on the frontier young George Simpson was warned to be wary of Black on his way to Lake Athabasca, Black's home ground. Simpson put up a bold front and kept on his guard: "I am however armed to the Teeth, will sell my Life in danger as dear as possible and never allow a North Wester [to] come within reach of my Rifle if Flint Steel & bullet can keep him off."[5]

The 1820–21 campaign fell short of such rhetoric. The trade war was heated, but violence was minimal. Even so, Simpson spent the winter apprehensive of what Black might attempt. When a party of Hudson's Bay Company trappers was overdue, Simpson speculated: "Suspicion points to the Villain Black . . . this outlaw is so callous to every honorable or manly feeling that it is not unreasonable to suspect him of the blackest acts."[6]

Three years later Simpson was cocky enough to write that Black "will never forget the terrors in which he was kept that winter."[7] From Simpson's own journal Samuel Black does not appear to have suffered terrors; rather it was Simpson who was constantly on the qui vive, ever wary of what Black might try. Black was like an evil specter, hovering over Simpson's operations the entire winter, wreaking no havoc, only his share of "terrors."[8]

In the spring of 1821 Black received the disastrous news that the North West Company, to which he was devoted, was to be taken over by the despised Hudson's Bay Company. George Simpson, his former foe and his junior in experience, was to command the Northern Department, while Black, Peter Skene Ogden, and another irreconcilable, Cuthbert Grant, were not even afforded a place in the new company. As Black retired from the Northwest at the age of forty-one, his old comrades presented him with a ring engraved with the sentiment "To the most worthy of the Northwesters."[9]

What he did for the next year is a mystery. Perhaps that in itself concerned the Hudson's Bay Company, for men as experienced as Black and Ogden could be potential rivals in the fur trade, while as members of the company they could be controlled. With such a view in mind Simpson recommended that Black and Ogden be admitted into the Hudson's Bay Company at the rank of chief trader.[10] It was one of the best moves that Simpson ever made.

It must have been quite an encounter when Simpson and Black met again in July, 1823, at York Factory on Hudson's Bay. The governor saw before him "a Donquixote in appearance, ghastly, raw-boned and lanthorn jawed, yet strong vigorous and active."[11] What fascinated Simpson was the inner character of this adventurer who until recently had been his foe. He thought Black "the strangest man I ever knew. . . . A perfectly honest man and his generosity might be considered indicative of a warmth of heart if he was not to be known to be a cold blooded fellow who could be guilty of any cruelty and would be a perfect Tyrant if he had the power . . . his word when he can be brought to the point may be depended upon."[12] Throughout their interview Black never once looked Simpson in the eye. The governor noted this, perhaps uneasily. In any event, Simpson elected to put some distance between himself and Black, and the Finlay River expedition served that purpose.

Samuel Black could not have been more pleased. He was a student of the history of exploration and familiar with the narratives of North America's great explorers. In his heart he had always harbored the ambition of contributing to geography a record of some unknown part of the continent. In 1823 the possibilities were swiftly diminishing. Therefore the Finlay River expedition suited Black's purposes also.

Black set to the task of preparing for the expedition with his characteristic energy. He spent the winter at Rocky Mountain Portage on the Peace River, where he would have easy access to the "Finlay Branch" when the ice went out in the spring. In addition to shaking down his outfit, he interviewed some of the Iroquois trappers who had traveled on the Finlay and inquired among the natives about the lay of the land west of the Rocky Mountains. Those inquiries stood him in good stead, for, rather than looking for a river that would flow northwest into the Arctic Ocean like the Mackenzie, he heard reports of a river that flowed westward to the Pacific. This information could have brought his quest into line with the realities of geography. He ought to have been searching out the headwaters of the Stikine instead of the Yukon or some imaginary stream.

If Black was getting a clearer idea of what lay beyond the known frontier in the mountains, Simpson seems to have been hopelessly lost among the box canyons and deadfalls of rumors and Indian reports. He gave Black the following orders. After Black had explored the upper Finlay, it was hoped that he would discover the headwaters of a river that paralleled the Mackenzie. Having achieved this, he was to turn east and cross the divide, where it was thought he would meet the headwaters of the upper Liard. He was to follow the Liard until he reached Fort Liard or Fort Simpson, where he and his party were to winter. By that time Black's party would have explored the entire length of one river, discovered the headwaters of a great inland waterway, and, upon crossing the Arctic Slope a second time, would have traveled the entire length of a river whose upper reaches were clothed in mystery. The total distance to be covered was about 750 miles. But that was not all. During the next summer Black, having wintered in the Mackenzie, was to turn back, travel the entire length of the Liard River (against its considerable current) and recross the Arctic Slope. Then he was to explore the great transmountain river (which existed only in rumor) to its mouth, pre-

sumably to the Arctic—"the Frozen Ocean will be the boundary of your researches to the North West."[13] The total distance
to be traveled was at least 1,500 miles, not a bad summer's
work.

All that was quite preposterous. Perhaps even Simpson realized it in his less exuberant moods. His orders were an example of the tendency that men have to imagine watercourses in
the unknown, map out terrain in lands yet undiscovered, and
give detailed advice to explorers venturing into areas beyond
the ken of even the wisest. In addition to Sir Alexander Mackenzie's report of a rumored river on the west and a few gar-
bled translations of confirmations of it by the mountain Indians, Simpson was basing nearly all his orders upon pure
conjecture. Such reasoning can be very persuasive: one has
merely to imagine the unknown in terms of what has already
been explored. For example, the quest for the Northwest Passage was sustained by the knowledge that a pathway was open
on the south, the Strait of Magellan; it was assumed that there
must be a similar route on the north. Geographers and explorers were also certain that a great river existed on the west, a
sister to the East's Saint Lawrence, which would open a trail
to the interior from the Pacific. Such imaginary geography was
based upon a sense of proportion and a balanced view of
physiography. Simpson ignored Sir Alexander Mackenzie's belief that the transmountain river flowed to the Pacific because
he knew that the Mackenzie, the great river of the North,
flowed into the Arctic Ocean and that its valley spread out on
a north-south axis; he believed that, if a great waterway lay
across the mountains, it would drain those mountains' waters
north, like the Mackenzie, to the Hyperborean Sea.

As the expedition prepared to set out in the spring of 1824,
Samuel Black and George Simpson had two completely different visions of what would be found north of the Finlay River.
Black thought that he would come upon the sources of a
Pacific-bound stream, while Simpson hoped that the expedition would discover a great Arctic-bound waterway. Perhaps
because of the personal differences between them, or merely
because of slow communications, the explorer and the sponsor
never straightened out this confusion.

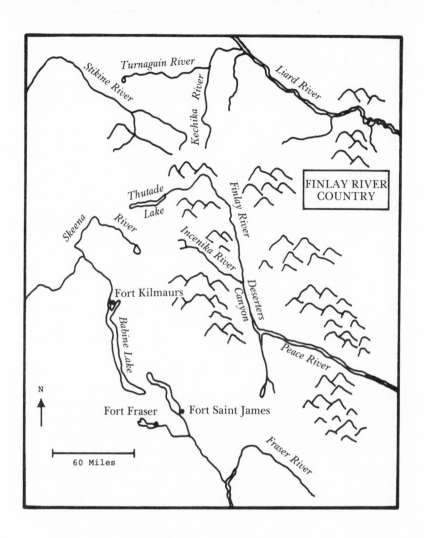

Turnagain River
Stikine River
Kechika River
Liard River
Thutade Lake
Skeena River
Finlay River
FINLAY RIVER COUNTRY
Incenika River
Deserters Canyon
Fort Kilmaurs
Babine Lake
Peace River
N
Fort Fraser
Fort Saint James
60 Miles
Fraser River

Finlay River Expedition

With Simpson's orders in hand, Black set off up the Finlay
River in the spring of 1824. His crew consisted of six voyageurs; an interpreter, who brought along his wife; and a clerk,
Donald Manson. From the time when they first entered the
Finlay, their North canoe felt the river's strong, steady current
nudging the birchbark with its silty water. Collections of driftwood, weathered logs, and uprooted trees gathered at the
mouths of the Finlay's feeders and at the heads of dry channels. The dense, tangled undergrowth of the forest pressed in
on the explorers and confined them to the stream, contributing to the Finlay's depressing impression.

The expedition's first major hurdle came at a difficult canyon where the Finlay is constrained by sandstone cliffs, creating a white-water hazard that renders upstream progress all
but impossible. To an old Nor'Wester like Black the word
portage had the hateful sound of surrender; he had to look
over the eddies and whirlpools a couple of times before he
would allow a portage trail to be cut. The party made camp
at the entrance to the canyon, and Black assigned two men to
the night watch. When morning came, the exploring party
was minus two canoemen; Louis Ossin and Jean Bouche, the
night watch, had deserted. Black was in a rage. The deserters
not only had robbed him of two strong backs but also had
plundered the expedition's food supplies. Black called together the remainder of his men and told them, as he recorded
in his journal, "that I expected better things from those that
remained; but if they had any plot to put a stop to the Voyage, they ought now to declare themselves, for that my determination was to get a sight of the Country pointed out by the
Concern, alone with the natives should I be reduced to such
an alternative."[14] The men responded heartily to Black's determination, and the party crossed the portage. The spot has
ever since been known as Deserters Canyon.[15]

On both east and west as they inched up the river, the explorers could see the dark-hued images of distant mountains.
On the east lay the Rockies, while on the west were the auxiliary ranges of the Coastal Mountains. The Finlay is flanked

by these dominating shadows for close to 150 miles, and it flows through a deep trough between them. This extraordinary geographic feature is known as the Rocky Mountain Trench; from Montana to the Liard River the great valley stretches nine hundred miles.[16] Where the Finlay flowed through the trench, passage upstream, though by no means easy, was just a matter of persistent effort. As Black put it, "by the united efforts of all hands," they managed to push up the unknown river, averaging about twelve miles a day.[17]

By the first of June the party had traveled about fifty miles above Deserters Canyon to a point where the Finlay veers westward and cuts a passage through the mountains of the cordillera. Black could see the river pouring through a gap surrounded by "high broken cliffs completely covered with snow."[18] The voyageurs knew that that meant rapids ahead.

To make matters worse for the explorers, they were suffering from unseasonably bitter weather. Snow, freezing rain, and frigid temperatures are considered bad spring weather even in the Northwest. This would have meant hardship for any party crossing the wilderness and sleeping out in the open, but it was felt all the more acutely because the voyageurs spent so much of their time in and out of the water. As they arose each morning, their buckskin trousers would still be damp, and in the frigid air their muscles, stiff and tired from weeks of work, would painfully protest the start of another day. Shivering, the crew was eager to push off, for paddling would at least stir some warmth into their bones. Then they would begin the frequently rehearsed ordeal of jumping into the arctic water, perhaps waist-deep, to prevent the canoe from being dashed against the rocks at a landing, or laboring along the bank with a towline, dodging the overhanging branches of alder bushes, stumbling over submerged rocks, pulling the canoe upstream. It is not surprising that Black heard his "men complain of numbness in their Arms their hands & wrists swelled & Galled by the Snow Water."[19]

Fourteen days and forty-five miles of such pain brought them to calm water. After the roar of the rapids the uneasy calm and the heavy, soundless air that hung over the river must have seemed eerie. The Finlay was at least temporarily

out of the mountains and flowing through a spacious valley. The landscape was much more open than on the lower
river, though low and swampy. Meadows of tall wild grasses
stretched along the river, broken by small duck ponds or
larger shallow, reed-choked lakes.[20] From Iroquois reports
Black knew this to be the section of the river known as the
Fishing Lakes. The area proved true to its name, as the explorers came upon some Sekani Indians netting fish along the
river.

The Sekani Indians were a miserable tribe who spent their
lives in the quest for fish, game, and roots, always on the
cutting edge of survival. Black, who lacked any genuine com-
passion for the rugged conditions in which these Native Americans lived, referred to the Sekanis as "these phlegmatic sheep-
ish looking Gentlemen." Their poverty, in Black's eyes, was
their own fault; he claimed that the Sekani "cares little about
tomorrow & [is] so lazie & indolent he will not move a step
when once his actual necessities are acquired."[21] At the same
time Black sized up the fur potential of the region, which
was not promising. He reported that the Sekanis' hunting
grounds "can by no means come under the denomination of a
Beaver Country in the common acceptance of the word on the
Waters of Hudsons Bay & Mackenzies River."[22]

The discouraging fur prospects of the upper Finlay did not
in any way reduce Black's determination to proceed as ordered to the river's source and beyond. He arranged with the
chief of the Sekanis, an old man whom he called Methodiates,
to rendezvous with the explorers at the source of the Finlay,
from which place Methodiates would guide them overland to
the northwestward. As they again began to push their canoe
upstream, the explorers were only about fifty miles from the
river's source, Thutade Lake.

Between Black and the lake were some of the worst rapids
on the Finlay River. The captain of the North canoe, when it
was in rapids, was the Iroquois foreman, or bowman, Joseph
La Guarde. It was his duty to map out the craft's route
through white water. La Guarde, though very skillful in a
rapid, was a cautious man by nature. He not only had once

made a vow not to drown in a rapid but also felt severely a responsibility for the canoe's safety. Black was of a much more daring nature, and by this time in the voyage he had begun to lose patience with his contentious canoemen. When they came to a rather treacherous rapid, where the Finlay is divided in midstream by a wooded island and is forced into two very small channels, La Guarde called a halt in order to investigate a safe passage. Black looked over the rapid and, probably slightly piqued at La Guarde's action, remarked in his journal, "The lofty brakers dancing majestically in the Sun beams before us have begun to dance in La Guards brain."[23]

Matters between Black and La Guarde came to a head four days later. At that time the expedition was within reach of the Finlay's source, with only one obstacle in the way. Black described it thus:

The River which falls 80 feet heavily over the smooth extended Bank with a hollow noise like distant Thunder . . . looks like a thin white sheet . . . the shelf part of the water fall is precipitated, oozing through the mass by small perforations & the whole body thus precipitated slowly recovering takes a second tumble into the Basin, at one part the water having freer Scope boils up furiously giving the Idea of the D——ls cauldrons.[24]

Black marked out a short portage past only the very worst of the rapid, figuring that his voyageurs could work the canoe up the rest of the white water. Unknown to Black, La Guarde also went ahead and blazed his own portage route, over three miles long, avoiding all dangerous water.

That night at camp Black did not press the matter, perhaps hoping that La Guarde would give up his planned portage. The next morning he found his "foreman being a little perverse & still talking about his Portage . . . having had a little too much his own way which may not answer in the future, I took this occasion to tell him some truths."[25] Few men could stand eyeball to eyeball with Samuel Black and remain defiant. La Guarde was no exception. He abandoned his portage and asked for a new towline for the canoe. Black had made his point; he was the boss. La Guarde soothed his wounded pride by muttering that "he was afraid of nothing living or of anyone, which if designed for me [Black] I was pleased to take no notice of."[26]

The next day, June 23, was one of celebration. As the canoe slipped into Thutade Lake, the exploreres "bade adieu to all the currents rapids shallow shelves Cascades & Falls in Finlays Branch."[27] Before them stretched a beautiful mountain lake, sixteen miles in length, yet only a mile in width. They had reached the source of the Finlay River, which also happened to be the source of the Peace River. In fact, Thutade Lake is the ultimate source for the entire Mackenzie River system. From that mountain sanctuary the lake's waters had a 2,362-mile journey to the Arctic Ocean.

The expedition had achieved its first goal, navigation of the Finlay River. Before them the explorers still had their secondary mission, their nebulous orders to proceed northwest toward the Arctic. Before embarking on so arduous a journey, Black elected to rest his crew and restock their provisions. This would also give the June sun a chance to melt the snow that the Sekanis claimed would block the mountain passes.

The expedition rested until July 8. Much of their time was spent fishing and hunting. They had particularly good luck hunting caribou. On one occasion Black spotted "5 young Rein deer frisking in the Lake near shore." This was too good an opportunity to pass up, and the traders plotted to get all five. Black dispatched two of his men to circle through the woods and prevent the caribou from escaping to land. Then with their hatchets ready the voyageurs in the canoe descended upon the unsuspecting beasts. The men on shore with rifles dispatched those who fled up the beach, while the men in the canoe had quite a chase before they could catch the caribou in the water. In fact, two of the caribou, panic-stricken and swimming like dolphins, nearly reached the other side of the lake, a mile away, before the hungry traders sunk their hatchets into the necks of the helpless stags.[28] There was meat aplenty, and Black ordered scaffolds erected to dry it over low fires. He also supervised the construction of two very strong caches; he wanted supplies to be laid up for their return journey, safe even from the wily wolverine, "the Most destructive animal in the Country."[29]

Black was in high spirits when they finally set out overland. Almost two months of hard travel had gone by since they had initially set out, but the Scotsman, who had read so much of the exploits of great explorers, was still keyed up by the idea of leading his own party into "the Bonny Glens of the Rocky Mountains." His brigade was a cosmopolitan crew, including English, Iroquois, French-Canadian métis, and Sekani men and women. When Black heard the babel of a half dozen different dialects and languages, it brought to mind "a set of itenerant Gipsies squabbling in their drunken fates."[30] What Black labeled squabbling may actually have been muttered oaths and groans, for the men labored with packs of 120 pounds, not to mention their personal gear. Black and Donald Manson did not feel the leather straps biting into their shoulders (or the tumpline burrowing into their foreheads), for their packs weighed a mere fifty pounds. There were certain advantages to being a "commissioned gentleman" in Rupert's Land.

The first two days back on the trail were marred by rain. The explorers made a difficult crossing of a small rapid-choked river by building rafts. From before dawn until dusk they marched on. The Sekanis lagged behind and griped about their burdens, while the sturdy voyageurs with "patient indurance" shouldered "the hated Loads" and set the pace. One can only admire the steady, methodical way in which the voyageurs went about their duties, even on land. On a particularly mild morning Black had "involuntarily indulged an hour longer than usual in morpheus chains"; in other words, he overslept. Looking about him, when he awoke, he found only Donald Manson; the rest of the camp was gone.[31] Had they deserted him? Not at all; the voyageurs had merely wakened at the usual time, packed up camp, and continued forward, carefully marking their trail so that their leaders could catch up when they chose to awake. What more could Black ask?

After a week of travel the Hudson's Bay men reached a

small mountain lake, where they met up with Methodiates. The chief had gone ahead to make contact with a neighboring Tahltan band, the Thloadennis, into whose lands the explorers were soon to enter. A council was arranged, and on July 15, in the twilight of a subarctic evening, a group of fifteen Thloadenni braves approached the lakeshore encampment. The strange tribe "arrived slowly singing harmoniously . . . dressed in their best apparel for the occasion." They were resplendent in white leggings embroiderd with porcupine quillwork. With their stout chests and strong shoulders bare, save for the long strands of their black hair, and with their heads crowned by an array of feathers, they looked the embodiment of the natural man. Their first stop was at the tent of Methodiates, who was "also in state to receive them with his War Cap on." The old chief joined the savage entourage as it moved toward Black's camp.[32]

The explorers had prepared the council grounds, over which flew the Hudson's Bay Company's scarlet ensign, the standard of the British Empire in the Rocky Mountains. Black greeted the Thloadennis like proper gentlemen "by shaking Hands & this mode of salutation they returned very awkwardly after giving the left hand in a Bear like manner."[33] With the introductions aside, Black gave each of the red men a plug of tobacco, and the council began.

Black made the first speech, giving the Thloadennis a history lesson. He spoke of how the fur trade had expanded into New Caledonia and told them that the two great warring parties, the Hudson's Bay Company and North West Company, were now "formed into one & one & the same People & that we were now come to see if there were any of their relations hereabout, pitiful & in want of a Kettle and a Gun a Hatchet a Knife or Fine Steel." All the good traders wanted in return were animal furs, beaver and marten, and information about the lay of the land and the course of rivers. Black also gave them a warning "to tell no lies, for the White People hated Liars."[34]

The Thloadennis marked what Black said and told the truth, but their replies to his questions were discouraging. In spite of their noble appearance—they were much more impressive than the Sekanis—the Thloadennis lived a precarious existence. Their homeland was the upper slopes of the rugged Stikine Plateau. They lived in fear of another Tahltan band, whom they called the Trading Nahannis. The latter were strong and populous and enjoyed an easy life on the banks of a large westward-flowing river, amply supplied with migratory salmon. They were all the more powerful because of secure trade contacts with white men along the Pacific Coast, whom Black took to be Russian traders. The Trading Nahannis, armed with rifles and an abundance of ammunition, harried the Thloadennis, keeping them from the salmon waters and forcing them into a wretched condition.[35]

So fearful were the Thloadennis of the Trading Nahannis that they refused to guide Black farther into the interior. They told Black that they were at war with the Trading Nahannis and would not risk venturing into their territory. The fur trader tried to explain to "these wild men of the Mountains" how the Hudson's Bay Company viewed the world:

War amongst Indians did not stop our Business from going on & would not in the present case stop me, that we had never done anything to the Nahannies, that if I saw them I would be kind to them and give them some of our Goods if pitiful & in want: if I found them bad Dogs & wished to quarrel with us; we would kill them, that we had Guns & Pistols Powder & Ball as well as the Nahannies & never all slept at one time in the Night, that we had come here to see the Lands & would not turn back on conjecture that the Nahannies would kill us.[36]

The Thloadennis were stirred by this bravado, but not enough to change their minds.

The expedition spent nine days among the Thloadennis, resting and restoring both their bodies and spirits. For the former there was caribou, ground-squirrel, and rabbit meat, while for the latter there were lovely "Thloadenni Sylvan Nymphs," fine "in shape & appearance, light and tripping, [possessing] a soft melodious voice with a timerous kind of underside look that says much without intending it."[37] Black also managed to secure information concerning a westward-flowing river, called the Schadzue, which was described as a mighty stream leading to the ocean and to a white man's fort.

On July 25 the explorers were again on the trail. Though they had failed to secure Thloadenni guides, Methodiates and his Sekani braves remained with the party. They followed a winding trail through the mountains, which Black called the Thloadenni Road. Such a flattering description hardly matches what he had to endure. Even Black, whose colorful pen was usually ready for any detail, could only note wearily at the end of a day, "[We] came through Roads passing description often to the knees in moss & water entangled in under Wood &c."[38]

That day had been too much for La Prise, Black's métis interpreter and chief hunter. At one point he begged Black to turn back, complaining "that he did not expect such a country" and that after the many hardships of the journey "he was knocked up & not able to walk & impossible to go any farther."[39] Black agreed to slow down the pace for the limping La Prise, but refused to turn back. Much more disabling for La Prise than a swollen ankle was his wife, who was "very much alarmed" with the reports of the Trading Nahannis. It seems that she kept "plaguing him" to turn back.[40] Finally, on July 27, La Prise capitulated to his wife and deserted the party, beginning the long trail home. Black's expedition had the dubious distinction of being the first in the history of the Far Northwest to lose a man to the rigors of a woman's tongue.[41]

On the heels of La Prise's departure Methodiates and his Indian packers also decided to head for home. They were far from their usual haunts and had no taste for the arduous service that Black was exacting. Black was able to induce one of the Sekanis, "the Old Slave," to remain with the explorers for another ten days. Their line of march was serpentine; first up along the tundra-topped slopes of high mountains, then down the tree-covered hills into the alder-choked valleys and swampy morasses. Black was trying to steer clear of both the Liard River drainage on the northeast and the Pacific-flowing streams that were blocking his passage. He was searching plaintively for the water communication that Governor Simpson had said would lead north.

It was unfortunate that Black and Simpson were not in closer communication before the start of the voyage, for Black kept running into branches of feeders of the Schadzue, the large Pacific-bound river of which he had heard before the voyage. It was also the river by which the Russians through the Trading Nahannis were draining furs from British North America. Had Black, who had already surmounted epic hurdles, been free to explore this river, which is now called the Stikine, he might have opened a great trade area to the British and dealt a deathblow to the Russian American Company. The name of Samuel Black would now stand with those of David Thompson, Simon Fraser, and Jedidiah Smith. This was not to be only because of Black's precarious status as a sheep recently let back into the fold of the Hudson's Bay Company. His relationship with the man in charge was strained, and he was bound by clear orders and in no position to violate them. As a result he ignored the westward-flowing Schadzue and continued "to the Northwestward." Because he did so, the Hudson's Bay Company was denied for ten years the key to the fur trade of the Pacific Northwest. The Schadzue, or Stikine, River is only a thin blue line on a modern map, but in the nineteenth century it determined the balance of empires.

Though Black missed his chance at greatness as an explorer, his journey must be recognized as a triumph of human strength. The expedition kept pushing deeper into country that even today defies the railroad builders and roadmakers. The crew's hardest problem was crossing the rivers and streams bound for the Pacific that intersected their line of march, but the voyageurs rose to those challenges admirably. Black said of one of them: "Perrault swims like a Duck & dashes in at the first place come to hand & the others not wishing to appear less adventurous follow the example & may some day drown some of us."[42] On another occasion Black resourcefully led his men across a swiftly flowing stream by forming a human chain, arm in arm.

Such zeal was too much for "the Old Slave," who, after his ten days were up, was quick to head for home.

Then only the bourgeois and his voyageurs remained. On

August 13, as they crossed the Pacific-Arctic Divide, they came upon an Indian hunter. He was bold enough to enter the explorer's camp, but, when he went back to fetch the rest of his band, his courage left him. The whole group panicked into headlong flight, fearful of contact with strangers. In the Indians' camp Black found a few signs of white contact: a button, a file, and a scalping knife, all of English manufacture. They waited a day, hoping the Indians would return. Although he was near the end of his strength, Black's pen was as lively as ever,

We are here camped on a sandy eminence or mount rising in the Valley covered with dwarfish Pines and moss & one of the most romantic sequestrations imaginable, the evening is fine calm & serene & clear moon light & the solitude of this Nocturnal scene is only interrupted by the lonely howl of the Indian Dogs prowling about the mountain sides in anxiety for their masters.[43]

The romantic scenery was not what the company wanted to find. It was not as valuable to trade as a major river valley would have been nor as important as a new beaver territory.

The entire area that Black had traversed, from the source of the Finlay River to his camp in the Cassiar Mountains, was poor beaver country. It lacked the extensive meadows, or stretches of flat land, that attract large populations of the furry dam builders. Furthermore, this massive stretch of country was very thinly inhabited by people. Black came across few signs of Indian encampments and met even fewer Indian hunters. Each day that they marched, Black was hit harder by the realization that this country, no matter how wild or how beautiful, was of limited value to the fur trade.

On August 17 Black and his companions found themselves on the banks of a large eastward-flowing river. Black was perplexed; he had taken care to keep his line of march out of the Liard River drainage, and yet here before him was an eastward-flowing stream. From his projected longitude and the river's direction he was forced to acknowledge that he had fallen upon a feeder of the Liard River. The river was a tributary of the Kechicka River, which enters the Liard near the turbulent Grand Canyon. The discovery of the river slammed the door in the face of the expedition: if the Liard River was on the north, Black was not near to any great Arctic-bound waterway. Either the great transmountain river did not exist, or its sources were north of the Liard.

After a short conference the explorers agreed to turn back and retrace their steps toward the Finlay River, rather than descend the as-yet-unexplored Liard River to the company's posts in the Mackenzie District. The short summer season was swiftly winding down; autumn would soon be upon them. Black bitterly dubbed the river that marked his farthest progress, the Turnagain River.[44] The return journey was dispatched with efficiency by the explorers, who after months on the trail were able to handle the rigors of travel almost mechanically. At the end of September, Samuel Black was back in the relatively civilized world of the Hudson's Bay Company's Peace River posts. Behind him was the hazardous and exciting existence of the explorer's life, while before him stretched the comparatively mundane existence of a fur trader.

Results of the Finlay Expedition

Black's findings were soon before Governor Simpson. The expedition's primary goal had been geographic discovery: "to promote science" and to discover west of the Rocky Mountains a river running parallel to the Mackenzie. All that Black had seen tended to deny the existence of such a river. Simpson failed to appreciate the significance of Black's discovery of the Stikine River. Although knowledge of this large river valley would have done much to explain geographically the river systems of the interior and to open to the Hudson's Bay Company the exposed flank of their Russian rivals, it was largely ignored. Simpson had his mind set on finding a western sister to the Mackenzie, and in 1824 he failed to appreciate the Stikine. The expedition's secondary purpose had been to "encourage mercantile speculation" by opening new frontiers to the fur trade. In this too the company was disappointed. Black's journal revealed that the northern part of New Caledonia was a poor country inhabited only by a small group of Stone Age tribesmen. Simpson noted that "a few active trappers might make tolerable hunts," but the area held no great promise.[45]

In fact, Samuel Black's whole journey was an exercise in negative discovery. He had traveled hard and far, only to have the company eliminate the country north of the Peace River from its plans for expansion. Governor Simpson granted that Black and his voyageurs had blazed their trail through "perhaps as rugged a country as ever was passed,"[46] but that was all that Simpson granted. After over five months of exploration Black and his men did not earn the company's approbation or the governor's appreciation.[47]

Failure of Further Exploration in New Caledonia

Governor Simpson's plans to expand the trade of New Caledonia into the Far Northwest entailed more than Samuel Black's Finlay River venture. Like Black's exploration the other ventures met with frustration and disappointment. It seemed in 1824 that all of the governor's plans for New Caledonia were doomed to failure.

South and west of the Finlay River country was a large yet narrow mountain lake. This clear body of water, which was not unlike a Scottish loch, was known as Babine Lake. In 1822 the company dispatched Chief Trader William Brown, an officer in the company since the union in 1821, to extend the fur trade to the Babine's shores. Near the north end of the lake Brown erected Fort Kilmaurs, which was named after the parish in which he had been christened in Ayrshire, Scotland.[48]

The location of Fort Kilmaurs was superb. Unlike so many of the posts in New Caledonia, it was well provided with foodstuffs. Large sockeye salmon, with their firm pink flesh, ascended to Babine Lake annually. Well-placed nets yielded catches that more than met the needs of the fur traders stationed there. The traders often exported the surplus to their less fortunate brothers at nearby Fort St. James and Fort St. George. The welcome presence of salmon alerted the fur traders that Babine Lake was connected to the sea. Flowing northward from the lake was the Babine River, a clear stream with a swift current and, to the fur traders, an intriguing destination. From reports of Indians they learned that the Babine continued to flow northwest until it joined a river known to-day as the Skeena, which emptied its waters into the Pacific Ocean. The same Indians rendezvoused with the coastal tribes, who every year journeyed up the river to exchange Russian or American guns and hatchets for beaver pelts.

Chief Trader Brown mulled over these reports, and he and Governor Simpson tried to speculate on the significance of what the Indians described. There was some thought that the Babine River might flow far to the northwest and be, in fact, the nonexistent Cook's River. Samuel Black suggested that possibility, though his own discoveries militated against its likelihood, and though Captain George Vancouver had proved in 1794 that Cook's River was merely an inlet of the sea.[49] John Stuart, a veteran of New Caledonia since Simon Fraser's days, thought that the Babine River eventually flowed into the Pacific Ocean at the Portland Canal, the present boundary between British Columbia and the Alaskan panhandle.[50] In general, the Hudson's Bay Company was confused about the Babine country.

The most obvious way to clear up the confusion was to outfit an expedition to descend the river to its mouth. In 1824 the Council for the Northern Department (that is, Simpson and his chief factors) ordered Brown to embark downstream to settle the geographic question and to crush the trade system of the coastal Indians.[51] Unfortunately, although the council proposed, God disposed (an idea that Simpson sometimes found hard to accept). The northern New Caledonia and Peace River areas were beset by a series of setbacks, some petty and others tragic, that prevented the exploration from taking place.

In the summer of 1823 two of the company's servants attached to Fort George were killed in a scuffle with the local Indians. This caused a brief panic at several New Caledonia posts, and Fort George was temporarily abandoned in retaliation.[52] Fort Saint John on the Peace River was even harder hit. The aggressive Beaver Indians murdered five of the company's servants before rifling the fort. Here again the fur traders were forced to abandon the post and strengthen their remaining establishments. Even Samuel Black's Finlay River voyage was nearly postponed. Some traders thought that it was too risky to send a small party into the hinterland and that Black would be a good man to have around if there was to be any more Indian trouble.[53] Coming as they did in the same year, these were severe blows to the company's very existence, which depended upon amicable Indian relations.

The Indian disasters rekindled some other problems. New Caledonia had never been a popular posting among the fur traders. It was a hard, rough country to travel through, and, once one was located in a post, the situation was seldom comfortable. The diet consisted mainly of dried salmon, which after a year or two became tiresome. Big game animals, such as moose or caribou, which might have provided fresh meat, were seldom found in the area. Even the salmon were erratic in their migrations, and, when they failed to ascend the Fraser River as far as the trading posts, starvation became a real threat. One historian referred to New Caledonia as the Siberia of the fur trade—a place where misbehaving employees could improve their character in the hard conditions of the country.[54] When Indian attacks were added to their hardships, the traders let their dissatisfaction be known.

Exploration was also handicapped by New Caledonia's chronic personnel shortages. In 1822 the entire district could boast no more than thirty-six servants and eight gentlemen.[55] Although Governor Simpson wanted expansion and exploration, a critical part of his strategy was also "Oeconomy," or frugality in handling the company's expenditures. He would eagerly order his men to push forward, but often, in the same breath, he curtailed the very means that would have enabled them to do so. Thus Indian trouble, employee dissatisfaction, supply difficulties, and personnel shortages all stalled further expansion in New Caledonia.

As the winter of 1824–25 descended on the Northwest, the fur traders had a chance to assess the accomplishments of the first two years of the company's expansion program. In the Mackenzie District, John McLeod and Murdock McPherson had begun to explore the Liard River. Since the Liard carves a passage through the northern Rocky Mountains, it seemed to offer the best prospects for westward expansion in New Caledonia. Contact had been established with the Nahanni Indians, most of whom reportedly dwelt along the upper Liard. Prospects therefore were very bright for expanding the trade in that region.

If relations between Governor Simpson and Samuel Black had not been so strained, Black's expedition might have opened the trade of the Stikine River to the company. Instead it accomplished very little. The tangled terrain that Black traversed, the poverty of the tribes whom he met, and the difficult access to the area persuaded the company to close the book on the Finlay River region. Black's survey of the region between the Finlay and the Liard rivers failed to uncover any trace of the great transmountain river that the fur traders, from Alexander Mackenzie to George Simpson, had expected to find west of the Rocky Mountains. The explorers were forced to conclude that, if such a river did exist, it had to be north of the Liard. Thus Black's expedition further increased the importance of the Liard in the company's future plans.

The fur traders realized that the explorations of 1823 and 1824 amounted to little more than a glimpse of the vast tracts of wilderness that lay beyond their ken. With the restlessness of energetic men, they shared the frustration that Samuel Black had expressed in his journal, as his eyes searched over the distant hills: "I wish I had wings to go & see."[56] That was for the hawks and eagles; as they gently floated on the winds' currents, they might see stretched before them the rivers, lakes, and trails that would later lead the Hudson's Bay Company into the Yukon and Alaska, the vast fur empire of the Far Northwest. Unfortunately, the Hudson's Bay Company would struggle through the deadfalls and defiles of a long and treacherous path before it reached the threshold of that empire, and in 1825 it had only begun to blaze the way.

Although exploration promised to be lucrative in the future, it also provided an ominous warning. As the Hudson's Bay Company reached into the Northwest, it was entering the domain of the Russian Bear. Both John McLeod and Black

had heard reports of Russian settlements, and the company
could see the material evidence that native middlemen carried
inland from distant tribesmen. As the fur trade pushed at the
geographic frontiers, it was also crossing an international frontier and entering a diplomatic rivalry.

The Coastal Trade

The Hudson's Bay Company did not learn the importance of
the Stikine River to the fur trade of the Far Northwest until
nearly ten years after Samuel Black's Finlay River expedition.
In 1824, Governor Simpson had no detailed knowledge of the
trade routes along the Northwest Coast. He suspected that the
Russians and the Americans were draining furs from the interior of British America, but he was not well informed about
his rivals' methods.[57] Because the company's operations were
restricted to the continent's interior, its officers were ignorant
of the geographic and commercial realities of the coastal
region.

This situation was changed by the Anglo-Russian Convention of 1825. The negotiations with the Russians excited the
company's interest in maritime operations. George Simpson,
however, had begun to plot this reorientation even before the
signing of the treaty. In his 1824 journal he noted that the
expansion of New Caledonia would be matched by an advance up the coast: "The Coasting trade must be carried on
in conjunction with the inland business."[58] This unified policy, balancing the explorations of the interior and the trade
rivalry on the coast, guided the Hudson's Bay Company from
1825 to 1839.

Governor Simpson did not intend to compete with the Russians, at least not initially. His plan was first to drive the
American merchants from the coast and then to let the two
monopolies slug it out (he had no doubts about who would
win the latter struggle). The Hudson's Bay Company began
to outfit ships to join the maritime trade. Their purpose was
to hound the Yankee ships, follow them wherever they went,
and undersell them at every opportunity. Not content merely
to ruin the Americans' fur trade, Simpson also made plans to

take over their profitable supply trade with the Russian settlements.[59]

In 1826, Aemilius Simpson, a Royal Navy lieutenant on half pay, was hired as superintendent of the Hudson's Bay Company's maritime operations. He was a distant relative of Governor Simpson, and the two had been school fellows in England. The governor dismissed any accusations of nepotism by writing, "I should not have introduced Aemilius Simpson to the Fur Trade, had I not known him to be a man of high character and respectable abilities."[60]

Lieutenant Simpson proved himself to be worthy of the governor's trust. He was given command of the small schooner *Cadboro,* and he set about the "dirty work of cuffing & thunking" the collection of "vagabonds" aboard into something resembling a crew.[61] In 1827, Lieutenant Simpson and his men helped erect Fort Langley at the mouth of the Fraser River, the first of a chain of posts that the company planned to establish on the coast south of the Russian territory.

Although operations on the coast were progressing according to plan, Governor Simpson was vexed by troubles inland. In 1827 he complained to the London office, "A succession of dissapointments and misfortunes have year after year prevented our extending the trade of New Caledonia."[62] In 1825, Indian problems had prevented Chief Trader William Brown from descending the Babine River to the ocean. A year later the governor dispatched ten additional men to Babine Lake, and Brown was again ordered to explore the river. Again the expedition never embarked. William Brown took ill, and the voyageurs spent the summer loafing about the lake. Simpson was incensed. If Brown was not up to the task, Simpson complained, "some other Gentlemen attached to the Expedition were surely capable of that duty otherwise they can have no pretensions to the rank and standing they have in the service; indeed we consider that a Trading Clerk . . . is greatly overpaid for his services if not qualified to undertake and accomplish any duty connected with voyaging."[63] The governor censured William Connolly, who shared control of the district with Brown; and Brown was granted a leave of absence for his illness.[64]

The Babine Lake area never achieved the importance that
Governor Simpson hoped for it. The post there shrank in significance after 1827, when Fort Connolly was established fifty
miles northeast of the lake. Fort Connolly was located at
Bear Lake, the source of the Skeena River. The Babine River
turned out to be just one tributary of the Skeena, a large
stream that entered the Pacific just south of the Russian
lisière.

The failure of the inland traders to explore the Babine or
Skeena rivers to the sea was the cause of a great deal of confusion for Lieutenant Simpson. In 1827, while cruising the coast
for furs, he learned from a pair of Yankee shipmasters of an
estuary where the Americans had always enjoyed a lucrative
trade. This was the mouth of the Nass River, which drains a
considerable portion of north-central British Columbia. It was
not then, nor is it now, an important route to the interior.
When Simpson learned of the Nass estuary, he mistakenly assumed that it was the mouth of the Skeena; or, as the traders
called it, the Babine River.[65] Lieutenant Simpson felt that a
post located at the mouth of the Nass would draw furs from
deep within the interior—furs that until recently had been going to the Americans. Investigation by the company confirmed
that "more Land Furs are traded at Nass than at any other
place along the Coast."[66] There was even hope that this might
be the source of all Russia's land furs, for, though the river's
mouth was in British territory, it was within a few miles of
the Russian zone.

The company was particularly interested in the Nass River
for another reason. Of the major rivers flowing into the Pacific from the company's territories, only the Columbia was
navigable for commercial purposes. The company's operations
on the Columbia were compromised by American claims to
that river valley. Simpson would have liked to have had a
route to the interior that was indisputably in English territory. In 1828, on one of his transcontinental tours, he even
investigated the Fraser River as a possible avenue inland. The
old Nor'Westers assured him that it was too wild a stream to
be worth consideration, but Simpson wanted to see for him-

self. The rapids, canyons, and whirlpools that he encountered during his descent might have driven any man mad. The governor's perfect composure allowed no outward show of alarm, although he might have made a mental note to believe it when a Nor'Wester says a river is unnavigable.[67] In any event, he reported to the London Committee, "From my own knowledge of Frasers River, I can positively say, that it never can be made a communication adapted for the purposes of inland transport."[68] His disappointment over the Fraser was mollified by the promise of what the Nass River might hold.

In July, 1830, the Council of the Northern Department ordered Chief Factor John McLoughlin, head of the Columbia District, to establish a trading post at Nass River.[69] Charge of the proposed post was to be given to Peter Skene Ogden, Samuel Black's old companion in devilry. Since he had been readmitted into the company, Ogden had been leading brigades of trappers through the mountains and deserts of present-day Idaho, Utah, and Oregon, stripping the Snake River valley of furs, and exploring the Great Basin. Like Black, Ogden was at his best when left to his own devices, at least semiindependent of his superiors. That had been Simpson's reason for assigning him to the Snake River brigades and for trusting him now with the far-removed post at Nass River.

Although Aemilious Simpson was able to scout out what seemed to be a good location for the post during a voyage up the coast that same summer, Ogden and his men were delayed and did not move up to the Nass River until a year later. A vicious malaria epidemic was sweeping the Columbia River valley. It struck down fifty men at Fort Vancouver alone, Ogden among them. Even Chief Factor McLoughlin, who had studied medicine for four years in Quebec, was pressed into service tending to the sick.[70] Aemilius Simpson and Peter Skene Ogden were not able to embark until April, 1831.

Lieutenant Simpson and Ogden headed an impressive expedition, including over fifty men and three schooners, the *Dryad*, the *Vancouver*, and the *Cadboro*.[71] It took the three little ships more than a month to work their way up the five hundred odd miles of coast to the Nass estuary. Simpson

helped Ogden begin construction of the post before setting
out on an additional exploration to the north, where he had
been ordered to sail into Russian waters and "to examine
Stikine and ascertain if as reported a large River falls into
the ocean at that place."[72] When he reached the Stikine harbor, 140 miles north of the Nass, he found that the estuary
was stained brown with silt and that the mouth of the Stikine
spread out into innumerable channels, which were clogged
with piles of driftwood. Simpson could tell at a glance that the
river drained a large section of the interior. Ignorant of the
inland geography, he guessed that the estuary was the mouth
of the Babine River, not the Stikine.

When Simpson returned to the mouth of the Nass, he found
that the post there was near completion. Unfortunately, the
lieutenant was unable to appreciate what had been accomplished. Bothered by back pains for a couple of days, he barely
had time to tell Ogden of his findings on the Stikine before
he lapsed into a serious illness that turned out to be an inflam-
mation of the liver. With no medical help available he suffered for a few days and then died at the age of only thirty-
eight.[73] In his honor the traders named the post that he had
helped establish Port Simpson.

Ogden was now weighed down with the dual responsibili-
ties of administering Port Simpson and supervising the maritime trade. Chief Factor McLoughlin dispatched Donald Manson, who had been Samuel Black's second-in-command on the
Finlay River, to assist Ogden at Port Simpson. In 1832, Manson made a valuable survey of the lower Nass River. After ascending the stream for four days, he found it an impractical
route for the fur trade. Like the Fraser, it would not be the
company's route to the interior.[74] Again the Hudson's Bay
men turned their eyes farther north, wondering whether the
Stikine—the river that Lieutenant Simpson had discovered on
his last voyage—was the stream that they sought. American
shipmasters told the company that they collected between
three and four thousand beaver furs annually at that river's
mouth.[74] The Stikine was, of course, the same river that Black
had found eight years earlier and called the Schadzue. Although in 1832 it was still unknown to the English traders, it

was to become the goal of the company's expansion, both on the coast and in the interior, during the rest of the decade.

Although Aemilius Simpson's death put a brake at least briefly on the company's campaign along the Northwest Coast, that campaign had been proceeding quite well. The Yankee merchants proved tougher to drive out of business than Simpson had first expected, but inroads were being made. In the early nineteenth century about fifteen American ships had traded along the coast each season, but that number dropped to five or six in the 1830s.[75] As Hudson's Bay Company's competition proved too much for Americans, Governor Simpson felt that it was time to begin the second phase of his attack and capture the Yankees' provision trade with the Russian settlements. Aemilius Simpson had made a preliminary visit to Sitka in 1829 and delivered the company's bid for the provision trade. The Russian governor had merely said that he would pass the note on to Saint Petersburg. The Hudson's Bay Company never did receive a satisfactory answer.

In the spring of 1832, Peter Skene Ogden followed up this initiative. As the *Cadboro* sailed into Sitka harbor, Ogden was met by Russian America's new governor, Baron Ferdinand von Wrangel. A short, active man, Wrangel possessed considerable acumen, as was demonstrated in his scientific and commercial accomplishments, and he drove a hard bargain. He said that the Russians were willing to contract for supplies from the Hudson's Bay Company, but he wanted the goods at "prime cost" and would only pay for them with notes redeemable in Saint Petersburg. Neither Ogden nor McLoughlin was impressed with this counterproposal. The crafty Russian did not appear to be negotiating seriously. It was now the Hudson's Bay Company's turn to smile politely and refer the decision to Europe, or, in this case, the London Committee.[76]

Wrangel was the most astute governor of Russian America from the time of Baranov to the Alaska sale. He had no intention of working with the Hudson's Bay Company in 1832. The American traders remained a nuisance to the Russian American Company, but, as the Hudson's Bay men stepped up their pressure on the Yankees, the Bay traders also put a dent in Russia's trade. Furthermore, Ogden had mentioned the Hudson's Bay Company's interest in the Stikine River area, which greatly alarmed Wrangel. He warned his company's directors in Saint Petersburg:

Although Mr. Aemilius Simpson's sudden death temporarily put a stop to this intention, it is probable that it will not be for long and in a year or two the English will occupy a post there also undoubtedly in prejudice of our own commercial relations with the Kolosh[Tlingit], For the excellent quality and abundance of the merchandise of the English constitute an attraction to the Kolosh which we have no means to compete with, and there is no doubt whatever that if the Board of Directors does not find means to supply the colonies with merchandise of such quality and in such quantity as to be able to hold out against the Hudson Bay Company this company will be in possession of the whole fur trade in northwestern America from Cross Sound or even from a more northern point south as far as the coast of California.[77]

The Hudson's Bay Company was a greater threat than the Yankee skippers had even been. Wrangel was not about to enter into an agreement that would only increase the Bay Company's power on the coast. In 1832 the Russian American Company did not want to replace the scavenging American eagle with the voracious British lion.

Governor Simpson, however, was not going to be so easily put off. Rupert's Land had been under his firm control for over a decade. In that time the man known as "the Little Emperor" had molded the company into a tight, efficient organization. He had laid the groundwork for territorial expansion and forged the successful maritime branch of operations. If the Russians would not cooperate with his plans willingly, then Simpson would use the company's muscle to force them into line. The maritime branch would carry on its offensive on the coast, directing operations toward the Stikine, while in the interior his traders were ordered to redouble their explorations westward toward Russian territory. The British lion was showing its claws.

CHAPTER 5

Up the Liard River Trail

CHIEF FACTOR Edward Smith, commander of the Mackenzie District, needed no encouragement to promote exploration. Since John McLeod's return from the South Nahanni River country in 1824 the district had been the scene of a continuing effort to expand the frontiers of the fur trade. The explorations were directed southwest up the alluring Liard River.

The Hudson's Bay Company followed up John McLeod's efforts among the Nahannis during the very next season. John Bell, a young clerk recently assigned to the Mackenzie District, was dispatched with two men in the summer of 1825 to set up a post among the Nahannis.[1] The establishment was not a notable affair—a bark shack or perhaps a tent cabin— and was probably located somewhere near the junction of the South Nahanni and Liard rivers under the shadow of Nahanni Butte. White Eyes, the head of the Nahanni band, visited the post a couple of times, but trade was minimal. In September, Bell closed up shop and advised White Eyes and his band henceforth to take their furs to Fort Simpson. Smith informed Governor Simpson of the disappointing trade and advised him not to expect much more from that group of Nahannis: "Altho' they inhabit a rich country, their wants few once completed they will not exert themselves."[2]

From 1829 to 1839 the Hudson's Bay Company traders in the Mackenzie District extended their explorations and trade along the entire length of the Liard River—a continuation of the advance begun in 1824. These explorations should be seen as part of the Hudson's Bay Company campaign to capture the trade of the Northwest Coast. As the Russian American Fur Company gradually revealed its unwillingness to cooperate with George Simpson's plans to drive the Yankee merchants off the coast, the Hudson's Bay Company stepped up its pressure on the Russians. A major part of that effort was to cut off in the interior the furs that heretofore had made their way to the Russian *lisière*. The center of this struggle was the Stikine River valley, toward which Peter Skene Ogden was driving from the coast, and which soon was to be the goal of the Mackenzie District traders.

Throughout the spring of 1828, Murdock McPherson, the clerk commanding Fort Liard, was visited by a distant tribe of Indians, whom he called the "Thekannies." By June these hunters had brought in over four hundred beaver, and they requested that the company open up a trading post in their hunting grounds "on the West Branch of the Liard River below the Falls—and in the Mountains."[3] The Thekannis were a branch of the Sekani Indians, whom Samuel Black had encountered along the headwaters of the Finlay River.[4] Chief Factor Smith felt that granting their wish for a post would not only bring the company a greater portion of their trade but also serve as "a beginning to open communication to the Westward of the Mountains—where there is such attractive Proofs of finding a rich Country—the Natives still unacquainted with the whites—and know not to use of European manufacture."[5] Governor Simpson, always interested in schemes to expand the trade, promptly gave his approval to the operation.[6]

Establishment of Fort Halkett

The job of establishing the new post was given to Clerk John Hutchison. This thirty-one-year-old Scotsman was probably not the best choice that Chief Factor Smith could have made. Governor Simpson, notorious for his harsh judgments, thought him "weak delicate and not adapted for severe or active Service."[7] In 1823, Simpson suspected Hutchison of "becoming addicted to private tippling." The governor said nothing to the man, "but appointed him to Mackenzies River where it is impossible to be otherwise than sober as no intoxicating liquor of any description has been admitted into that District since the Year 1824."[8] Perhaps Edward Smith felt that the young man, who had been manipulated in such a petty manner by the governor, deserved a chance to prove himself.

Hutchison left Fort Simpson on June 27, 1829. With four men, an outfit of trading goods, and a North canoe he headed up the Liard River. The original plan of building the post west of the Rocky Mountains had been modified. The Thekannis portrayed the upper Liard as unnavigable and devoid of the big game needed to provision a post. At their request Hutchison was directed to build a post on the East Branch of the Liard, known today as the Fort Nelson River.[9] What the voyageurs called the West Branch, or the Courant Fort ("strong current") , is today the Liard River proper.

Hutchison traveled up the Liard, most of the time tracking the canoe against the current, until three wooded buttes came into view. These hills marked the junction of the East Branch with the West Branch. From the forks Hutchison could look up the West Branch through the clear northern air and see the distant uplifted shadows of the Rocky Mountains.[10] His course lay to the south, however, and the North canoe turned up the East Branch, or Fort Nelson River. Although the river's current was not as strong as the Liard's, travel continued to be tedious. The Fort Nelson wound its way into the interior in broad-looped bends, each meander increasing the frustration of the voyageurs. A half day's paddle brought the Hudson's Bay men to great sandstone cliffs, rising precipitously from the riverbed, a pleasant change from the dense banks of forest that bounded the river's lower stretches. The voyageurs would later call the spot "Roche qui Trempe a l'Eau."[11] Still farther up river they passed the location of old Fort Nelson, abandoned since the Indian massacre of 1812. Hidden by thick shrubbery and trees were the ruins of the North West Company's former post, the all-but-forgotten remains of the first attempt to open up trade on the East Branch.[12]

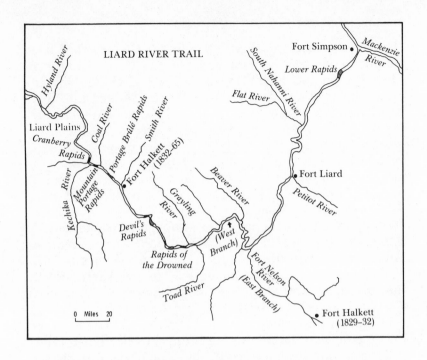

The Hudson's Bay traders continued up the Fort Nelson River for two days after passing old Fort Nelson and then turned to the west up a stream that the Thekannis called the Buffalo River. After two more days of travel up the Buffalo River, Hutchison began building his post.[13] His site was probably in the general vicinity of the present settlement of Fort Nelson on the banks of the Muskwa, or Prophet, River. The new post was named Fort Halkett after John Halkett, one of the more active members of the Hudson's Bay Company's governing committee.[14]

The trade of Fort Halkett never lived up to expectations. The first winter was "severe in the extreme." Many of the Indians were diverted from trapping by the painful necessity of finding enough food to survive the season.[15] In 1830, Chief Factor Smith sent Charles Forester, an enterprising servant of the company, to winter with the Thekannis in their hunting grounds in the Rocky Mountains. Forester was to "incite them to industry," in order to increase their fur harvest, and collect additional information about the transmountain region.[16] The company was heartened by reports that the Indian tribes of the mountain area were planning to visit Fort Halkett. One of those tribes was the "Touchtochoctinne" Indians, who lived west of the Rockies along the upper Liard River.[17]

Nonetheless, Chief Factor Smith was becoming impatient with the vague and often contradictory information that was filtering down to the fur traders from Indian trappers. It was time that the Hudson's Bay Company had a look at its position on the upper Liard River. Edward Smith and John Mc-Leod had spent much time in past years discussing what kind of country might lie hidden west of the Rockies. Smith was a man of broad interests and always had an eye open to advance his knowledge. At Fort Simpson he tried to begin a small natural-history collection, only to be confounded by the lack of means to preserve his specimens.[18] Even though, as he confided to a friend, all that he knew of the upper Liard was "what we can glen from Indian report," he felt sure that in the hunting grounds of the western tribes "the curious traveller would find among them an enexhaustible store of still unknown plants, flowers, Birds, and quadrupeds etc. etc."[19] Smith's interest in the Liard frontier was matched by John Leod's, and, following the lead of his superior and friend, McLeod volunteered to lead an expedition to the source of the Liard River.[20]

Before the expedition was official, Smith had to communicate with Governor Simpson, not only to secure his permission for McLeod's exploration, but to clear up some problems that had hamstrung the Mackenzie District's expansion efforts. Although the Hudson's Bay Company had given its formal approval to the long-term expansion of the Mackenzie District, the means necessary to complete the task were seldom at hand. District commanders, such as Edward Smith, were left with tall orders and limited means to execute them. This tendency crippled the company's expansion efforts because the district commanders' small resources seldom allowed them immediately to follow up any success.

One of Smith's major complaints was the quality of the men who were sent to him. Strong, tough men were needed in the Mackenzie District, and too many of Smith's employees complained when they were assigned to active service.[21] To complicate matters, the good men in the district seldom wanted to renew their engagements. The annual outfit of goods that was sent north to the Mackenzie was so slim that there was little enough for the Indians, not to mention the needs of the company's servants.[22] The severe winters often aggravated this situation, as they caused ration shortages and hardships. The Mackenzie District was not the most popular posting in Rupert's Land.

That was something that George Simpson found hard to understand. In fact, he thought, "MacKenzies River is the most advantageous wintering ground in the Indian Country."[23] Still, he was not disposed to argue with Edward Smith, who was one of his most efficient assistants. He informed him that "all the assistance you may require in men or goods will be forwarded."[24] When it came to McLeod's proposed exploration, Smith and Simpson were of the same mind. Edward Smith wrote, "This voyage may open to the Company a Second Caledonia."[25] Simpson viewed it not only from the vantage point of the interior trade but also for what it might mean to the struggle on the coast:

This would be the first step towards establishing a communication between the Settlement of Nass, which is now about being formed and the interior, and would be the commencement of a District which in due time would deprive the Russian Fur Cop., our rivals in trade on the North West Coast, a valuable branch of their business, to which they have no claim as the greater part of their Land Skins are drawn from British Territory in that quarter.[26]

Simpson gave the expedition his full backing.

Just when all factors seemed to assure the prospect of exploring the upper Liard, plans for the expedition were threatened from an unexpected quarter. The winter of 1830–31 began calmly and from all evidence promised to be a mild one, but, though the thermometer did not reveal any threat to the fur traders, the fur returns did. Inexplicably, there were very few lynx furs that winter, whereas the year before they had been plentiful. That was bad not just for the company's profits but also because the lynx population was closely dependent upon its main prey, the rabbit, and the rabbit was also one of the main foodstuffs for the Hudson's Bay men and their Indian trappers. The disappearance of the lynx was a tip-off to the absence of rabbits and to a winter of hunger and suffering. Austerity became the watchword at Fort Simpson, and food supplies were closely rationed, as the traders tried "to scrape every thing together that we could catch to oust famine."[27] For the Indians the situation was even worse. Although Smith tried to help them by "dividing our little pittance with the needy and unfortunate," eleven Indians attached to Fort Simpson "perished from want of Provisions."[28] Spring brought no relief, only redoubled troubles. Its warmer weather turned every small stream and creek into a rushing torrent. The melting ice on the Mackenzie River could not give way fast enough before this flood, and the water charged over the banks, inundating the countryside. Fort Norman was destroyed and its inhabitants nearly went with it, while John Bell and the men at Fort Good Hope escaped into the flooded woods in a boat.[29]

As the summer began, there was more than enough work in the district merely trying to recoup after the spring's disasters, and the district could not handle an expansion program at such a time. Nonetheless, Smith was determined to have the upper Liard investigated, regardless of other more pressing concerns. An expedition such as those that John Franklin had led would have been impossible because the privations of the winter had prevented any stockpiling of pemmican. For John McLeod and his voyageurs, however, this was no serious matter. They would travel light with just a handful of provisions, a limited collection of trade goods for the Indians whom they might encounter, and their rifles; they would live off the land for much of the voyage. The Hudson's Bay Company's explorations seem much less impressive than the elaborate government-sponsored efforts of John Franklin, George Back, and John Richardson, but they reflected the company's orientation. It was after all a commercial concern, not a geographic society. Its explorers were interested primarily in the fur trade and were interested in geography only insofar as it affected business. Also the unpretentious outfit of McLeod's expedition was admirably suited to the rough terrain to be traversed, where the distance a man could travel was determined by the weight of his burden.

Exploration of the Upper Liard River

McLeod was given permission personally to select his crew from the district's employment rolls, and he drafted six of the company's *engagés* and two Indians as hunters.[30] His "faithful dog," Spring, also joined the expedition. On June 28, 1831, the party pushed off from Fort Simpson, turning the nose of their durable North canoe into the swirling brown current of the Liard River. By July 3 they had reached Fort Liard, where McLeod's old friend Murdock McPherson was no doubt happy to see him. McPherson advised McLeod that the Liard was running high, still swollen from the spring thaw, and that, if he waited a few days, the river would drop and upstream travel would be much more practical.[31] During the week spent at Fort Liard, McLeod had an opportunity to hear for himself what the Indians of the area had to say about the upper river. In an animated style they told him of the Liard's terrors, how dangerous it was, and how its navigation was "insurmountable."[32] McLeod expected that the Liard would be dangerous, but he shrugged off the idea that it was insurmountable as one of "the paliating measures adopted, many from interested motives," by the Fort Liard Indians, who were not anxious to see the trade extended to their neighbors.[33]

On July 10, McLeod was again on his way. The Liard River rolled toward him from the southwest, spilling from the unknown country ahead. In spite of the Indian reports that he had received and what he knew of the lower Liard River, McLeod was probably not prepared for what awaited him. Today we know the Liard River to be one of the great rivers in western North America and one of the more dangerous. Its headwaters lie well west of the Rocky Mountains, about eight hundred miles southwest from Fort Simpson. It has managed, like the Peace River, to force its way through the mountains, but the struggle has left the face of the river scarred by scores

of rapids and canyons.[34] In the late nineteenth century Father
Emile Petitot, missionary to the northern Athabasca Indians
and a noted anthropologist, wrote of the Liard:

All the travellers who have navigated it agree in giving a terrifying
description of its peaks, gulfs, and whirlpools which the velocity
of a current constrained by the rocks makes in its water. To come
down this dizzying river safely metis helmsmen tie themselves to
the deck of their craft so as not to be hurled into the frightful
waves.[35]

The Mackenzie River has often been called the Mississippi of
the North. The Liard may be regarded as the North's equivalent to the Missouri.[36] Physically the Liard and the Missouri
share many characteristics, including principally their driving
currents. Even when free of canyons and rapids, their currents
seldom slacken; they push relentlessly on, sweeping up fallen
trees, ripping away sections of riverbank, frustrating the voy-
ager. The Liard, in its descent to the Mackenzie, drops more
than 1,700 feet, thus enlisting even gravity as a weapon in opposing any upstream progress.[37] Like the Missouri the Liard
became an avenue of western exploration, a fur trade route,
and the road to the Rocky Mountains.

McLeod's first week on the river was marred by poor
weather. Head winds, which can be quite substantial on the
half-mile-wide river, whipped up heavy waves that allied with
the current in slowing travel. Lead-colored clouds, laden with
moisture, periodically unleashed rainstorms, damping the
explorers' spirits and raising the river's volume. The wet
weather was made all the more uncomfortable by the constant presence of mosquitoes. The dreadful drone and the
pesky stings of the insects were only a nuisance during the
day, but at night they made sleep nearly impossible.[38]

On June 16, McLeod met Baptiste Contret, an *engagé* from
Fort Liard, who together with a party of Indians had been
sent ahead of the explorers by McPherson to hunt for and
otherwise aid the expedition. Contret's presence was welcome;
John McLeod's provisions had been just about exhausted, but
with the addition of more hunters the larder soon boasted two
hundred pounds of meat.[39] As their hunting fortunes changed,

so too did the conditions of the river. Travel became easier, as
the current slackened. The explorers were occasionally able to
make their way upstream by their paddles. The voyageurs welcomed the relief from towing the canoe from shore. The Liard
occasionally split into two or more channels, and frequent
sandy beaches, shadowed by forests of spruce and aspen, gave
the river a serene countenance. In the distance, drawing ever
closer, were the rounded heads of the northernmost ranges of
the Rocky Mountains.

Taking advantage of the favorable conditions, McLeod had
his party moving early. By 4:00 A.M. the North canoe would
push its way through the morning mists that hung heavily over
the river. On one such day, after two hours of travel, McLeod
encountered "some difficulty in doubling a point of rock
about 200 yards high and [so] perpendicular that the men
could make no use of the towing line, the current too strong
for the Paddle, and too great a depth of water to make use of
the pole."[40] He was, however, equal to the challenge. After
"some time and difficulty" the voyageurs made it through the
canyon by pulling the canoe upstream, handhold by handhold
along the rocky walls. They named the spot Slate Point because of "the color of the Rock and number of the pieces resembling slate."[41]

The next day's march was delayed because McLeod sent out
his hunters to restock their provisions. The voyageurs, who
seem always to have had energy to spare, spent the time erect-
ing a "temporary chimney." Presumably the rude structure of
mud and rock was designed to speed the process of drying
meat. In any event, before pushing off, McLeod named the
spot, which was near the mouth of a small river, Chimney
River.[42]

Travel conditions on the Liard continued to improve; the
river, which was now a mile wide in some places, seemed to
be losing its strength. On July 19 the explorers traveled the
entire day by paddles alone, the first day since leaving Fort
Liard that they had not been forced to use the towline.[43] On
the south McLeod noted the mouth of an important tributary
of the Liard, the Toad River, which flowed into the larger
river from what one explorer called "a deep gloomy valley."[44]

McLeod noted in his journal, "Toad River is the boundry line of the Fort de Leard and Sandy Indians, the former (altho' seldom) come across land for the purpose of making provisions about the entrance of this river."[45] The Toad River was also the boundary between the navigable regions of the Liard River and the dangerous canyon country ahead.

At first there was no noticeable difference. The explorers passed by several high cliffs with steep rock faces reaching down to the river's bank, but they came across none of the deep canyons that they had been warned about. After passing by one minor riffle, they entered a large, deep lakelike section of river. High hills ringed the water, creating the impression that the Liard had disappeared. It was quiet and peaceful, hardly the cauldron of foaming water that the Indians had described.[46] The North canoe glided across the peaceful pool. The only sounds were the methodical movements of the voyageurs' paddles. Then suddenly, as the canoe rounded a point, Hell Gate was before them. Three hundred feet of weathered limestone, its sheer face resembled aged bronze doors because the golden stone was streaked and disfigured by black and green patches of lichen. It was the gateway to the worst rapids in Rupert's Land and the future grave of many a voyageur.

The canyon was a mile long. The water constrained by the walls of the Gate, which were 150 feet apart, boiled and twisted until its fury was spent in the calm pool below. McLeod and his voyageurs after some difficulty made it through the canyon. The first hurdle was behind them, but what lay ahead?

The real battle with the Liard had begun. McLeod, realizing this, decided to strip his expedition of unessentials and prepare for action. On July 22 he built a cache, in which among other things he put way a store of moose meat. These provisions would serve as an emergency backup in case the expedition met disaster in the rapids ahead. The explorers would later have reason to appreciate this prudence.[47]

After passing through Hell Gate, McLeod and his men had to push their way up a series of strong riffles. These gave way to even more dangerous water at the Rapids of the Drowned. The Liard at this point veers sharply from the north, but the massive flow of the river has difficulty changing direction so suddenly. The result is that the full force of the current collides violently with the high sandstone banks. The river, furious and foamy white from its unexpected collision, then spills over the rapid's second feature, a ledge of rock extending boldly from the north shore. The Rapids of the Drowned are among the most lethal hazards on the Liard.[48] Their macabre name dates from a tragic mishap in 1840, when five voyageurs and a Hudson's Bay Company clerk were to perish there. McLeod led his party up the south bank of the rapids, where there was room to track their canoe.

After such an alarming stretch of river the explorers needed a break, and unexpectedly the Liard gave it to them. The river valley widened, and the stream spread itself out again, flowing among tree-covered islands and sandy beaches. The current, still unrelenting but less constrained, was much easier to manage. Since passing the Toad River four days before, McLeod's men had been tested severely. Ascending the Rapids of the Drowned had required every skill that the voyageurs had acquired in their years of canoe work. From their constant jumping in and out of the canoe, tracking through shallows, and pushing up rapids, the explorers were constantly wet, and by nightfall they were bone weary. When they lay down to sleep, the clouds of mosquitoes about their heads were barely noticed. On the evening of July 24 their much-needed sleep was startlingly disturbed:

Shortly after we retired to rest that night my faithfull dog (Spring) gave us notice by his frequent ranging into the woods and occasionally barking that there were some strangers lurking not far from our camp, in which opinion we were soon convinced by being assailed with a shower of stones thrown from an iminence a short distance from our fire, but could plainly perceive with no intention to injure any of the party, as every stone fell some distance in front of our camp, my Interpreter hailed several times both in Slave and the Kenzie language, but no answer returned.[49]

This was indeed an alarming situation, but, rather than push recklessly into the dark of the forest, McLeod kept his men in camp and set up a watch to guard as the others tried to sleep.[50] He elected to let the Indians initiate contact with him when

The Upper Liard River valley. Photograph by the author.

they felt that the time was right. It was a difficult plan to follow, for, whatever the men did during a day's march, they
knew that the eyes of a strange tribe were following their every movement; they would look into the brush and see trees,
but know that the Indians were there.

Fortunately the waiting game did not last long. The explorers continued their river voyage at the usual early hour. Good
progress was made until, in the afternoon, they came to a
strong riffle. It proved impossible to overcome with the fully
loaded canoe. The explorers then adopted the expedient of
what was called a "*décharge.*" Their provisions, guns, ammunition, and the entire cargo of the canoe was portaged while a
couple of the voyageurs pulled the empty canoe up the riffle.
McLeod blazed the portage trail up "a high precipice." He
reached the top ahead of the others and was proceeding across
a small clearing when he was "surprised to perceive an Elderly
Indian comming towards me armed with a gun and spear."[51]
The Indian had not yet spotted McLeod, but, rather than
drop out of sight until the voyageurs came up the trail, the
explorer advanced toward the Indian. McLeod was to within
"10 or 15 paces" of the Indian before he was seen. The Indian
was startled and raised his gun. Coolly, McLeod put down his
gun and continued walking toward the Indian. This gesture
allayed the red man's suspicions. He also put aside his weapons "and stepped forward with both arms extended."[52]

The old Indian was of the Sandy tribe, probably a branch
of the Kaska nation. He spoke a version of the Slave Indian
language and had been staying near the banks of the Liard,
hoping that the Slave Indians would come upriver to trade.
The Indians never used the Liard for travel, preferring instead to travel overland. He was plainly impressed that the
Hudson's Bay men had fared so well on the river: "He never
harbored the least idea, that the whites could have surmounted the many dangerous parts of the River now behind
us, but was highly gratified to perceive we had so far succeeded in comming up a stream [which] until now appeared
to him impossible."[53] Upon ascertaining the peaceful intentions of the white men, the old Indian called his family out
of their hiding places, and a general council ensued. From

Interior of a Cree Indian tent, 1820. Illustration in Franklin, Narrative of a Journey to the Shores of the Polar Sea in the Years 1819, 20, 21, and 22.

their appearance McLeod could tell that they had only recently been in contact with whites, for they still had the outward appearance of a Stone Age people:

Like all other Indians inhabiting the Mountains, smart and active in their motions, they make hardly any use of wearing apparel, further than a pair of Leather Stockings, and a Moose or Badger Skin Robe, hanging loose over the shoulders, and tied with a leather thong under the chin; the females are smart and good looking and wear a similar garment with the men, with the addition of a piece of leather of about 10 or 12 inches broad, the end of which is formed in below a Girdle round the Waist and extends loose in front to about half the tigh and only when in an erect posture serves partially to cover their nakedness.[54]

The rest of the Sandy tribe was spread out along the upper Liard in small parties. They were particularly apprehensive that year because they had heard from the Mackenzie Indians that the feared Crees were going to launch a raid against them.

It was their hope to lie low through the summer and then rendezvous "by the falling of the leaves" when the Cree danger
had passed.[55]

When the interview focused on the Sandy Indians' trade
connections, McLeod made an interesting discovery. The Indians had recently visited Fort Halkett, where they had bartered for three guns, but they complained that they were destitute of ammunition, save a small quantity of cannon powder
which they had got from the "Nahany, a tribe West of the
Mountians who traded at or near some of the Russian Establishments."[56] McLeod gave them a small quantity of powder
and some other gifts. To his amazement the old Indian countered by giving to McLeod a new cotton sail. This was further
proof that the explorers were now entering the Russian zone.
The sail, which was rather useless to the Indians, had been
gotten from the "Nahanys," who, McLeod surmised, probably
had "pillaged or stolen it near some Russian Establishment."[57]
The "Nahanys" of whom the old man spoke were actually
Tahltan Indians, the same tribe that Samuel Black had heard
described as "Trading Nahannis." The interesting interview
lasted the remainder of the day, after which both parties went
their separate ways.

The Hudson's Bay men were now entering the impressive
Grand Canyon of the Liard. This stretch of the river is between thirty and forty miles long and is really a series of short
canyons. Throughout its length the current is extremely fast.
Later in the nineteenth century two men claimed to have run
the entire Grand Canyon in two hours. If they are to be believed, their average speed was a remarkable eighteen miles
an hour.[58] The most difficult navigation that McLeod experienced in the Grand Canyon was in a dark, narrow gorge with
steep, black walls, where passage was complicated by a series
of small rocky islands that divided the current and increased
the intensity of the riffles.[59] Fortunately, the voyageurs' skill
was equal to the test, and the explorers were able to press on,
forcing their way through the canyon.

Successful navigation on the Liard only means fresh challenges. With the Grand Canyon behind him John McLeod
was immediately faced with the Devil's Rapids. This hellish

cauldron is located where the river makes a large U-shaped bend to the southwest to avoid a high mountain ridge; in its impatience to reach the Arctic Sea the Liard at that point tires of the detour and turns southward, tearing a passage through the mountains.[60] The battle between the river and the rock has been going on for centuries, as the sheer canyon walls indicate. As the Liard deepens its path, the mountain holds on doggedly, restricting the river in places to a defile only 150 feet wide. John McLeod struggled for two days through rain and mud, making long portages, before he was able to circumvent the rapids.[61] Later the fur traders would hack out a four-mile trail up a 1,000-foot mountain ridge to avoid this hazard.

After what he had just come through, McLeod thought that the river above Devil's Rapids was much calmer and even-flowing. The terrain also took on a more pleasing appearance as the high canyon walls gradually receded and gave way to tree-covered shores with long gravel beaches. It was the end of July, and the headwaters of the Liard did not appear to be close. At this point McLeod decided that it was best to send back Baptiste Contret and the Fort Liard Indians, who were after all only temporarily assigned to the expedition. He had an Indian guide with him, and it appeared that the major rapids were behind.[62]

The explorers were now in the midst of the mountains. On the south was the Muskwa Range of the Rocky Mountains; prominent peaks, such as Mount Prudence and Mount Rothenberg, dominated the wooded, rounded heads of the neighboring hills. The Liard River marks the northernmost extension of the Rocky Mountains; from here southward, for over one thousand miles, the great range stretches out. The continent's backbone continues north through the Mackenzie Mountains, but they are not a branch of the Rockies proper, as they begin their march to the Arctic Sea eighty miles east of the Rockies in the vicinity of Hell Gate. This distinction, however, is a mere technicality, as the entire upper Liard region is extremely mountainous, and it is difficult to determine where one range begins and another ends.

Continuing up the Liard, McLeod reached the Smith River on August 1. Heretofore the old Nor'Wester had named the

notable places that he had passed as their appearances war-
ranted, or because of some incident on the journey. Slate
Point and Chimney River are good examples of this practice.
Beginning with the Smith River, which he named after his
superior and friend, Chief Factor Edward Smith, McLeod began to adopt the practice of his acquaintance, Sir John Franklin, and dotted the landscape with the names of personal
friends and prominent people who might advance his career.
McLeod was attracted to the area about the Smith River. It
had every appearance of being an excellent location for a
trading post. His Indian guide, who left the expedition at this
point to visit relatives, reported that the upper section of the
Smith River abounded in beaver and that the river drained
a lake that was an excellent source of fish. McLeod himself
ascended the river a short distance, until he encountered some
rapids. Turning back to the Liard, he made a mental note on
this promising location.[63]

The already dangerous voyage now became spiced by an
added element of destruction, a forest fire. The banks of the
Liard on both sides were ablaze. Hundreds of miles of magnificent spruce and poplar forest were transformed into smoke
and ash. Even on the river, away from the flaring fires of the
forest, the explorers were beset by the conflagration's side effects. Thick, heavy clouds of smoke embraced the river, dark-
ening the sun and choking off all fresh air save for the sultry
drafts escaping from the fire. McLeod could see no more than
three hundred yards ahead of his canoe. To make matters
worse, he had been informed by his guide to expect three
miles of cascades in this section of the river. Fortunately, when
the bowman spotted a rapid ahead, the party had already gone
past the heart of the fire. The banks adjacent to the rapid
were covered with smoking gray ash and tangled charred trees,
while the rapid itself was a difficult two-mile canyon strewn
with hazards. McLeod elected to play it safe and portage
around the canyon. It was an easy carry, over level ground
except for the head of the trail, which was directly up a
sharply rising rock one hundred feet high. The voyageurs
were forced to unlimber their towline, rig a sling for the
canoe, and haul it up the slope after them. The carrying place

has appropriately been known ever since as Portage Brûlé, or the Burntwood Portage.[64]

Embarking again, McLeod passed the mouth of a clear-flowing river about three hundred yards wide. The explorer dubbed the stream Charles River, after Chief Factor John Charles, who commanded the Athabasca District.[65] It is known today as the Coal River because of the scattered deposits of lignite coal near its junction with the Liard. McLeod, however, had no time to muse on geological features. He soon found himself battling up Whirlpool Canyon. Here treacherous crosscurrents produced by the restraining limestone walls of the canyon create a series of whirlpools, which alternate between sucking the water deep into their vortices and throwing it up, with a sound that a later voyageur described as "resembling the rumbling of distant thunder."[66]

The party continued to inch its way upriver, sometimes by tracking and sometimes by poling, taking each hazard as it came. Near nightfall on August 4, they came to the foot of Mountain Portage Rapids, where they set up camp since everyone was dead-tired after a long day of toil. Then one of the men discovered porcupine tracks along the muddy bank, and the whole company was aroused. Suddenly a supper of grilled porcupine, rather than dried moose meat, seemed in the offing. Also there was another good reason for ridding the area of porcupines: under the cover of darkness the quilled prowlers would often sneak into a voyageurs' camp and gnaw at the canoe paddles or tumpline straps—anything that might have a salty taste from human sweat. McLeod's men, armed with cudgels and with the dog, Spring, barking furiously, hunted down five of the slow-moving creatures,[67] which they placed whole in the white-hot coals of the campfire. Broiled in their own fat, the animals provided a rich and tender, if greasy, feast for the explorers.

The next morning McLeod spurned the portage trail and risked the dangers of the rapid. As he emerged from the white water, he noticed a large river flowing into the Liard from the south. Its waters were dark and silty, though it was a broad three hundred yards wide. McLeod correctly surmised that this was the same river whose upper reaches marked Samuel

Black's farthest progress during his 1824 expedition. This was confirmed by the "written inscription nailed to a tree, and other marks left of which the Indians make particular mention."[68] McLeod named the waterway Black's River in honor of his fellow explorer.[69] The rest of the day was spent in the usual upstream struggle; the voyaguers, wading through the shallows with the tracking line over their shoulders, pulled the canoe up the nameless riffles created by every bend in the river. They were wet and battered from stumbling over sunken rocks, weary of the Liard's unending obstacles.

McLeod's voyageurs were nearing the end of their rope. Since passing through Hell Gate, they had ascended a series of rapids such as were not to be found on any canoe trail in Canada. The white-water ladder by which the Liard climbs over the mountains had sapped their usually buoyant spirits. On the evening of August 5, McLeod noted in his journal that "the danger in many places, and hard duty of the day began to form some discontent in the bosoms of some part of our crew." Most of the men kept their complaints to themselves. "One, however, more daring than the others could resist no longer," and he proceeded to tell McLeod what he thought of canoeing on the Liard and the expedition in general. John McLeod knew this man as a barracks lawyer; west of the Rocky Mountains in unknown country was not the place to let him stir up emotions. In order "to check a future repetition" of the insubordination, McLeod thought that "a little corporal chastisement was the best medicine that could be applied." He dealt this out quickly and dispassionately so that there would be no future platform for complaint, but closed the incident by noting in his journal, "I must however do them the justice to say, that since we left Fort Simpson, today was the first instance of discontent."[70]

The party awoke the next day to a cold, gray rainy morning. After the incident of the preceding evening John McLeod realized that it was best not to push his men. Rather than send them out into the dreary weather, he kept the weary canoemen "snug to our encampment." Later in the day the hunters shot a moose, and around the evening fire the whole party feasted on tender moose tongue and deer heart. Their duties were kept light the next day as well, as they dried and packed the bulk of the moose meat. John McLeod knew the character of the voyageurs: after a day and a half of light duties and a full stomach had transformed their outlook on the world, they were ready to proceed with the journey.[71]

On August 8, McLeod had his men back at their usual pace, breaking camp at 4:00 A.M. Fog obscured the Liard that morning, but through its veil they could hear the rumble of rapids ahead. These were the Cranberry Rapids, the last major obstacle that the Liard would hurl at the explorers. Directing the canoe up the south shore of the river, McLeod was able to ascend the hazard by poling the canoe through the eddies and by tracking up the riffles.[72] In 1968 two Russians, who were expert slalom canoeists, heard that no one had shot the Liard from its headwaters to Fort Simpson and decided to show the North Americans how it was to be done. Cranberry Rapids was their first major challenge—one drowned and the other returned to Russia.

Above Cranberry Rapids the Liard valley stretches out; mountains and defiles are replaced by gently rolling hills. The river itself slows down; there is no foaming white water from rapids and falls as the current slips smoothly between wooded islands. The multiple channels at this point confused McLeod, who thought that the Liard was two miles wide here. Certainly it was superb hunting country. On the morning of August 10, McLeod shot five beaver from the door of his tent. The beaver were so abundant and unused to human predators that throughout the day the explorers were able to chase them in their canoe. It was a fur trapper's paradise.[74]

On August 14, McLeod reached a major tributary of the Liard, which he named after a friend, Peter Warren Dease, a chief factor in the company.[75] He pushed up the new river for a couple of miles before his progress was blocked by a rapid that flowed through a canyon "with high perpendicular rocks on both sides." This rapid and the diminished size of the river convinced McLeod that it was not one of the main branches of the Liard, but, as he turned back to the larger river, he noted that the Dease was a promising road to the interior.

The Hudson's Bay Company's explorers continued upstream for another week. Daily the Liard's current diminished in strength, and the riverbed became smaller. The men in the canoe were aware of the significance of these signs. McLeod wrote, "Such sudden changes and other circumstances induces me to suppose that we are now drawing near the termination of our voyage."[76] It became increasingly difficult to differentiate between the main body of the Liard and its tributaries. As a result McLeod made a significant error in navigation. While passing through an island-crowded section of river, he directed the canoe up what he thought was the main branch of the Liard, because it veered sharply to the north. In reality he had entered the Frances River, the last major tributary of the Liard. If the explorers had continued on the Liard, they would have discovered an ever-shrinking river fed by insignificant creeks. The Frances and the Dease rivers were the only commercially important affluents of the Liard and both would figure prominently in the later exploration and exploitation of the region.

McLeod ascended the Frances for about thirty-five miles up a rapid-filled canyon, a maneuver that the voyageurs now did as a matter of course. The river's thickly timbered banks restricted the explorers from any general view of the country ahead, which McLeod needed to see in order to ascertain the Liard's main sources. On the evening of August 21 the party camped near the base of a low range of mountains. Early the next morning McLeod decided to climb the closest peak to steal a view of what lay ahead:

At 4 AM we began to ascend the Mountain and after several rests we obtained the summit at 1pm. from which I had a good prospect of the country on both sides of the River, a short distance ahead the Country is level, in which is situated a pretty large lake from which a River flows into the West Branch, at the north end of the Lake is another much higher Range of Mountains, extending in a NE direction, and as far as the eye could extend, distant summits appeared towering much higher, and all covered with snow, from the different cuts and Valleys, I had a fair view of the number of small Rivulets, which form such a body of water as the West Branch, all combining on the NE side of the Lake in sight; being now satisfied that the object of the Voyage was fairly accomplished, I dispatched one of the Hunters back to where I had left the men, with orders to the Bowsmen to leave all our luggage, in order to lighten the canoe, as I intended to visit the Lake in sight in expectation of finding some natives.[77]

They set out for the lake at noon the next day. Pushing a short way up the Frances, the explorers noted that the current was slack. Since it was "bordering on stillwater, the men with cheerful countenances threw aside their Setting Poles, and with a lively song plyed their paddles, with some Spirit."[78] With the words of "La Claire Fontaine" or some other *chanson* on their lips the voyageurs steered the canoe up the small stream that connected the Frances River with the large lake ahead. Unfortunately, the character of the stream took all the joy out of their song. Fallen trees blocked its channels, and McLeod continually had to send men ahead with hatchets to clear a path. As darkness spread out of the forest, they were forced to camp short of their goal. It was not until late the next morning that the explorers finally pushed their canoe into the smooth waters of the lake. As the voyageurs rested their paddles on the gunnels of the canoe, they saw before them a beautiful lake about twelve miles long and two miles broad. McLeod recorded, ". . . in honor of our worthy Governor called it Simpson's Lake, on each side of the Lake is a high mountain, and in honor of two respectable Gentlemen called them Garry's and McTavish's Mountains."[79]

As far as John McLeod was concerned, they had reached the end of their voyage: "Simpson's Lake I consider one of the principal feeders of the West Branch, where along it's margin lay dormant the fortunes of many."[80] McLeod proceeded across the lake, hoping to meet some local Indians. All he found was an abandoned fishing camp on one of the lake's islands and a not too carefully hidden cache. "Being anxious to know if they had any European manufacture," McLeod ordered his men to break into the cache, "but found nothing that could convince me they had ever seen whites."[81] The fur traders took three beaver skins from the cache and left behind knives, fire steel, and other goods to inform the Stone Age Indians that nineteenth-century fur traders had reached Simpson Lake. Before leaving the island, the interpreter lopped off the branches of a high Pine Tree, on which I cut my initials, Day and Date, number of my crew and date of my departure from Fort Simpson H.B. Co and by request of my crew named the spot McLeod's Island, after thanking my crew for their uniform good conduct and egarness in bring the voyage to a satisfactory close, which I now considered fully accomplished, and I hope to the satisfaction of my Honorable Employers, we embarked with 3 cheers and began to retrace our steps.[82]

It was late August, and they were a long way from Fort Simpson. The cold season was swiftly approaching. At least the homeward journey would be downstream all the way; after an entire summer of bucking the current it was a relief to have it on their side. Back on the Liard they made good progress. On August 28 they were at the mouth of the Kechika River, where they met a group of Indians. After trading for twenty beaver skins and holding a brief council, the explorers were again on their way. Perhaps they were in too much of a hurry. Arriving at the brink of Mountain Portage Rapids, McLeod made a hasty decision to run the cataract. This, he later admitted, was a mistake: "We for our impudence nearly paid our folly, with our lives, we ran aground on a sunk rock, the blow breaking about 2 feet square of the bottom of our canoe."[83] It was touch and go, as the waters of the rapid poured into the fractured canoe and the voyageurs, paddling for their lives, struggled to maneuver it toward shore. They just barely made it; the canoe was loaded to the gunnels with water.[84]

This was merely a prelude to the tragedy that beset the party at the Portage Brûlé Rapids. The voyageurs thought that they could run the rapid. To lighten the North canoe and increase its maneuverability, McLeod and four other men took the portage trail around the rapids. The bowman, the sternman, and two middlemen were left to pilot the canoe. They started down the rapid in fine style, as McLeod and the four others shouted encouragement from shore. The canoe slipped between the small islands and rocky outcroppings that obstructed the channel and all seemed to be going well. Then suddenly, as they neared the end of the rapid, the voyageurs found their path blocked by a limestone ledge reaching out into the river. The water spilled over the rock, creating a foaming cascade. The bowman had no choice but to point the canoe down the chute. The waves broke over the birchbark hull, first filling the canoe and then tearing it into three pieces. Two of the men, Thomas Corin and Antoine Brilliant, were immediately sucked beneath the swirling waters and dashed against the sunken ledge. They were probably killed instantly; their bodies never reappeared. Louis Briant and Pierre Paul were more fortunate. They managed to hang onto a section of the canoe and, using it as a life preserver, floated safely through the rest of the riffles. Their problems, however, were not over as the Liard was flowing at about ten miles per hour toward another smaller rapid two miles farther downstream. Briant and Paul struggled with all their might to push the ruined canoe toward shore, while McLeod and the rest of the crew scrambled along the bank trying to lend assistance. At the very brink of the second rapid the two voyageurs, fighting panic and the cold water, which was sapping their strength, mustered a final effort and were able to reach the shore "completely exhausted."[85]

The expedition was now in critical straits; "entirely destitute of means of getting back to any hospitable quarter, every party was now quite discouraged, and sorely lamenting the loss of our companions."[86] Their very survival now depended on McLeod's abilities as a leader. The Scotsman was equal to the occasion: "seeing that no time was to be lost to ensure our future preservation we gathered up the remaining part of our canoe, and [made] as shifts to patch the pieces together."[87] The task of rebuilding the canoe was confounded by their lack of an axe. In fact, their only tool was a crooked knife. McLeod would have considered abandoning the canoe entirely and proceeding to Fort Simpson overland, except that most of his men lacked shoes.[88] The voyaguers, calling upon their great skill, were able to fashion a canoe of sorts with the crooked knife. John McLeod dubbed the vessel "our crazy craft," but on it they again headed downstream, hugging the shore, for obvious reasons.

The rest of the voyage held no further adventures. They made it out of the canyon country, carefully navigating the

river and subsisting on the provisions that McLeod had pru-
dently cached on the upstream voyage. When they reached
Fort Simpson on September 9, John McLeod had completed
his exploratory survey in seventy-four days.[89]

Edward Smith was enthusiastic about the success of Mc-
Leod's expedition. He boasted to a fellow fur trader that
"since the coalition such a field has not yet been opened for
commercial undertakings."[90] Smith had been at Fort Simpson
for nearly ten years and had always been interested in expanding the fur trade up the Liard River; now he finally had some
results. The "old spirit of the Northwest" shone in his eyes
when he penned:

I am now pleased in having something more substantial than indian report to lay before Council of this long talked of Country—
and my ambition now ceases—and when the day comes that I
turn my back to McKenzie River not to return—it will be one of
those trying moments when the mind is neither cloudy with sor-
row or cheered with joy—I have done my duty let those that follow me—keep to the path that is now open—and extend it right
and left and I now pronounce the District to be still on the pro-
gressive and will continue so for many years to come, sometimes I
would wish to possess younger days to finish what is begun.[91]

Old Daddy Smith, as the chief factor was affectionately
called, made an additional contribution to the advance up the
Liard in 1832. He ordered Fort Halkett to be moved from its
unsuccessful location on the East Branch, or Fort Nelson
River, to the heart of the mountainous upper Liard near the
Smith River. That, however, was a parting gesture. In 1832,
Governor Simpson granted Edward Smith a year's leave "to
visit the civilized world, from which he has been absent for
upwards of 30 years."[92] With Smith's exit the expansion up
the West Branch lost its guiding hand.

The Dryad Affair

Governor George Simpson did not fully appreciate the new
area of operations that had been opened up by John McLeod.
He was preoccupied with the myriad of personal concerns that
close in around a newly married man, having returned to Ru-

pert's Land in the summer of 1830 after a furlough with a demure young English bride. When he was again free to concentrate on the company's business, his interest centered particularly on the Northwest Coast fur trade. There the Hudson's Bay Company had successfully crippled the American maritime trade, but had failed to secure the Russian support that it needed to complete the campaign. In retaliation Simpson proposed to step up the pressure on the Russians. The Stikine River was to be the center of this program, since the Russian traders were reaping huge harvests of land furs from British territory by that route. John McLeod's 1831 journey had revealed that the Russian influence had penetrated far up the Liard to the doorstep of the Mackenzie District. Simpson hoped to disrupt the flow of furs to the Russian American Company by seizing control of the Stikine River.

Responsibility for the new venture was given to the commander of Port Simpson, Peter Skene Ogden. Following Simpson's directions, Ogden fitted out the brig *Dryad* with thirty-eight men and an ample allotment of trade goods. The plan was for Ogden to sail the *Dryad* to the mouth of the Stikine River and then proceed upriver until he passed the limits of Russian territory. He was then to establish a new trading post in British territory to intercept the inland furs before they reached the hands of the Russian American Company.

Baron Ferdinand von Wrangel, however, was not going to let his operations be subverted so easily. He knew that the British had the right to navigate all of the rivers, such as the Stikine, that flowed through the Russian territory to the coast. That right had been secured by the Anglo-Russian Convention, which was due to expire in 1835. Although the free navigation privilege had been granted in perpetuity, Wrangel could hope for renegotiation. The problem was, as he explained to his Saint Petersburg superiors, to delay the British thrust:

The greatest trouble I have now is the Hudson Bay Company which is allowed by the convention to navigate freely on rivers falling into the sea in our possessions, for it is the region neighboring upon the rivers which furnished us with beavers and not the coast, and I beg of you that should any other convention be

signed (the term of the old ones having expired) you should so-
licit that free navigation on the rivers should at least be limited
by the condition that free navigation to the British from the interior to the sea should not be forbidden, while free navigation
from the sea up the rivers should be prohibited. Of course it
would be best not to allow any navigation whatever, though I
think that it will not be possible to manage it. However, this circumstance will depend on diplomatic transactions and until further instructions I will hinder the British by force from sailing up
the Stachin [Stikine] river.[93]

Wrangel still needed some legal justification for blocking
the British. Studying the 1825 convention, he came upon an
article vague enough to suit his purpose, which stated in part:

Subjects of his Britannic Majesty shall not land at any place
where there may be a Russian establishment, without permission
of the Governor or Commandant; and, on the other hand, that
Russian subjects shall not land, without permission, at any British
establishment, of the Northwest coast.[94]

All that he would have to do was build a post near the mouth
of the Stikine River and then forbid the British access to the
waters about the establishment. This was, of course, confound-
ing the original intent of the article and it was in itself convo-
luted reasoning, but it would serve the purpose.

In the fall of 1833, Wrangel dispatched Lieutenant Dionysius Zarembo with the fourteen-gun brig *Chichagoff* to begin
construction of the post, or redoubt. The site selected was ten
miles south of the mouth of the Stikine River off Etolin Island, at the present-day settlement of Wrangell. Unlike most
Hudson's Bay Company posts, Fort Dionysius, as the new
post was named, was fortified with cannon and well prepared
for action.

On June 15, Peter Skene Ogden set out with his Hudson's
Bay Company expedition. Three days out of Port Simpson he
approached Point Highfield, where he was surprised to spot
the Russian fort. Although he did not think it a formidable
installation, calling it a "shapeless mass of logs and planks," he
knew it did not bode well for his operation. Ogden anchored
the *Dryad* off the Russian post and prepared to meet a whale

boat that was beating toward his ship from the shore. Lieutenant Zarembo came on board the *Dryad* and presented Ogden with Baron von Wrangel's order prohibiting British vessels from the vicinity. Ogden would have none of this; he quickly dashed off a short note informing the Russians that he had the right to proceed upstream and reaffirming his intention to do so. Zarembo took the note and returned to shore.[95]

Shortly thereafter a second boat pulled alongside the *Dryad*. Out of it stepped a "short thickset goodnatured vainlooking man," Zarembo's interpreter. Ogden invited the gentleman into his cabin, hoping to get some clarification of what was going on. As the Russian belted down brandies, he tried to make clear to Ogden what would happen if he disregarded Wrangel's decree. Unfortunately the interpreter knew only a few English words, and his use of those was not facilitated by the half pint of spirits that he had consumed. Ogden, who knew no Russian, tried to speak with his guest in French, but to no avail. The two greatest empires in the world, Great Britain and czarist Russia, were on a collision course, and neither side could understand what the other was saying. Before the encounter was over, Ogden had tried English, French, Spanish, and Latin on the Russian authorities, but all he learned was that the Russians insisted on preventing his ascent of the Stikine. If he attempted to pass Fort Dionysius, their orders were to "boxum," which Ogden took to mean to stop him "by violence."[96]

Eventually Zarembo agreed to send Ogden's note to Sitka, and at the same time he appealed to Wrangel to confirm his previous orders. This meant at least an eight- to ten-day delay in Ogden's plans. Trying to make the best of a bad situation, he moved the *Dryad* into the Etolin harbor, where he was surprised to see the *Chichagoff* and her fourteen guns.[97] The Russians used the waiting time well. At every opportunity Zarembo lectured the local Tlingit Indians about how a successful British post upriver on the Stikine would destroy their trade as middlemen with the interior tribes. This soon had its effect. On June 19, Ogden received a visit from a powerful Tlingit chief, named Seix. The chief represented a trading party that was as powerful on the frontier as the English and the Russians. The Tlingit warriors had defeated the white merchants on previous occasions, and they were prepared to do so again. Seix told Ogden that he could build a post at the mouth of the Stikine, but he would not be allowed to establish a post upriver.[98]

The Russian courier finally returned from Sitka on June 28. Wrangel was not able to respond to Ogden's assertion of British rights because he was absent from Sitka for the summer, a very diplomatic move. His second-in-command, Captain Adolf Etholine, merely reaffirmed Zarembo's opposition to the Stikine venture.[99] It was time for a showdown. Ogden had nearly forty men and an armed brig at his command. Governor Simpson had described him as "a very cool calculating fellow who is capable of doing anything to gain his ends."[100] He was not a man to shrink from violence; his career in the fur trade was checkered with incidences of overaggressiveness and strong-arm tactics. Still, on this occasion Ogden was forced to back down. If it had been simply a matter of facing the Russian brig, Ogden most likely would have pushed on and damned the consequences. The determined opposition of the Tlingit Indians was a more serious consideration. It would be impossible to found a trading post if the local Indians were opposed to it. Ogden did not have to look far to see what the Tlingit would do if he persisted. Their 1802 massacre at Sitka was still well remembered on the coast. Therefore he decided "it would be highly imprudent to persist in the undertaking."[101]

Returning to Port Simpson, Ogden decided to try to make use of the abundant resources that had been allotted to the Stikine venture and relocated the site of Port Simpson. As it was, the post was overly exposed to winds and gales blowing in from the North Pacific. For the rebuilding Ogden needed wood for spars. Since the area around the post did not have the proper trees, he sent a small party across the channel into Russian territory. The Hudson's Bay men had no sooner started gathering the wood than a group of Russians sortied out of the nearby settlement of Tongass and drove them off.[102] This was too much for Ogden, who was in no mood for the petty harassments of a cold war. He expedited the rebuilding of Port Simpson and then re-embarked in the *Dryad* for Sitka; he was going to give Wrangel a piece of his mind.

When Ogden finally reached Sitka on September 27, his anger had dissipated somewhat, and he was ready to play the role of a diplomat. After entering Sitka harbor, he ordered his men to fire a nine-gun salute to Baron von Wrangel. The Russian shore batteries returned the tribute, and Ogden proceeded to Baranov's Castle, a large wooden building that served as the governor's residence. Although the two parties shared dinner and vodka toasts, the interview had its unpleasant moments. Ogden officially protested Russia's obstruction of the Hudson's Bay Company's trade. Wrangel, who stuck to his interpretation of the convention, countered by accusing the English of plotting to destroy the Russian American Company's trade. Ogden tried to obscure that fact by telling Wrangel that the Honorable Company's only purpose in advancing up the Stikine River was to provide a line of communication between the coast and the company's posts at the headwaters of the Stikine. This was a barefaced lie, as the company did not even have any posts at the headwaters of the Stikine in 1834. Wrangel knew this and felt justified in countering with falsehoods of his own. The Russian blockade of the Stikine, he claimed, not only rested on firm legal grounds but also was motivated by humanitarian considerations: a Hudson's Bay post would strip the land of furs and ruin the livelihood of the poor Tlingit Indians. Piously Baron von Wrangel claimed that the Hudson's Bay Company's strategy resembled "the robbery of a band of brigands who trample on the rights and property of the aborigines." In this tedious, superficial manner the negotiations with Wrangel dragged on until the chief trader realized that he was not going to get any satisfaction from the Russian governor.[103]

Ogden left Sitka and filed a detailed report with the Columbia district commander, John McLoughlin. The Hudson's Bay Company then contacted the Foreign Office in order to protest Baron von Wrangel's blockade, claiming damages of £22,150.10.11. Lord Palmerston, then foreign secretary, gave the Hudson's Bay Company his full support. The resulting diplomatic fracas became known as the *Dryad* Affair. It was a charmingly nineteenth-century dispute; the conflict on the exotic fringes of the two empires, although treated seriously and with some dispatch, was not allowed to disrupt the general flow of foreign policy.

Lord Durham, Britain's minister in Saint Petersburg, put pressure on the Russian government for "redress and compensation."[104] The czar's case was again represented by the urbane Count Nesselrode, who with suave ineptitude immediately destroyed Baron von Wrangel's defense by admitting that the Russian American Company's interpretation of the Anglo-Russian Convention was erroneous.[105] The directors of the company were shocked by Nesselrode's concession; they had never suspected that their position would be subverted by their own government.[106] The British then tried to obtain compensation for the Hudson's Bay Company, which, even by Nesselrode's admission, had been wronged. The Russians, however, balked at that point, claiming that they had not threatened forcibly to prevent Ogden's passage. The British, of course, thought otherwise. The negotiations broke down into a series of counter claims asserting what Zarembo, who spoke no English, had said to Ogden, who spoke no Russian. The comedy dragged on for years.

The Inland Route to the Stikine River

The Hudson's Bay Company was not content to wait patiently for the diplomats in Europe to clear up the frontier crisis. Although operations on the Pacific Coast were cut back to reduce tension with the Russians, this did not constitute acquiescence to the Russians' strength; instead, Governor Simpson was foregoing obvious frontal assaults on the Russians in favor of a campaign on his enemy's flanks. Inland operations were for the first time given priority over those on the coast. Simpson's sudden optimism concerning expansion from the interior was a direct result of a new exploratory survey by John McLeod, who in 1834 again headed up the Liard to extend the company's frontiers.

Exploration in the Mackenzie District had stalled temporarily after 1832, when its major patron, Chief Factor Edward Smith, left the Northwest for a year's furlough. His duties at Fort Simpson were assumed by Chief Factor John Stuart. Fur trader J. G. McTavish remarked, "McKenzie River made a very bad exchange a Smith for a Stuart—regularity & system for Confusion and Nonsense—It must be disgusting to the Young expectants in that quarter to see an old useless hunky good for nothing but waisting Tobacco sent as their leader."[107] Governor Simpson was even harsher in his judgment of Stuart:

Is exceedingly vain, a great Egotist, swallows the grossest flattery, is easily cajoled, rarely speaks the truth, indeed I would not believe him upon Oath . . . fancies himself one of the leading & most valuable men in the Country, but his Day is gone by, and he is now worse than useless being a cloy upon the concern . . . (May be considered in his dotage and has of late become disgustingly indecent, in regard to women) .[108]

It would, however, be unfair to dismiss John Stuart with these biting judgments. He had joined the North West Company in 1799 and had spent most of his career in New Caledonia. He served as Simon Fraser's second-in-command on the notable descent of the Fraser River in 1808. As late as 1829, Simpson himself referred to Stuart as "the Father or founder of New Caledonia" and singled him out for his "unwearied industry and extraordinary perseverance."[109] John Stuart ran afoul of Simpson and McTavish in 1831. Both of those gentlemen had cast off their "country wives"—the Indian women with whom they had lived—and married English girls. Stuart, who was commanding the Winnipeg District, was given the responsibility of caring for the former wives. He assumed this uncomfortable task, but gave both McTavish and Simpson a piece of his mind, censuring them for heartlessly discarding their former wives and leaving the poor women "stigmatized with ignominy."[110] It was under these circumstances that Stuart earned the sharp characterizations by McTavish and Simpson quoted above. Stuart's transfer to the Mackenzie District may be regarded as a banishment, as Simpson would have wanted the sharp-tongued Scotsman removed from earshot. Although this was convenient for the governor personally, it was not in the best interests of the district. Stuart was no longer at the height of his powers, and he lacked the energy to continue the march up the Liard River.

The impetus for continuing the explorations came from the Council of the Northern Department. In 1833 they ordered, "That John McLeod, Clerk, be employed Summer 1834 with 5 men employed in discovering the countries situated on the west side of the Rocky Mountains from the sources of the East Branch of the Liard."[111] Governor Simpson, the most influential member of the council, did not initially agree with this decision. He had soured on the Liard as a trade route, perhaps because of the intially poor fur returns from the first Fort Halkett, or because of the hazardous navigation that had marred John McLeod's 1831 journey. Writing to Edward Smith, who had returned to the Northwest as commander of the Athabasca District and had remained involved in the affairs of the Liard, Simpson made his views quite clear:

Missions of this description are generally attended with heavy expense and inconvenience, and as it does not appear to us that much benefet is likely to be gained by following them up in that quarter, where their progress has been miserably slow for some years past, you need not keep up an establishment of people for that object, on the contrary we beg that you will reduce the complement of servents in the District.[112]

The governor's opinion was to change radically after John McLeod's return.

John McLeod had passed the winter of 1833–34 deep in the Rocky Mountains at Fort Halkett, at the mouth of the Smith River. In accordance with the council's orders he left the post on June 25 with a North canoe, five voyageurs, and two Indian hunters. McLeod, however, had no intention of exploring up the East Branch, or Fort Nelson River, as the council had suggested. His goal was the Dease River. Having discovered and ascended that river a short distance in 1831, McLeod felt that it was a potential avenue into the interior.[113]

The Liard was running much higher than it had in 1831. The pushing upriver from Fort Halkett proved rather difficult. Where during his first journey McLeod had made only a single portage between the Smith River and Cranberry Rapids, he now was obliged to engage in twelve separate portages.[114] Still, on July 10, he was at the mouth of the Dease.

After two miles of smooth, steady current on the Dease McLeod reached the first rapid on the new river, which, appropriately enough, is known as Two Mile Rapid. The river spills over a rocky ledge and through a narrow gap between a rocky bank and the steep wall of an overhanging cliff. After the Liard's rapids this presented McLeod with no difficulties. The same was true of a second cataract, called Four Mile Rapid, a couple of miles farther upstream. This rapid lacks the canyonlike appearance of Two Mile Rapid, but the innumerable boulders that congest the stream are formidable obstacles. McLeod would have proceeded up the west side of the rapid, where a relatively clear channel is afforded.

After this unfriendly beginning the Dease settled down, flowing pleasantly between banks of poplar and willow. The current was steady, about three or four miles per hour, but the water was not deep, and the voyageurs, using their poles, made excellent progress. Poling was a delicate art. The voyageur stood up in the canoe, carefully trying to position his eight- or ten-foot pole, known as a *perche*, while at the same time keeping his balance.[115] It took a cool head to execute such a maneuver in the middle of a dangerous riffle. During the day McLeod stopped several times to light tangled piles of driftwood, hoping thus to notify the local Indians of the traders' approach.[116]

The hunting along the Dease was excellent; on successive days the Indian hunters brought down a moose and a caribou. On July 16 McLeod passed a smooth-flowing river entering the Dease from the southwest, which he named for the hearty commander of Fort Simpson, John Stuart.[117] The river's course began to vary, weaving in great bends to the east and to the west. Toward the end of the day the party approached a high, barren ridge of mountains well back from the river that dominated the landscape. This was the Horse Ranch Range, a twenty-five-mile-long crest of ancient granite reaching to 7,300 feet at its highest points.

John McLeod was anxious to open communication with the

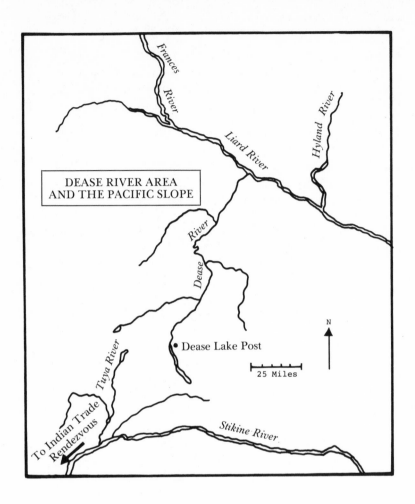

DEASE RIVER AREA
AND THE PACIFIC SLOPE

Frances
River

Hyland River

Liard River

River

Dease

Tuya River

N

• Dease Lake Post

25 Miles

To Indian Trade
Rendezvous

Stikine River

natives of the Dease River. When he saw the Horse Ranch Range, he supposed that they might be spending the summer in the high country, hunting wild mountain goats. Acting upon this hunch, he spent the next day climbing the slopes of the range. Unfortunately, he was unable to locate any of the Dease area's inhabitants or gain any significant knowledge of the land ahead.

Continuing upriver, the explorers encountered the difficult Stoney Island Rapids, where the Dease flows through a narrow, canyonlike constriction framed by impressive outcroppings of granite. It is a picturesque spot. The rock cliffs are speckled by mosses and lichens burnt orange and black by the sun; a spruce forest provides a somber crown for the canyon. It is also a dangerous spot, for whirlpools shift from side to side about the rapid, their yawning dark mouths suddenly appearing in what seems to be calm water. The boulders and rocky islets that give the rapid its name can, all too quickly, produce disaster. The voyageurs had to track their canoe up this rapid. Probably they chose the west bank of the river.[118]

One of the landmarks that McLeod passed on the Dease was McDame Creek, where forty-one years later, in 1874, gold was to be discovered. A settlement sprang up where the McDame joins the Dease, and the creek became the center of the entire Cassiar mining district. The Hudson's Bay Company, which had preceded the prospectors into the area, probably made the most money out of the rush, bartering the miners' gold for beans and bacon, the necessities of life. After McDame Creek the Dease begins to weave in long looping bends, meandering with a slack current.

On July 19, McLeod came upon another set of rapids. The voyageurs had no difficulty tracking up the boulder-strewn hazard, but the Cottonwood River, which enters the Dease at the head of the rapids, proved to be more of a difficulty. At the junction the Dease and the Cottonwood are both no more than a hundred feet wide with steady, smooth currents. McLeod camped at this spot for the night and tried to guess which river was the main branch of the Dease.[119]

On the next morning the expedition embarked up the "west fork," or Cottonwood River. After a few miles, however,

this river became progressively shallower and frequently interrupted by small rapids. McLeod called a halt; it seemed
that there had to be a better route to the interior. With his
two Indian hunters and the interpreter he left the Cottonwood, determined to climb one of the nearby mountains.
Upon reaching the summit of a nearby peak, the explorer was
afforded a fine view of the surrounding country. On the east
he could clearly make out the Dease River, which, clear of
rapids, was the route that he wanted. He and the interpreter
headed back to the canoe on the Cottonwood, while the two
hunters were left to search the treeless slopes for mountain
goats; they would rendezvous with the main party the next
morning on the Dease.[120]

McLeod had no difficulty shooting the North canoe down
the Cottonwood and proceeding up the Dease, but, as they
approached the selected rendezvous, the voyageurs noticed
that only one of the hunters was present. McLeod recorded:

I was sorry to learn that his Companion he left on the adjoining
Mountain his left hand, from the bursting of his Gun in firing at
Goats, mangled in a shocking manner, and from the loss of blood
in too weak a condition to be able to proceed onto meet us, I
made all possible expedition accompanied by the Hunter to the
spot, and after dressing his wounds in the best manner possible
reached back at the canoe at a late hour.[121]

In unknown country a Hudson's Bay Company officer had to
be not only a fur trader and an explorer but also occasionally
a doctor.

On July 23, McLeod came upon an Indian camp that was
perhaps three days old. If the Indians were a hunting expedition, they might still be in the area. McLeod, who was very
anxious to open up trade relations with the natives of the
Dease River, elected to follow their trail. He set out with the
two hunters, the interpreter, and a voyageur, and had no
trouble picking up the Indians' trail. After a short time it became obvious that they were quickening their march, fleeing,
McLeod suspected, from the fur traders. The chase continued
for the "remainder of the day and night" before McLeod
finally gave up the effort. During the inland trek McLeod

could see in the distance a very large body of water, which he suspected must be the source of the Dease River.[122] The remaining few miles of river that separated McLeod from the lake were extremely beautiful. The Dease's current was again alive, and the water was clear; as the river, a mere thirty to forty feet wide, flowed through thick forests and passed gravel bars of shiny white rock. Because the river was only a few feet deep, the voyageurs were able to make excellent progress placing their poles in the transparent stream.[123]

McLeod reached the source of the Dease River on a gray, rainy day. In such weather heavy clouds rest upon the high hills that ring the lake, presenting a scene dismal to any observer except a Scotsman like McLeod, who must have noticed the lake's striking resemblance to the lochs of his native land. On the next day Dease Lake revealed a more pleasant face, and the explorers were justifiably impressed with their discovry: "Deases Lake is a magnificent body of water 43 Miles in length and from 1½ to 3 Miles broad by compass SE & NW, and surprising that in such a body of water not an Island is to be found, the country on both sides the lake is hilly but well wooded, and running parallel on both sides is a mountain but not high."[124] Today the mountain on the west side of the lake is known as Mount McLeod. In his enthusiasm the explorer overestimated the length of the lake, which is about half as long as the forty odd miles that he jotted down in his journal. Such a mistake is understandable. On a calm, clear day the long, narrow lake presents distant, miragelike vistas to a canoeist, giving the traveler a static feeling, as if, in spite of every exertion, no progress is being made.

Near the close of that day McLeod's party reached the south end of Dease Lake. McLeod had now traveled over two hundred miles into a new country and had seen rich beaver territory. He might have turned back or, since he had reached the source of the Dease, he could have spent his energies trying to open up contacts with the Indians of the area. His journal reveals that he had something quite different on his mind:

A complete stop being now put to our further advance by water, my intention is to secure our canoe and baggage at this place, and

The Dease River valley and Cassiar Mountains. Photograph by the author.

proceed for some days in the same direction overland, and as no
Mountains of any great Magnitude approach before us, I have
every expectation some of the streams flowing to the Pacific can be
no great distance, and before long anticipate the hope of drinking
their waters.[125]

McLeod was not blundering in the dark. He had a clear idea
of what he hoped to find. He was familiar with Samuel Black's
accounts of the Trading Nahannis, and from the tribes of the
upper Liard he had heard of a trail that led from a large lake
to the Nahannis' homeland. Dease Lake, he surmised, was that
large lake, and, after making camp on July 25, he discovered
a well-beaten path leading into the interior. McLeod hoped
that this would lead him to "the large River west of the Mountains" upon whose banks the Trading Nahannis dwelled. The
explorers also found "a Wooden Canoe sufficiently large to
carry six Persons and made in much the same model as a
Boat."[126]

On the next morning McLeod put his men to work constructing a cache to secure their supplies and make safe the
canoe. He then distributed a five days' ration of food and a
small allotment of trading goods among his crew. With these
small bundles on their backs the explorers set out overland.
The Indian trail took them through forested terrain, up and
down small hills and ravines. In the evening they camped
near a southward-flowing stream, probably the Tanzilla River.
After a decade of effort the Mackenzie District explorers had
finally breached the Pacific Slope. McLeod wrote, "with satisfaction did the whole of the Party quench their thirst of the
first Water on the West of that Barrier, through which we
have been penetrating for such a length of time."[127]

The next day's march led them into difficult country. The
trail began to drop down into lower elevations and eventually crossed a swampy stretch of muskeg. Every step sent them
ankle-deep into the cold water and sphagnum moss, and they
did not reach firm ground until sunset. Two more days of
travel, marked by morning rains and "beautiful and hilly
country," brought the explorers to a swiftly flowing river. So
fierce was this stream's current, and so boulder-strewn were its
channels, that any attempt at fording or rafting to the oppo-

site shore would have been suicide. The situation was further confounded by the river's steep banks, which McLeod described as "perpendicular precipices." In short, the whole party was "put to a complete stand how to cross."[128] After they reconnoitered the river farther downstream, however, the explorers came upon what promised to be a way across the torrent:

We spied a bridge, errected by the natives for which we made the best of our way, it was constructed of Five Trees 22 ft in length resting on projecting points of rock on both sides of the River, and 15 feet from the surface of the Stream, which rolled in a white foam; with some difficulty we all succeeded in obtaining the opposite shore.[129]

This grim crossing proved to be just a prelude to what the Hudson's Bay men were to face at the end of the day:

At a late hour we reached the border of another River, but frightful to look at, a similar Bridge with the one of the morning was thrown across by the natives, but so very slender was its construction, that only one of the Men (John Norquoy) would venture across, it is 40 feet long and 4 feet broad, and from the surface of the foaming stream below 27 feet.[130]

The river before them was the Tuya River, a tributary of the Stikine. The problem was to get across. The rickety log span perched precariously above the raging river must have looked doubly bad in the deep shadows of twilight. Rather than force the issue that evening, McLeod called a halt, and the crew began to set up camp. McLeod hiked up the river bank, hoping to find a safer crossing. He came upon "a beautiful perpendicular Water Fall of upwards of 100 feet," which he named Thomas Falls after Thomas Simpson, kinsman and secretary to Governor Simpson. With the roar of the falls in their ears the explorers spent an uneasy night.

On the following day they attempted to cross the bridge. Norquoy again nimbly made his way to the other side. McLeod, no doubt anxious to set a good example for the rest of the crew, followed him over the uncertain log span. Others in the crew tried to follow suit, but only one could bring himself to hazard the entire forty feet. The more the voyageurs saw of that bridge the less they cared for it; orders or not, they were staying on terra firma. McLeod was forced to proceed with Norquoy and the other light-footed *engagé*, while the rest of the crew followed as best they could from the opposite shore.[131] A few hours of such travel brought McLeod to an Indian camp, which had been only recently abandoned. The fur trader poked about in the tents, trying to detect any signs of white contact. From a few scraps of cloth and other implements McLeod deduced that the Indians had some contact with whites, but no heavy exposure to white trade goods.[132]

Also found in the Indian camp were some fishing spears. McLeod thought that the Indians used them to spear sturgeon, but actually they were used for salmon fishing, a delicate art that is still practiced today by some of the denizens of the Stikine River valley. The fisherman stands poised at the riverbank, with his spear resting in the rapid water, until he feels the salmon. A quick turn of the spear secures the fish on a sharp gaff attached to the shaft. Twenty- and thirty-pound salmon, which are not uncommon in these waters, can provide a different ending to the story by pulling the off-balance fisherman, spear and all, into the river.[133] John McLeod avoided that indignity, but neither he nor any of his men was "dexteroris enough in being able to grapple" the salmon.[134]

Eventually McLeod and his crew followed the Tuya River to a point where it was joined by two other streams, which together formed "a considerable River, equal in magnitude to the rocky parts of the West Branch Liard River."[135] This was the Stikine, whose headwaters Samuel Black had discovered in 1824, and at whose mouth Peter Skene Ogden had been repulsed by the Russians only a month before. Now a third Hudson's Bay Company explorer had succeeded in reaching the river. McLeod realized its significance. He wrote in his journal that he had found the stream "so much and so long spoken of by which the Coast Indians annually come up in boats on trading excursions with the Nahany and other Indians of the interior."[136]

Reaching the Stikine was the climax of McLeod's 1834 expedition. He had more than fulfilled his instructions, which were merely to explore the region west of the Rocky Mountains. He also accomplished his personal goal of reaching Pacific waters:

Being now fully convinced, that for these four days past, we have proceeded through the country West of the Main range of Rocky Mountains and on frequent occasions quenched our thirst of the waters flowing towards the Pacific: I have determined on now retracing our steps back to where we left our canoe, which intentions I communicated to my two Companions, and in the best possible manner to the remainder of my Party who had taken up their quarter for the night on the opposite shore.[137]

In a final attempt to discover something about the Stikine valley, they climbed a nearby hill, but saw nothing but the Stikine, rolling through its canyon walls toward the sea. McLeod turned his back on the great river and headed up the Tuya.

By July 31, John McLeod was again faced with crossing the unstable Indian bridge. Luck and good balance were with him and his companions, and they were reunited with the rest of the crew. Once safely across the Tuya, McLeod decided to name that stream the Frances River, "in honor of the Governor's Lady."[138] The return march to Dease Lake had to be made on reduced rations because their original five-day allotment of supplies had been exhausted. Hunting as they hiked, they were unable to find even a trace of beaver or a single moose or caribou track. Their success in hunting was limited to a single partridge, which could not have provided more than a taste of meat for each of the eighteen men, and a wolverine, which was hardly a culinary favorite. Finally, on August 4, the party was once again at the head of Dease Lake, where they rested a day, eating their fill of "the best of Whitefish, and the richest Trout." The excellent fishing, McLeod noted, would recommend the south end of the lake as a site for a trading post.[139]

Bad weather, heavy rain, and dark skies made their departure from Dease Lake unpleasant. The voyageurs resourcefully took advantage of the gusting winds to put up a sail on the canoe, so that the explorers yachted across the lake in style. Then, as they entered the narrow upper reaches of the Dease

River, the North canoe suffered a puncture from a sunken log, and repairs had to be made. The bad weather continued to plague them, and the larder, away from the whitefish of the lake, again began to run low. While delayed by a particularly violent storm near the Cottonwood River, the hungry voyageurs spotted a huge flock of Canadian geese. Every weapon in camp was utilized as the explorers crept close to the great birds before opening fire and then massacred the majority of the flock. Twenty-two geese were bagged in all, and the rich, fatty flesh of the waterfowl kept them well fed for many a day.

The only noteworthy event during the return voyage occurred on August 10 when McLeod finally made contact with the Dease River Indians. They were regular customers of the Trading Nahannis, but McLeod's party were the first whites that they had seen. McLeod described the Stikine River to them, and they expressed their familiarity with it, claiming that after four days' march from the mouth of the Tuya the Stikine was clear of rapids to the sea. After trading twenty-three beaver skins, and persuading the Indians to visit Fort Halkett in the spring, McLeod continued on his way,[140] reaching Fort Halkett himself on August 17.

McLeod was welcomed back to the Mackenzie District by good news. Edward Smith, McLeod's former bourgeois and old friend, had been given the dual command of the Mackenzie and Athabasca districts. Another longtime friend, Murdock McPherson of Fort Liard, was assigned to supervise affairs at Fort Simpson. And, to top things off, both McPherson and John McLeod were granted promotions and brought into the Honorable Company as shareholders with the rank of chief trader.[141] Both of the promotions were the work of Edward Smith, who knew both men well and had made use of his influence with Governor Simpson and his fellow chief factors. Of John McLeod he wrote:

To the Majority of the Council he is a stranger—with his actions during seven years residence with me you are better acquainted they have been conspicuous . . . you will pardon the freedom and last effort of one of your Honorable Council, in recommending him to your unanimous support for a speedy Promotion—you will not allow me to Plead in Vain for the man that has such strong claims in service and in merit—and who has in a modest and Gentlemanly manner conducted the Parties whose labours have extended the limits of your favourite McKenzies River District as far beyond its usual boundaries—introduced to our acquaintance seven tribes of Indians—with whom we had intercourse in 1824— and laid open a rich Country to the future pursuits of the Honorable Company.[142]

The promotion brought with it a transfer. Although he had earned this reward and could leave the district with his head held high, McLeod must have regarded his departure as a mixed blessing. He had after all spent eleven years of his life in the Mackenzie, extending its boundaries, enduring hardship, and surviving long, cold, and hungry winters there. Such experiences make emotional bonds with the land. He was now ordered south to the Oregon country, where the winters were mild and the frontier was already explored.

The success of the 1834 Dease River expedition proved to be a rallying call for a redoubled Hudson's Bay Company effort to expand up the Liard River. Only weeks before, Governor Simpson had been planning to reduce the Mackenzie District in the interests of economy and had complained of the futility of such exploratory probes. Now he was suddenly enthused. News of McLeod's success on the Stikine followed the reports of the *Dryad* affair. Although the Russians had slammed the front door to the Stikine trade in the face of the Hudson's Bay Company, John McLeod redeemed all by unexpectedly presenting Governor Simpson with the key to the back door.

CHAPTER 6

The Drive Toward the Stikine River

THE MAN who replaced John McLeod in the vanguard of Hudson's Bay Company explorations in the Far Northwest was a broad-shouldered young Scotsman named Robert Campbell. A religious man, fond of psalms and given to meditation, he carried a Bible with him for guidance and comfort on all his explorations. He was also a man of action, able to endure great physical privation—a hardy traveler whose epic marches have seldom been duplicated. In the annals of the Northwest he was like Job, because his operations were stalked by an unlucky star. Each time that he was within reach of a goal for which he had carefully planned through toil and danger, some unforeseen disaster disrupted all his schemes. Yet, in spite of all, he stuck doggedly to the path of duty and service.

Robert Campbell was born on February 21, 1808, in Perthshire, Scotland. His father was a sheep farmer, and young Robert assisted him with the flocks and farm chores. At age twenty-two, when most of the other lads in his parish were casting about for wives and settling down in the timeless stream of rural life, Robert Campbell's career took an abrupt turn. Chief Factor James McMillan, a hardy old Nor'Wester, returned to Scotland in 1830. Making the rounds among friends and relatives whom he had not seen for decades, McMillan visited the home of his cousins the Campbells. From him Robert heard tall tales of adventures in the Rocky Mountains, thundering herds of buffalo, and exotic tribes of red men. These wild scenes went to the young man's head like the whiskey of the Highlands. In a few days he began to feel an "irresistible" urge to see for himself Rupert's Land, the domain, he fancied, of romance and adventure. Chief Factor McMillan had been assigned the charge of an experimental farm that the Hudson's Bay Company was planning for the Red River Colony. Through his influence Robert Campbell was taken into the service of the company as a submanager of the farm.[1]

The most difficult moment for any recruit of the Hudson's Bay Company was the departure from home. Robert Campbell, who left as a young man of twenty-two, later wrote, "I faced the ordeal with what composure I could muster." A good many of those entering the service were of much tenderer ages. Robert M. Ballantyne was sixteen when he left Scotland as an apprentice clerk contracted to five years' work overseas.[2] Nor was his case an exception. Fifteen- and sixteen-year-old apprentices were common in the company throughout its history. Many of them never returned to their homes, at least not as the lads who had left them.

Campbell embarked for North America from Stromness in the Orkney Islands on June 29, 1830. With him aboard the company supply ship *Prince Rupert* were his cousin, Chief Factor McMillan, Chief Trader Donald Ross, and some apprentice clerks and other servants. The voyage was uneventful except for a delay in Hudson Strait because of heavy ice. The passengers beguiled that time away playing football, taking target practice, and hunting seal. On August 15 the *Prince Rupert* reached York Factory, the company's principal depot. There all was bustle and business. The short shipping season had to be taken advantage of, before winter again froze the bay. At York Factory, Campbell first met the motley population of the Northwest: "Indians, Half-breeds & French Canadian Voyageurs, all different in appearance, a dress & language to anything we greenhorns had ever run across before."[3]

The second leg of Campbell's journey was by York boat to the Red River. A York boat was a broad, shallow rowboat that was capable of carrying very heavy loads while drawing no more than three feet in the water.[4] Governor Simpson had sponsored the adoption of this craft instead of the old North canoe, which, while lighter, was not capable of handling a burden anywhere near the size of a York boat's cargo. Also, the York boat, largely propelled by oars, required less expertise than a canoe—a strong back was sufficient.

Although the York boat spread in use throughout the Northwest, the traditions of the voyageurs, even without their canoes, lived on. Each day before dawn the rousing wake-up call of the guide, "Leve! Leve! Leve!," set the whole camp about its duties. The daily voyage was still divided up into "pipes," distances of ten or fifteen miles, after which the boatmen would rest their oars and indulge in a smoke. And the boatmen's supper was likely to be *robbiboo*, a boiled mixture of flour and pemmican that had been concocted by voyageurs decades before. Fur-trade rituals and traditions such as these had been handed down by traders, coureurs de bois, and voyageurs for almost two hundred years. It was in this world that Campbell would spend most of his adult life.[5]

The Red River settlement was the heart of Rupert's Land. Located in Manitoba at the site of present-day Winnipeg, the settlement had been founded in 1811 by Lord Selkirk to provide farms for the destitute rural folk of the Highlands. After the amalgamation of the two great fur companies in 1821, it had served also as the home base of the half-breeds, or métis, who roamed the frontier during the summer, hunting buffalo and pounding the slaughtered flesh into pemmican for sale to the company. Other métis served the company as boatmen and voyageurs. In the period after 1821, Canada gradually ceased to be the main manpower pool of the fur trade, having been replaced by the Red River settlement.

The purpose of the experimental farm was to encourage the development of agriculture in the settlement by discovering the best grain seed and animal breeds for the area. Campbell ran the farm for the most part on his own, with daily visits from his cousin and an occasional appearance by George Simpson. The governor took a liking to the young man, perhaps because he was influenced by Chief Factor McMillan and Chief Trader Ross, Campbell's traveling companions on his voyage from Scotland. When the agricultural effort proved less than a success, it was Simpson who suggested that Campbell join the fur trade. Thus in the spring of 1834, at age twenty-six, Robert Campbell put away forever the tools of a farmer and headed for York Factory and the life of a fur trader.[6]

Simpson assigned Campbell the rank of postmaster (which made him the equivalent of a noncommissioned officer in the Hudson's Bay Company) and dispatched him to the Mackenzie District. The governor's last words to him were, "Now, Campbell, don't you get married as we want you for active service."[7] Traveling with Campbell on the long York-boat voyage up the Churchill River was Chief Factor Edward Smith, who no doubt gave the young man a full account of the Mackenzie area. Arriving at Portage la Loche, they spent a week at the great carrying place, while the heavy packs of trade goods were transferred from the Hudson's Bay to the arctic drainage. Campbell, like so many travelers before him, was impressed by the wild beauty of the place, particularly the magnificent vistas afforded from a high hill near the end of the portage. It "reminded me of the Scottish highlands," he wrote. Finally, on October 16, he reached Fort Simpson.[8]

Chief Factor John Stuart was still the commander of the Mackenzie District when Campbell arrived. The buoyant old veteran made the novice fur trader welcome and set him about his duties. During the winter Murdock McPherson came downriver from Fort Liard to assume charge of Fort Simpson. With him came John McLeod, who marched the five hundred odd miles from Fort Halkett for a bit of company. McLeod was still brimming over with tales of his journey to the Stikine River the previous summer. Campbell listened attentively as McLeod described the canyons of the Liard, the serene beauty of Dease Lake, and the climax of the adventure at "Terror Bridge." When McLeod returned to Fort Halkett, Campbell was sorry to see him go and remembered him, even years later, as "a most genial man."[9]

Robert Campbell spent most of the summer of 1835 at Fort Liard. Chief Factor Stuart left the district for Scotland, and John McLeod left for the Columbia Department (where he would continue his active service) leading the Hudson's Bay

Company brigades to the Rocky Mountain Rendezvous. Except for those departures the affairs of the Mackenzie River post continued as usual; the summer crop of garden vegetables was harvested, and the Indians visited the fort for their winter outfits of supplies.

The Council of the Northern Department, meanwhile, was actively making plans to follow up on John McLeod's 1834 discoveries. At their annual meeting the council ordered Murdock McPherson to prepare to open up communication with the Northwest Coast via Dease Lake. The first step would be again to move Fort Halkett farther into the interior, this time to Dease Lake, where it would be a stepping-stone to a new post called Fort Drew. Fort Drew was to be established as soon as possible "at least 200 miles distant in a direct line from the height of land towards the Pacific"—in other words, on the border between Russian and British territory.[10] McPherson was also promised an additional fifty "pieces" of trade goods (each "piece" weighed about ninety pounds) to support the new endeavor.

As it turned out, McPherson was distracted from preparing for this venture by Indian trouble at Fort Norman, one of the district posts on the lower Mackenzie River. While traveling to a winter fishery to secure provisions, three of the company's servants attached to Fort Norman had come upon an Indian band. Two of the men, both métis, had had an altercation with these Indians before because of their designs upon the Indian women. McPherson described the atrocity to his friend James Hargrave:

The poor unfortunat Indians were still in the vicinity of the Fishers and our Bucks paid them this hostile visit. They seized upon the arms of the poor unsuspecting Indians and then had them at discreation. [At this point the métis opened fire, killing] 3 men, 1 women [sic], and 7 children . . . The lives of two Women were spared to crown the villany of the atrocious murderers.[11]

News of the murders riled the Indians of the area. Their support in both the fur trade and the provisions trade lagged. McPherson dispatched Robert Campbell to Fort Norman with four men to resupply the post, make a show of strength, and "fetch up to discipline Cadieu the principal acter" in the massacre.[12] Campbell arrived at Fort Norman and with the help of William Mowat, who was in charge of the post, did his best to restore normal relations, promising justice to the Indians. He then made the nine-day march back to Fort Simpson to surrender Cadieu to McPherson. Although Fort Simpson did not have a jail, Cadieu was secured "in a manner that he will have no opportunity . . . to shed more blood."[13]

McPherson laid the blame for the grim affair on the unstable character of métis employees: "Some misfortune of this kind has been long since apprehended from the number of Indian & half Breed Servants that were sent to this District."[14] John Bell, at Fort Good Hope, echoed this sentiment when he wrote: "It was a very bad piece of policy to have introduced so many of these profligate and infamous characters into McK. River, where they are with justice detested by the Natives and disliked by the Whites."[15] It may have been such complaints that prompted the Northern Department Council to resolve that "in future European servants only be sent into McKenzies River."[16]

In spite of that incident, plans for expansion to Dease Lake continued in the summer of 1836. Originally the charge of the enterprise was to be given either to John Bell or John Hutchinson, both of whom were clerks. Then, in a later correspondence, George Simpson seems to have changed his mind: "Mr. Hutchinson is inactive . . . the choice must therefore be between Mr. Bell and Mr. Campbell the latter only requires a little experience to become a very useful man."[17] Unfortunately this letter did not arrive in time for McPherson to effect the shift of responsibility, and John Hutchinson was given the honor of expanding the company's operations to Dease Lake. He was not particularly anxious to assume the duty. In February, 1836, he advised McPherson that he wished to retire from the service because of "the repeated and urgent solicitations of my friends at home." McPherson reminded Hutchinson that he would not be allowed to leave until the Council of the Northern Department had reviewed his application, which would take another year. A few months later

Hutchinson was again making noises about his inability to carry out the Dease Lake expansion. This time the problem was insufficient means, complicated by the supposed bellicosity of the Nahanni Indians, who threatened to destroy the English if they entered their lands.[18] Faced with such a mixed bag of excuses, McPherson might have realized that Hutchinson was not the man for a task that required energy and determination, but he did nothing to alter the situation before he left Fort Simpson to deliver the year's fur returns to Portage la Loche. He assumed that Hutchinson was on his way to Dease Lake.

Robert Campbell was left to supervise Fort Simpson during the summer of 1836. His routine was fairly leisurely, as there was not much to do about the fort. Occasionally *engagés* would be sent a short distance down the Mackenzie to a swampy section of the river where tall grass grew. The weeds would be cut and used to feed the few head of cattle at Fort Simpson. Sometimes one of the local Indians would "cast up" and trade a few fish or a beaver pelt for a small amount of powder and ball. On one particular early August morning, however, the peaceful rhythm of the summer was unexpectedly disrupted. John Hutchinson and a North canoe of voyageurs landed at the fort. Campbell was surprised by Hutchinson's appearance, as the entire district had thought that he was at Dease Lake. By way of explanation Hutchinson told a tale of near disaster.

According to Hutchinson's report he had proceeded up the Liard from Fort Halkett to Portage Brûlé. Arriving at the portage in the later part of the day, the men were able to transport the outfit only a short distance up the trail before dark. On the next morning they discovered the footprints of someone who had circled their camp during the night. Fearful of a Nahanni ambush, Hutchinson sent two Indians to scout the trail ahead. At the end of the portage they spied a large Nahanni war party with their faces fiercely painted black, "attired in blue cloth capotes and red leggings." Each of the warriors was armed with a stout lance and a trade gun. After a while, the warriors, who were over one hundred strong, left their hiding place and began to move to the attack. Hutchinson's scouts reached the camp in time to warn the traders of the approaching enemy. The clerk tried to make an orderly retreat, but when the voyageurs saw the Indians, a panic ensued, and all fled to the canoe just before the attack commenced. So great was the danger that Hutchinson did not feel safe in maintaining Fort Halkett; he and his crew did not stop fleeing until they reached Fort Simpson.[19]

This incident became the main subject of discussion throughout the district. Most agreed that the traders had been lucky to escape with their lives. Hutchinson announced that he would no longer take risks and would quit both the district and the company's service the next spring. Robert Campbell's reaction was completely different. He notified Murdock McPherson that he would volunteer to lead another attempt to settle Dease Lake.[20]

In the meantime, Governor Simpson had made a careful study of Hutchinson's retreat. He had never thought highly of Hutchinson's abilities, which in 1826 he had described as "being rather beneath mediocrity."[21] He did not believe a word of Hutchinson's tale about the Indian war party: "The whole is a tissue of misrepresentation arising from his own imbecility, the formidable and hostile array referred to being nothing more or less than the production of a timid mind."[22] After Hutchinson left the Hudson's Bay territory, the whole incident became clearer. As Murdock McPherson wrote, "there can be only one opinion of his unprecedented story regarding his shameful flight from the West Branch. He was affraid of going to pass a winter in such Country and invented a story to avoid that."[23]

Whatever his reasons, Hutchinson's retreat was extremely debilitating to the Hudson's Bay Company in its trade war with the Russians. Not only was the expansion from Dease Lake delayed but also the abandonment of Fort Halkett marked a step backward for the company. It would take the Mackenzie District two years to redeem a setback that need never have occurred. The delay was all the more galling to Simpson and the Northern Department Council because each

year that went by without an English establishment on the
Stikine River, or at least on Dease Lake, was a year of steady,
profitable trade for the Russians based on furs from English
territory.

Robert Campbell was promoted to clerk in return for his
"spirited tender" of his services for the Dease Lake extension.
In March, 1837, he left Fort Simpson on snowshoes, journey-
ing to Fort Liard, which was a convenient jumping-off place
to the upper Liard River. The abundance of birchbark at Fort
Liard made it a good location to construct the canoes necessary for the summer's voyage (the scarcity of good birchbark
on the upper Liard and later in the Yukon was one of the
many difficulties that complicated the advance into those regions). The canoes were constructed and gummed before the
ice broke up on the Liard. That left Campbell plenty of time
to select his crew. He would need all the time he could get.
Hutchinson's graphic, if apocryphal, account of the Nahanni
war party had stymied the spirit of adventure among the engagés in the Mackenzie District, who believed that, if they
managed to elude the Nahannis, their reward would be the
formidable natural barriers of the Liard's rapids, climaxed by
the Terror Bridge over the Tuya.

In spite of this timidity Campbell—by cajoling, playing on
their pride and probably pulling rank—was able by mid-May
to form a crew of sorts. He did not have much faith in the
sixteen men whom he had bullied into going: "I could see
that they went into the enterprise in a half-hearted way & were
animated with anything but the proper spirit."[24] At their
third camp up the river the Indian hunters deserted the enterprise. Nor were the engagés who remained very enthusiastic.
Still, Campbell roused them to their duty at an early hour,
and the canoes embarked. As was usual, the canoemen took a
rest from their paddles for breakfast in the midmorning.
About half the crew took this opportunity to stand together
and refused to continue upriver. Campbell must have been
in a Highland rage. There "was no use waisting time espostu-
lating with such a timid crowd"; he resolved to return to Fort
Liard to find some stouter souls.[25]

When he arrived at the fort, Campbell called together all the men at the post. In a cool, determined manner he explained:

The trip *had* to be made; that the men who engaged would like myself have to go through to the end of the journey; that there was to be no turning back or flying from an enemy before he was seen; that when seen I would not ask any of my men to go before me to face the enemy; that I would be kind to, & do all I could for, my men; but that if any of them showed signs of insubordination, it would be at the peril of his life.[26]

Campbell's frank declaration won him the support of the voyageurs, and the next morning he again pushed up the Liard.

The return to Fort Liard had cost Campbell a week's time. During the delay the river waters continued to rise, as the warmer weather melted the mountain snow, flooding the creeks and multiplying the strength of the already turbulent river. The difficulties of river navigation made Campbell apprehensive that his men might lose heart. He was constantly trying to calm their fears, "as the croak of a frog or the screech of a nightowl was immediately taken for an enemy signal."[27]

By the time when the expedition had reached Devil's Portage, some of the voyageurs were deeply regretting ever having volunteered for such risky service. They would have welcomed a panic like that which overcame Hutchinson's party. On the night when they arrived at the three-day portage, their campfire conversation was interrupted by the barking of the expedition's dogs. The voyageurs right away assumed the worst, crying "there must be enemies prowling round." Campbell assured them that it was merely a bear or some other animal ambling past the camp. In a short while the dogs were again quiet, and the party was able to get to sleep. Early the next morning Campbell rose before the rest of the crew and, taking his gun, went ahead to scout the portage trail. A short distance from camp, he passed some pieces of trade goods which had been brought up the evening before. Sometime later, while returning from his hike, Campbell passed the same bundles and noted as he did that they had been rearranged and that one had been cut, as if by a knife, in a corner. Back at the camp Campbell found most of the voyageurs crouched behind cover with their guns ready, cowering from an enemy, who they claimed had surrounded them. Campbell scolded his men for their idleness and ordered them to get about their duties. They offered as proof of the Nahannis' dangerous presence the torn bale of trade goods. Campbell, however, had been up too early in the morning to accept that story:

I immediately answered that this had been done by one of themselves; that I had seen the bale that morning before they were out of their blankets, but had seen no enemy or trace of them; that I had noticed the altered position of the bale on my return & that it was not the work of enemies, as they were not in the habit of leaving clumsy marks of their presence to betray them; & that in short I was not to be taken in by such a transparent imposition.[28]

In this manner the voyageurs learned that the man whom they were dealing with was no John Hutchinson, but a worthy successor to John McLeod. Perhaps they were shamed by their conduct, or just at a loss for further devices to defer the expedition. They gave Campbell no more trouble.

Because of the delays encountered, Campbell decided it was too late in the year to risk establishing a new post. He therefore set up winter quarters at Fort Halkett, which the voyageurs were surprised to find exactly as Hutchinson had left it, undisturbed by marauding hordes of Nahanni Indians. This prompted Campbell to make a visit to Portage Brûlé, where Hutchinson had encountered the enemy. As he expected, the pieces of trade goods meant for Dease Lake were scattered about the portage landing just where the men had left them; "of course everything was spoilt, except such articles as ball, shot, &c, & the provisions eaten by wild animals." The sight had a sobering effect on Campbell's men, who now realized the "folly of their fears."[29]

During the winter the fur traders were able to make contact with the Indians of the region, who, with the desertion of Fort Halkett, had been deprived of the white men's goods on which they had just begun to depend. Campbell also received dispatches from Fort Simpson, including a personal note from Governor Simpson. The governor was continuing to take an interest in Campbell's career. He exhorted him to try to open up operations on the Stikine River, closing the note with the overconfident assertion: "Robert Campbell is not the man I take him to be unless in due time he plants the H.B. Standard on the shores of the Pacific."[30]

In the spring of 1838, as Campbell prepared to set off for Dease Lake, he received reinforcements under the command of A. R. McLeod, Jr., an apprentice clerk. McLeod was the métis son of Chief Trader Alexander R. McLeod, who had briefly commanded the Mackenzie District. The younger Mc-Leod, although educated in Canada, was a dissatisfied man. In 1836 he had joined "General" James Dickson's Indian Liberating Army, which was supposed to conquer California and set up an Indian and half-breed state. McLeod had served as a captain in this crusade, before it died for lack of support. He was not the able second-in-command that Campbell needed.[31]

Campbell's journey from Fort Halkett to Dease Lake was accomplished without incident, though he was impressed by the snow-covered mountains along the Dease River. He climbed one of them and named it Ben Lawers after a mountain in his native Perthshire, Scotland. Upon reaching Dease Lake, he put the majority of his men under the command of A. R. McLeod, Jr., with orders to construct a wintering post. Campbell wanted to explore the country along the Stikine. With him were three men who would be among his faithful retainers in the years ahead: Francis Hoole, the interpreter, and Lapie and Kitza, two young Indian hunters.

In two spruce-bark canoes the four men crossed Dease Lake and followed the trail that McLeod had discovered four years earlier. The trail took them uphill and down. Because of the changes in elevation Campbell experienced each of the four seasons in a single day: winter in the snow on the top of the ridge and spring in the young grass on the upper slopes, and the thick vegetation of summer climaxed by a patch of berries as ripe as in autumn. On that same day they reached the native bridge that McLeod's men had aptly named Terror Bridge. Approaching it, they spotted the smoke of an Indian campfire on the opposite side. Hoole, the interpreter, "though very handy, a splendid hunter & canoe maker, & most ingenious at all kinds of work, was exceedingly timid & afraid of strange Indians." Only after some discussion would he agree to continue.[32]

Terror Bridge had not improved during the four years since Hudson's Bay Company explorers had faced it last. It had developed, in addition to its former flimsiness, a distinct list to one side. Hoole would have no part of it. While he waited on the opposite bank, Campbell, Kitza, and Lapie crossed the bridge—which swayed and bent under their weight—and proceeded to the Indian tent. Whoever had dwelt there made a hasty departure when the explorers drew near. Campbell found the campfire burning brightly, and in the tent they found three metal pots, a sure sign of the fur trade. One of them contained some salmon. Since Campbell and his Indian companions were hungry, they helped themselves to the fish and left as payment a knife and some tobacco.[33] When they recrossed the bridge and joined Hoole, they no doubt told him about the fresh fish that they had for supper. They then turned in for the night, leaving the interpreter perhaps to munch on a tired piece of pemmican and to muse on the old adage that "fortune favors the bold."

Very early the next morning Campbell was awakened as one of his young hunters cried out, "Indians!, Indians." Through the faint light of dawn they saw on the far side of the river a group of sixteen Indians making their way toward Terror Bridge. Hoole's reaction was to throw off his blanket and grab his gun, saying, "Let us run for our lives." Only Campbell's own threat of violence kept him from turning tail. Campbell himself remained cool. He hoisted the Hudson's Bay Company flag, which was a red ensign with a small Union Jack in the top corner and the initials "H.B.C." prominently displayed. After some hesitation the Indians crossed the bridge, and a council ensued. The chief of the band presented Campbell with a peace pipe, which was then passed around the fire. It soon became clear that the Indians were Nahannis. They had been informed of Campbell's presence by the resident of the tent that the explorers had visited the evening before. The tribe was at that time taking part in a great Indian tribe rendezvous on the Stikine, at which the Tlingits and many other tribes were present. The Nahannis had always been told that, if they met white people from east of the mountains, they should kill them because they were enemies. Fortunately for Campbell, this chief was friendly, and he soon took a liking to the Scotsman.[34] He became alarmed, however, when Campbell made it clear that he intended to visit the rendezvous site. The Nahanni chief claimed that a great Tlingit chief, Shakes, would be the lord of the assembly and that, if Campbell fell into his hands, "Shakes will kill you, & though I & my band would be willing to protect you, we could not do so as Shakes' men are as the sands of the beach."[35] This did not deter the explorer, who was determined to visit the rendezvous.

Campbell's little party and the Nahanni chief set off down the trail to the Stikine. These Nahannis were the same as those whom Samuel Black had called the Trading Nahannis. They were actually Tahltans and had in precontact times been enemies of the Tlingits, fighting many battles for control of the Stikine River.[36] The Tlingits' trade with the Russians and Americans on the coast had made them too formidable as foes and too valuable as trade contacts for the Nahannis to risk their hostility. Trade goods, especially fire arms and steel knives acquired from the Tlingits, had allowed the Tahltans in turn to dominate the poorer tribes of the interior, such as the Sekanis and Kascas. Anthropologist Catharine McClellan, who has studied the oral traditions of the southern Yukon Territory, has found a similar relationship between the Tlingits and the Tagish Indians.[37] The Tahltans and the Tagishes are both Athapascan tribes of the cordillera region. Early anthropologists, like the fur traders, grouped the two tribes into one large group, calling them Nahannis.[38]

The relationship of these tribes to the Tlingits was ambivalent. They suffered humiliations at the Tlingits' hands; their camps were raided, and their women kidnapped. At the same time, because of their close commercial relations, the Tagishes and Tahltans often intermarried with the Tlingits, forming family alliances.[39] This ambivalent attitude was also demonstrated in the Tahltans'—or, as Campbell called them, the Nahannis'—reaction to the fur traders' presence. It seems as if some Nahannis welcomed meeting him as an opportunity to throw off the Tlingit influence, while others viewed him as a threat to their own dominance of the interior tribes.

The Hudson's Bay Company never fully grasped the significance of this complex intertribal trade system. George Simpson, Murdock McPherson, and even Robert Campbell thought only about the Russian competitors on the Northwest Coast, not the Indian traders who actually transferred the furs from the British interior to the Russians.

As Robert Campbell neared the rendezvous, Nahannis came up in twos and threes and tried to dissuade him from continuing. Sometimes they pushed at him or tried to turn him around; always they said, "If you persist, you will never return, Shakes will kill you." This did not deter the explorer, but it did alarm him. If he were slain, McLeod and the men at Dease Lake would be left open to a surprise attack. To prevent this, Campbell told Hoole and one of the young Indians to return to Terror Bridge and wait there for two days for him. If he did not appear, they were to assume that he was dead, cut the bridge down, and return to Dease Lake. Hoole "was much pleased" by this new plan; he had not been too anxious to meet Shakes, who by all accounts was an unpleasant character. His deliverance, however, was short-lived. Neither of the young Indian lads, Lapie and Kitza, would agree to leave Campbell's side. They swore that they would rather die with him than turn back; "Their fathers they said had told them that if they ever deserted me in danger they need never come back themselves." The tears in their eyes persuaded Campbell of their earnestness, and he scrapped the emergency plan. The Hudson's Bay men therefore pressed on together. Poor Hoole was unable to hide his disappointment and distress.[40]

Their first view of the rendezvous was from a high hill overlooking the Stikine River. Campbell later wrote: "Such a concourse of Indians I had never seen assembled. They were gathered from all parts of the Western slope of the Rockies & from along the Pacific Coast."[41] The rendezvous would last for weeks, with hundreds of Indians living on the plentiful salmon of the Stikine. It was a time for trade and games and an opportunity to exchange news.

Descending from the hill, Campbell was immediately im-
mersed in a sea of curious red men, who were eager to see the
audacious stranger. Escorting the Scotsman was an Indian,
named Jack, who spoke a bit of English. As the Indians ad-
dressed question after question to Campbell, Jack translated
the fur trader's replies, which were in turn "taken up & yelled
by a hundred throats till the surrounding rocks & the valley
re-echoed with the sound."[42] Then suddenly the ranks of half-
naked Indians opened, and through the lane came Shakes, the
despotic overlord of the rendezvous. The tall, muscular Tlingit gravely shook Campbell's hand and led him to his tent. In
the tent, much to Campbell's surprise, were four Russian
American Company officers. The leader of the group was a
Mr. Monrobe, who, although polite, was unable to hide his
jealousy at Campbell's appearance.[43] Shakes served his guests
a cup of whiskey, which Campbell only tasted. He wanted to
keep his wits about him. Outside the tent there was a great
deal of noise. All at once the cover of the tent was ripped off
by the Nahannis, who suspected that Shakes was planning to
murder Campbell. They warned the Tlingit that, "If the
White Chief is killed, there will be plenty of blood spilled
here!"[44]

Campbell himself was well aware of the great danger that
he was risking when he entered this great Indian concourse.
He had surrendered hope of escaping, but, armed with a
double-barreled rifle, pistols, and a dagger, he intended to sell
his life dearly. He thought his moment might have come when
Shakes asked him to give a demonstration of his rifle, which
was not only double-barreled but also a new percussion gun,
unlike the flintlocks of the Tlingits. Campbell thought that it
might be a trick on Shakes's part to have Campbell empty his
rifle and thus disarm himself. The whole crowd of Indians
loudly exclaimed each time Campbell fired. Between their
screams and the gunfire it must have sounded like hell on
earth. Shakes, however, was unable to take advantage of the
situation, as Campbell always had a fresh charge ready in his
hand each time that he fired.[45]

Among the Indians with Shakes were some who claimed to
know Dr. John McLoughlin, the chief factor of the Columbia

Department. Campbell took this opportunity to dash off a short note to the doctor and entrusted it to one of the Indians. Remarkably this note, dated July 22, reached the Hudson's Bay Company post at Port Simpson by August 10. The Indians had a great deal of respect for the written word.

After a time Campbell was able to break away from Shakes and the throng of Indians about him and return to the hill above the rendezvous site. There he was reunited with Kitza, Lapie, and Hoole. Also present was a remarkable person, the chieftainess of the Nahanni Indians:

She commanded the respect not only of her own people, but of the tribes they had intercourse with. She was a fine looking woman rather above the middle height & about 35 years old. In her actions & personal appearance she was more like the Whites than the pure Indian race. She had a pleasing face lit up with fine intelligent eyes, which when she was excited flashed like fire.[46]

With her was her husband, whom Campbell described as a "nonentity." The chieftainess soon demonstrated her influence, when she noticed that Campbell was vexed by the theft of "a gun, fire bag, small kettle & axe," all of which were needed for the tramp back to Dease Lake. She climbed down to the great encampment and in a short while returned with the stolen objects.[47]

Before departing from the rendezvous, Campbell "hoisted the H.B.C. flag & cut H.B.C. & date on a tree, thus taking possession of the country for the Company,"[48] as Shakes and the Russians looked up from the plain below. There was no time for further ceremony; the Nahanni chieftainess had informed him that his life depended upon a quick departure. She escorted the explorers for several miles, warning them not to stop until they crossed Terror Bridge, because Shakes was sure to have stirred the young braves to violence. As a parting gift Campbell gave the chieftainess his handkerchief; in return she took from her wrists two silver bracelets and put them in the Scotsman's hand. It was the beginning of a friendship that eventually would save Campbell's life.

The four explorers made their way back to Dease Lake, brimming over with elation at their success, not to mention their safe exit from Shakes's camp. A. R. McLeod, Jr., had meanwhile begun construction of the fort. He had done a good job, but the work was hampered by food shortages. The fishnets yielded only small catches, and the Indian hunters had been unable to bring in any moose. Campbell realized that, if the larder was bare in summer, winter would be no better. He resolved to go to Fort Simpson. This would allow him to report what had transpired on the Stikine, as well as to fetch up additional food supplies and trade goods.[49]

Campbell, together with Lapie, made the long journey down to Fort Simpson. The Dease Lake post could afford no provisions for them, and they had to live off the land on the entire journey. They must have both been excellent voyageurs to navigate the Liard in just a small bark canoe. They did run into some trouble near Hell Gate, where in heavy rapids, surrounded by sheer canyon walls, the canoe inconveniently sprang a leak. It quickly began to fill with water, and they would have been swamped before passing through the gate. Their lives were saved only by the fortuitous discovery of a small landing at the bottom of one of the cliffs. They got the canoe ashore and, with luck again on their side, found a pine tree with pitch so that they could repair the rupture.[50]

Lapie and Campbell arrived at Fort Simpson on August 20. McPherson was pleased with Campbell's success. By encountering the Russians and the Tlingit Indians, Campbell conclusively proved that the river that McLeod had discovered in 1834, which Governor Simpson insisted on calling the Pelly River, was indeed the Stikine. McPherson was not sanguine, however, about the trade prospects of the Dease Lake post. He thought of it as "a region of eternal snow & barren rocks, and I do believe, literally of nothing else."[51] He refused to grant Campbell any additional trade goods and, in spite of Campbell's every entreaty, allowed him only a small amount of provisions (not even enough for the return trip to Dease Lake). Risking his life, Campbell had journeyed to the depot only to return empty-handed. He was beset by snow storms on the return voyage to Dease Lake, which he reached on October 12, completing a summer's travel of over two thousand miles.[52]

Campbell was not to be allowed a winter of rest. When he

surveyed his situation, he realized that there would be hard-ship ahead.

The buildings were ready for our use, but our prospects were very gloomy. The produce of our nets, on which we depended princi-pally for subsistence, was inadequate to our daily wants, & the hunters were unable to add anything to our slender means. We were now thrown entirely on our own resources, a long dreary winter approaching, ten men, one family [probably Hoole's], a clerk & myself to provide for, a distance of about 600 miles be-tween us & the nearest Company's Post (Fort de Liard), shut in by barren mountains surrounded by a host of Indians rendered by Shakes' instigations & our high tariff, anything but amicably dis-posed towards us. We exerted ourselves to the utmost, trying every plan to increase our stock. Several fisheries were established along the Lake and our hunters searched far and near for game, but all in vain. It was not without reason that I looked forward to the winter with apprehension.[53]

To increase the possibility of survival for all involved, Camp-bell dispersed his men. Some were sent to the south end of Dease Lake, where Lapie and Kitza had found good rabbit hunting, and others went down the Dease toward the Liard, where it was hoped that they might find some big game. The latter party was given the option of trying to make their way to Fort Liard, and Campbell gave them a message for McPher-son if they decided upon that course.

Hunger proved to be only one of several trials that the Hudson's Bay men had to endure that winter. Most trying were the harassments of the Nahanni Indians. During their first visit to the post they were on their best behavior because of the presence of the chieftainess. When she saw the pitiful condition of the fur traders, she ordered her slaves "to cook the best they had for our use, & it was served under her direc-tions." The feast placed before Campbell consisted of salmon steaks and caribou meat, "a sumptuous repast." The Nahannis remained at the post the rest of the day. During the evening, a group of young warriors burst into the dwelling house, catching Campbell and McLeod unprepared. Screaming their war cries, they seized the traders' guns and would surely have killed them, but for the chieftainess, who had been sleeping at the other end of the house. She thrust herself into the middle of the fray. The warriors were immediately silent and still. Then she "found out the instigator of the riot, walked up to him, and, stamping her foot on the ground, repeatedly spat in his face, her eyes blazing with anger."[54]

Unfortunately, when the chieftainess returned to the Stikine, these warriors stayed in the Dease Lake area. Without her "controlling presence," they began a campaign of terror and intimidation. It was an old custom for Indians coming to trade at a post to fire shots into the air as a salute. The Nahannis gave a new wrinkle to this practice on one occasion, when they came towards the post firing their guns right at the buildings. Campbell said to McLeod, as they both took cover, "I have often heard it said that a ball passing through one feels like an icicle; we will soon know."[55] Luckily the Indians ceased fire and contented themselves with roughing up the fur traders. A few weeks later another band of Nahannis burst into the post. They seized hold of Louis Lapierre, a veteran voyageur, who asked Campbell uneasily, "Are we to yield to them or are we to sell our lives as dearly as we can?" Campbell feared that resistance might spark a general massacre. Trying to stall for time, he picked up his Bible and read out the first lines he came upon: "Have I not commanded thee? Be Strong & of good Courage, be not afraid, neither be thou dismayed, for the Lord thy God is with thee whithersoever thou goest." The words were a tonic to Campbell's spirit and disconcerted the Nahannis, who were awed by both the book and the grave tone of the fur trader's voice. Campbell then defused the crisis by a few presents and asking a Nahanni to deliver a note—a task they enjoyed—to A. R. McLeod, who was told to bring the men from the rabbiting area at the south end of Dease Lake to the main post.[56] With these reinforcements Campbell was able to rid the post of the marauders, though not before they had plundered the storeroom of its contents. This constant humiliation was bitterly accepted by Campbell only because "to resent the outrageous conduct of the Indians would have been suicidal folly." Campbell could only relish the thought that, if "we had been in a stockaded fort with plenty of provisions & all our men inside, I venture to say we would have taught these aggressive gentlemen a wholesome lesson."[57]

The Indians of the Fort Halkett region, with whom the company had good relations, tried to help Campbell, bringing food and furs to Dease Lake. This traffic was stopped after only two or three visits by the Nahannis, who threatened to kill anyone who gave aid to the English traders. In late February, Campbell set out on snowshoes to see how the men he had sent toward the Liard were faring. After three days' travel over the snow he came upon the first of several camps in which the men were living. The winter there had been as difficult as at Dease Lake, except that the rabbit hunters were spared the presence of the Nahannis. On one occasion the nine men shared a single squirrel for their only meal of the day. Two of the *engagés* and an Indian despaired of surviving the winter in such a fashion, and set out for Fort Liard. They were in too weak a condition for the lengthy trek; the *engagés* perished en route, and only the Indian was able to stagger safely to the fort.[58]

As spring began, Campbell and his men were found scraping their empty larder for anything edible. With the snow melting, they tore off the webbing of their snowshoes and boiled it up for dinner. Their last meal at Dease Lake was the boiled parchment of the post's windows, which had the savory consistency of glue. Then on May 8 the Hudson's Bay men left the scene of their wretched winter and headed down the Dease River, which was now free of ice and flowing clearly toward the Liard. Ducks and geese flying to their nesting grounds in the Arctic provided the first good meal that the fur traders had known in many a day. Farther downstream they came upon the camp of one of the Nahanni bands who had bullied them all winter. The Indians "were much alarmed at seeing us in such force, & were now as abject & submissive as they had formerly been bold & arbitrary." Campbell's men thought that this was a perfect opportunity to pay back the savage treatment that they had suffered in the past season; it took all the trader's influence, not to mention his own Christian patience, to stop the men from killing the Nahannis. Instead the English satisfied themselves with retrieving some of their stolen property and continuing downriver in peace. Campbell reached Fort Halkett at the end of May. He sent some men down to Fort Simpson with the few furs that they had collected during the winter. He would reestablish Fort Halkett and await further orders.[59]

Robert Campbell in the spring of 1839 was physically and mentally exhausted. In the past year he had endured constant and considerable danger, unrelenting privation, and despair. The Dease Lake operation, which was his responsibility, had failed. Two of his men had died of starvation. Little had he realized, when he returned in triumph from the Indian trade rendezvous a few months before, that in so short a time he would be routed from the area. His mind must have returned to Chief Trader McPherson's refusal to increase his supplies. Perhaps a little more support would have made the difference. Nor were Campbell's spirits lifted when in September, 1839, he received word from Governor Simpson that all his efforts had been for naught. While Campbell had been battling Russian influence and starvation in the Dease Lake region, Simpson had come to an amicable agreement with Baron von Wrangel concerning the Stikine trade and intercompany relations in general. There was no longer any need for the Hudson's Bay Company to push toward the Stikine from the interior.[60]

The Contract of 1839

The agreement to which Governor Simpson referred in a letter to Robert Campbell was a unique document known as the Contract of 1839. It was a direct result of the Dryad Affair and the continuing trade war between the two companies. After Count Nesselrode had admitted that the Russian American Company based its blockade of the Stikine on an incorrect interpretation of the Anglo-Russian Convention, the negotiations had bogged down on the issue of reparations, which the Russian government tried every excuse not to pay. Although the British Foreign Office tried to maintain pressure on the Russians for compensation, the explosive Eastern Question was heating up, and because of the conflict with Russia on the Persian and Afghan frontiers the Stikine River was necessarily regarded as a minor matter.

In August, 1838, the Hudson's Bay Company decided to settle the matter independent of the two governments. While its servants, such as Robert Campbell, were maintaining the pressure on the Russian trade on the frontier, George Simpson and John Henry Pelly, the London governor of the company, journeyed to Saint Petersburg to wave the olive branch, hoping to solve the company's dispute with the Russians by some head-to-head business meetings. It proved difficult. Neither Simpson nor Pelly spoke Russian, and the British consulate was unable to help them make contact with the Russian American Company's officials. Pelly, almost in despair, wrote that "so much involved in mystery are the affairs of that Concern, that none of the English residents in Saint Petersburg with whom we had communication could give any distinct information respecting its affairs, altho many of them were Stockholders."[61] Patience and persistence in the end carried the day, and a series of meetings were arranged with von Wrangel.

During the negotiations the Hudson's Bay Company used the claims of the Dryad Affair as a bargaining chip for further concessions. Simpson and Pelly went back to the proposal that had first been made almost ten years before when Aemilius Simpson had visited Sitka: they wanted to secure a contract for provisioning the Russian American Company's settlements. Thus the Hudson's Bay Company might drive out the Yankee traders, who were still making profits from that business. The departure of the American traders would reduce the United States's influence in the Northwest—an important consideration in the rivalry for Oregon—and at the same time the Russian American Company would become dependent upon their English rivals for supplies. After much dickering over price, the Russians finally agreed to the Hudson's Bay Company's proposal.

The provisions agreement was merely the springboard for a much broader scheme to reduce tensions between the two monopolies. Baron von Wrangel proposed leasing to the English control of the Russian American Company's southern coastal territories. The rent was set at two thousand beaver skins annually, and the lease was to run for ten years. The proposal promised something to both parties: the British would have complete control of the Northwest Coast, while the Russians were guaranteed the land furs that had made the Stikine so important to them.[62] The formal provisions of the contract between the two monopolies were drawn up in January, 1839, and the document was signed on February 6 in Hamburg. The Hudson's Bay Company had assumed the supervision of a large portion of the Russian empire as a matter of routine business.

The Contract of 1839 marked the end of the Hudson's Bay Company's attempts to push through the mountains of the interior and exploit the trade of the Pacific-bound waters. With the coast under British control the furs of the interior, even if acquired by Tahltan or Tlingit middlemen, would still eventually fall into the hands of the Hudson's Bay Company. There was no need for such costly and dangerous posts as Dease Lake while the company held the Russian lease; the trade of the Pacific Slope would best be conducted from the coast. That is not to say that the Hudson's Bay Company was abandoning its western expansion, particularly in the Mackenzie District. Instead the direction of expansion was deflected from the Stikine on the southwest toward the northwest and the as-yet-undiscovered upper Yukon River. The English, having achieved control of the southern coast of Russian America, were beginning a campaign to capture the undeveloped trade of Russian America's northwestern frontier as well.

Discovery of the Peel River

The drive for the Stikine River, including the expeditions of Samuel Black and John McLeod, had been an exercise in negatively motivated expansion: the Hudson's Bay Company's aim had been simply to thwart its trade rivals.[63] The furs of the Stikine River valley could be most easily acquired either at the interior posts of New Caledonia and the upper Liard River in the Mackenzie District, or along the coast by company trading ships. The Stikine itself had only been important when Russian or American rivals were in a position to interrupt the flow of furs into English hands. Thus the explorations there had been not so much to open a new area as to protect a commerce that had already been developed.

After the successful resolution of the Northwest Coast trade rivalry the Hudson's Bay Company did continue its westward exploration program, but the purpose of the explorations had changed. The company's aim was no longer to subvert the trade of a rival but to develop a new trade and to discover the geography of an unknown area. It had been aware of these goals during its explorations toward the Pacific Slope, but they had been in the background, subordinate to the struggle with the Russians.

Thus in the 1840s the English turned their attention to the area northwest of the Liard, to the headwaters of the Yukon River. At the same time an entirely new exploratory front was also opened up on the lower Mackenzie River along the Peel River.

The new orientation to the northwest had been prompted by the discoveries of the Arctic explorers. Between 1825 and 1827, Captain John Franklin had been in the Mackenzie District continuing his survey of the northern coastline of America. His second arctic land expedition was a much more successful endeavor than his first journey. Over twelve hundred miles of new coast were surveyed from Return Reef on the north coast of modern Alaska to the Coppermine River.

Besides adding to geographic knowledge, the second Franklin expedition had two very pragmatic purposes. The first was to thwart any attempt by Russian explorers to complete the mapping of the Arctic Coast and thus to impress upon the Russians that the north was a British sphere of influence (an aim in keeping with the hot international rivalry of the 1820s). The second purpose was to scout for British commerce, particularly the Hudson's Bay Company, the commercial opportunities west of the Mackenzie River delta.[64]

In pursuing the second aim, Franklin made a valuable find. During the return voyage along the north coast, a band of Eskimos warned Franklin that a band of western Kutchin Indians planned to ambush the exploration party as it entered the main branch of the Mackenzie River. These Indians traded with interior tribes who were in contact with Russian American Company posts. The Kutchins took the goods that they received from the middlemen and in turn traded them for a healthy profit to the Eskimos.[65] By entering the Mackenzie River via the seldom-used west channel, Franklin avoided any trouble. In doing so, he discovered a large tributary of the Mackenzie, which he named for Sir Robert Peel, then secretary of state for the British Home Department.[66] Since the Peel River enters the Mackenzie River from the southwest, the Hudson's Bay Company saw it as a potential source of new furs and a route to the transmountain region. Unfortunately, early efforts to exploit the Peel's promise were thwarted by poor planning.

A continuing theme in the Hudson's Bay Company's explorations of the Far Northwest was the inconsistency displayed by the administration of the company. Time and time again, the officers in the field were given orders to explore or expand their district only to be denied the men and supplies needed to execute those orders. It was this problem that prevented the early exploration of the Peel River.

In 1827, and again in 1828, the Northern Council ordered Chief Trader Peter Warren Dease, who had served with the Franklin expedition, to acquire information about the furs and the Indians of the Peel River in order to ascertain if a post should be built there.[67] Owing to a "scarcity of men," Dease was not able to investigate the river personally, but he did inquire among the Indians who traded at Fort Good Hope, the northernmost post of the Mackenzie District, and was able to gain some significant information about the Peel River country. He wrote Governor Simpson that, according to the eastern Kutchin Indians,

no other tribe but themselves frequent that Stream, they generally remain to the westward between it and where the Mountains dip into the Ocean which is their hunting grounds, They tell us that toward the sources of that River, Beaver is to be found Pretty numerous, but the distance great for them to hunt and bring their hunts to this Establishment, that was a Post established for them they would be able to make better hunts, But at the same time the Whites would require to be strong, as they would be the subject to the Visits from the Esquimaux who they represent as very treacherous and hostile people.[68]

Again shortages in the district prevented any attempt to extend the trade. This time there was a shortage of trade goods along the Mackenzie River. Far from being able to found a new post, the company was forced to go into debt to the Indians and exchange furs for credits on the next year's outfit.[69] In the face of this problem the company's interest in the Peel River dissipated, and its energies were directed toward the upper Liard and Stikine rivers.

Finally, in 1837, arctic exploration once again stirred the company's commercial interest in expansion from the lower Mackenzie valley. This time the company itself instigated the exploration. A team composed entirely of company employees was outfitted in the Mackenzie District to survey the unmapped sections of coastline remaining after Franklin's explorations. The command of the team was divided between Thomas Simpson, a cousin of the governor, and Chief Factor Peter Warren Dease.

The explorers descended the Mackenzie River and proceeded westward along the coast, reaching Franklin's farthest point, Return Reef, a month earlier than Franklin had. While surveying the unmapped coast between Return Reef and Point Barrow, the expedition discovered the mouth of a large river. The main channel was over two miles wide, and the river itself spread out into an even larger delta area. This impressive sight convinced Dease and Simpson that they had discovered a major river which, if its mouth was a fair indication, drained a considerable portion of the interior. They named their important discovery the Colville River, after Andrew Colvile, an important Hudson's Bay Company executive.[70]

The Dease and Simpson survey team operated in the Mackenzie District for two additional field seasons, but their explorations were confined to the Arctic Coast east of the Coppermine River. In terms of the ongoing exploration of the interior their most significant find was the discovery of the

Colville River. Although the Hudson's Bay Company never erected a single trading post along the Colville, the mere knowledge of its existence determined later events. Governor Simpson and other company officers envisioned the Colville as one of the great rivers of western America, a sister of the Mackenzie. The fact that the Colville entered the Arctic Ocean west of the Russian border and was therefore out of British territory was not even noted as an obstacle to expansion. The Colville was what the fur trade had hoped to find since Sir Alexander Mackenzie's 1789 journey, a large river west of the Mackenzie Mountains divide.

The Colville River raised the known, but still unexplored, Peel River to a new level of importance. Because the Peel entered the Mackenzie River from the southwest, it was believed that the Peel might lead to the headwaters of the Colville. Thus the discovery of the Colville, though a small incident in the history of arctic exploration, was of paramount importance in the Hudson's Bay Company's expansion into the interior of the Northwest. For over ten years the Colville was destined to be the elusive goal of the company's western explorers.

CHAPTER 7

Westward of the Mountains
The Peel and Pelly Rivers

IN 1838, Fort Good Hope on the Mackenzie River was the northernmost post in Rupert's Land, located less than four hundred miles from the mouth of the Mackenzie. The post had been moved only two years before. The old site on Manitou Island near the right bank of the river was subject to frequent inundations when the spring floods swelled the river, and in the spring of 1836 this nuisance turned into a dangerous hazard. On May 23 the water spilled quickly over its banks, and Fort Good Hope was engulfed by the rising tide. Nearly twelve feet of swirling brown river flooded the buildings, swept away the stockades, and undermined the bastions. The stands of spruce covering Manitou Island were ripped from the ground and hurled downriver. John Bell, the clerk commanding the post, managed to crowd his men and most of the post's valuables into a York boat. For two days they lived as if at sea, confined to the boat and exposed to wind and rain. They had continually to dodge heavy blocks of ice, though for a time they found one ice floe large enough to camp on. Eventually the boat became so entangled in the ice that they were unable to maneuver the craft, and they would have been crushed if the water had not begun to subside.[1] Returning to the mud-encrusted remains of the fort, Bell was understandably despondent.

At the age of nineteen John Bell had left his native Isle of Mull. Having turned his back on the Scottish coast, he en-

tered the service of the North West Company and after the
Union of 1821 became a clerk in the Hudson's Bay Company.
He was "a quiet, steady well behaved Man," who shrank from
the overbearing and brusque manner of address some officers
used to order about the voyageurs and *engagés*.² Bell instead
offered a much more reasoned approach to leadership, based
on respect and example. He was good-natured and generous,
sometimes at his own expense.³ He was also a bit of a musi-
cian, fond of playing his fiddle as a comfort during a long
winter night or as an accompaniment at the exuberant fur-
trade parties, where dancing was transformed from a social to
an athletic activity.⁴

In 1824, Bell was assigned to the Mackenzie District. He
spent the summer of 1825 at Fort Simpson and trading along
the South Nahanni River. When stationed at the posts of the
lower Mackenzie, Bell found the isolation numbing. For ten
years at Fort Good Hope his only personal contact with the
outside world was the twice-yearly boat from Fort Simpson,
which would pick up the year's fur returns and later deposit
the next season's trade outfit. Needless to say, these visits,
which lasted scarcely a day, and the winter mail packets were
greatly relished by Bell. James Hargrave, who had served as a
clerk with Bell earlier in his career, was the fur trader's source
for news of the outside world. Bell's own letters were brief
and sparse of information. As he explained, "I am as usually
the case with me in this miserable and distant part of the
country, a bankrupt for news of any kind. Where My friend
shall I glean any? from the Indians, animals or Fowls of the
air."⁵ As Bell began the difficult task of rebuilding Fort Good
Hope in 1836, his despair was at its deepest. He was thirty-
three years old and faced no prospect of advancement or,
seemingly, any relief from his castaway existence.

John Bell did receive at least a break from his gloom in
1836, when he was allowed to spent part of the summer at the
district depot, Fort Simpson. The company of Murdock Mc-
Pherson, Robert Campbell, and the other men at the headquarters proved to be a mild tonic for Bell, broadening his
lonely world. In 1838, Bell's prospects, though still linked to
the "dismal and secluded" Mackenzie River District that he

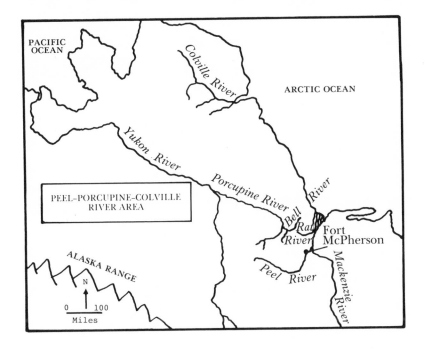

detested, began to improve. Governor Simpson advised the Mackenzie commander, Murdock McPherson, that the company wished to expand the district toward the newly discovered Colville River:

The Governor and Committee are desirous that Mr. Bell, or any other active experienced leader, should proceed with a small party (say 4 in all) across country to the westward, by ascending any of the streams in the neighborhood of Fort Good Hope, and endevour to fall on the waters of the Colville River at a distance of 150 to 200 miles from the Coast, and select a good situation for an Establishment to be formed there Summer 1840.[6]

Later the company decided it would be best first to explore the Peel River and thereby open up a possible route to the Colville. In the summer of 1839 Bell was ordered to

proceed down the Mackenzie River in a boat manned by 5 servants and 2 hired Indians and ascending Peels River from its mouth endeavour if time & circumstances will admit to trace that stream to its source. Your principal aim will be to select a commodious situation for an Establishment, and to acquire knowledge of the resources of the country in its vicinity for its support. These objects attained your utmost endeavour must be directed towards ascerting [sic] whether a practicable communication exists between the Peel and Colville Rivers.[7]

On June 25, 1839, John Bell embarked for the Peel River, and three days later his party reached the river's mouth. The Peel was about four hundred yards wide and flowing with a smooth, steady current of about four to five miles an hour. The profile of the terrain along the lower river was low; stretching out from the level banks of sand and clay were plains of thick forest, broken only intermittently by lakes and stretches of muskeg.[8] Bell traveled up the Peel for three days, covering about sixty miles. He encountered a minor rapid, where the Indians of the vicinity "had constructed a barrier of basket-work, which extended entirely across the stream, sufficiently open however to permit the water to pass freely through its interstices, for the purpose of catching fish which ascend from the sea during the summer."[9] The Peel then began to pass through the Mackenzie Mountains, and Bell noted that the river became "narrow and shallow with a strong currant which descends with a rapidity I have not seen in any other river in the country."[10] He continued with his York boat as best he could until August 8, when the boat had to be abandoned because the river began "descending with great velocity."[11] They passed through canyons that were later described as "bold, romantic defiles, so steep and lofty as often to hide the midday sun from view."[12] Bell tried to proceed on foot, but was soon stopped by an unfordable tributary. He then hiked back to the boat for a small bark canoe, which allowed him to cross the larger tributaries. The country through which Bell was traveling was fine beaver country. Although he did not see many of the animals, the great number of gnawed sticks and fallen trees revealed their presence. As the going became more arduous, Bell was forced to abandon the canoe. When the party came to creeks and streams, they now had to wade through the arctic water, whose frigid temperatures numbed the limbs of some of the men.[13]

Bell, however, was coming to the end of his upstream journey. He had reached a section of the river where the stream was only forty yards wide. His guide told him that beyond this place the Peel's "source is lost in the innumerable streams and rivulets which descend from the mountains and that late in the season it becomes dry."[14] There was no point in proceeding, as the river did not promise to be an important avenue to the interior or an access point to the Colville. In reality, Bell had only ascended the Peel for about one hundred and eighty miles, before turning up the Snake River, an insignificant tributary. The error was not critical, for, though the Peel is second only to the Liard among the Mackenzie's feeders and is navigable for another hundred miles past the mouth of the Snake, it is not, nor would it have been, an important route to the Yukon.

Turning downstream on the Peel, John Bell was finished with the first part of his voyage. He had traced the Peel as near to its source as he thought practical and had noted a good location for a trading post about a day and a half's march from the Peel's mouth. He now hoped to scout out a route to the Colville River, or at least make contact with the tribes who dwelt in the Colville valley. Near the mouth of the Peel, Bell had an interview with the Indians of the area, the Loucheux, a tribe that modern anthropologists call the Kutchins (the earlier name appears to date from Sir Alexander Mackenzie's voyage of discovery in 1789). These Indians, who are among the most numerous of the Athabascan peoples in northwestern America, had often traded on the lower Mackenzie River. They described themselves to voyageurs as "the people who keep both eyes alert for enemies." For this reason they were called the squinters or, in French, the *loucheux*.[15] The Loucheux were anxious to have a trading post of their own, and they were helpful to Bell. They told him of a small tributary of the Peel that flowed down from the mountains and could be followed to a portage across the height of land. They themselves used the river to travel to the portage, where they traded with a branch of their tribe, the "Tramontane Loucheux."[16]

It was the Rat River that the Kutchins described to Bell. Bell elected to trace it to its source in the mountains. He must have left his boat on the Peel, for only a canoe can ascend the Rat River. The first fifteen miles of the river were slow and sluggish. Willows and an occasional spruce tree leaned over the quiet water. Then the first rapids were encountered, and, as the Rat climbed higher into the mountains, it was reduced to a white-water chain of falls and riffles. Although Alexander Isbister, who joined Bell on the Peel River in 1840, described travel up the Rat as "smooth," most travelers on the river would find that statement difficult to reconcile with the actuality. Progress upstream can only be accomplished by relentless effort, pulling the canoe by its gunnels up the riffles, wading in the frigid water in order to catch the tail end of an eddy, stumbling with a tracking line through mosquito-infested bushes, which snag the tracking line and disguise the boulders that bruise and fell the traveler. After a few days of this sort of abuse Bell finally reached a broad meadow with thick, luxuriant stands of grass. This was the head of the portage. There he met a large band of western Kutchins. He did not profit much in the way of geographic knowledge from his encounter with them, but was able to do a fine trade in beaver.

It is unfortunate that Bell did not appreciate the significance of the rendezvous site. It was located at the head of McDougall Pass, a break in the great western divide which is only a bit more than a thousand feet in altitude. It would have been a natural gateway to the fur country of the Mackenzie Mountains. Sir Alexander Mackenzie's route through the mountains at Summit Lake was at 2,500 feet; Lewis and Clark crossed the Continental Divide at the 8,000-foot Lehmi Pass; and the South Pass on the Oregon Trail was 7,500 feet above sea level. Because of the difficulties of the Rat River, the access offered by McDougall Pass went unappreciated for some years. Bell returned to Fort Good Hope on August 3, after spending more than a month in the Peel River area.[17]

Bell's report of the fine prospects for trade on the Peel River started up the Hudson's Bay Company's machinery of expansion. An outfit of goods was assembled at Fort Simpson, and additional men were assigned to the lower Mackenzie. Governor Simpson had slight reservations about supplying the

Peel River area directly from the Mackenzie. He would have preferred a route through the interior that avoided contact with the Eskimos, who were known to frequent the mouth of the Peel.[18] The Hudson's Bay Company was understandably apprehensive of conflict with the Eskimos, in the light of Sir John Franklin's several altercations with them during his second expedition, not to mention the massacre of Duncan Livingston's Nor'Westers in 1799. Dease and Simpson, however, had put up a bold front when dealing with them, and Thomas Simpson had written, "The display of our arms was sufficient for Exquimaux stomachs." Their experience convinced the company to risk the encounter and open Peel River.[19]

On June 3, 1840, John Bell set out from Fort Good Hope to put the Peel's prospects to the test. His party, traveling in York boats, consisted of Alexander Kennedy Isbister and twelve Orkneymen and Canadians, as well as four Indian families, who would serve as the post's "home guard," hunting, dressing skins, and doing other chores about the fort. When they arrived at the mouth of the Peel three days later, they met a large group of Kutchin Indians. The war party's intention was to provide an escort for the fur traders, protecting them from Eskimo attack. Bell, however, trusting in the size of his party and perhaps distrusting so many Indians about his trade goods, gave the Kutchins a gift of tobacco and graciously declined the escort. They camped that night about thirty miles up the Peel, within sight of the Richardson Range of the Mackenzie Mountains.[20]

On the next morning the Hudson's Bay men reached the spot that had been selected for the new post. The Indians in considerable numbers had already gathered in expectation of trade. Bell was not especially pleased with the post site:

Its elevation above the present level of the River is considerable, but not withstanding I entertain some fears of the waters rising in the spring. That is perhaps the only objection which can be urged against it as a site for a Fort but that objection from the uniformly Low & swampy Country through which this River flows is unfortunately impossible to be obviated.[21]

The new post was called simply Peel River Post, though later it was named the name it has today, Fort McPherson. It consisted of a trading shop, the post commander's residence, and living quarters for the *engagés*, all surrounded by a wooden stockade. By September the post had been completed, and trade commenced. Not only the Indians of the Peel and Rat rivers visited the post but also some trappers from far west of the mountains. Bell interviewed them all about a water communication to the Colville River, but never with much success.

Bell's assistant at the Peel River Post, Alexander Kennedy Isbister, was a bright and able young man. Though of métis descent and born in Rupert's Land, he had been educated in Scotland. With the active disposition natural to an eighteen-year-old, he was excited by the prospect of opening new country. While at Fort Simpson in 1839 he had been given a pocket sextant by Thomas Simpson. The clerk used the instrument to make a chart of the Peel River area, which he published in the *Journal of the Royal Geographic Society* in 1845. Throughout the winter of 1840–41 he explored the post's hinterlands, making snowshoe journeys many days long. Isbister's initiative and curiosity would have cast him in a large role in the Hudson's Bay Company's westward explorations if he had cared for the life of a fur trader, but, when his contract ran out in 1841, he elected to leave the company and furthered his education in Europe.[22]

On Isbister's final journey before leaving the district he managed to cross the Continental Divide. This occurred in March of 1841, when the post was short of food. Three Kutchin Indians arrived at the post with the news that the Indians west of the mountains had plenty of meat in their camps. Bell dispatched Isbister and three men to accompany the Indians back to their camp and trade for provisions.[23] They followed the valley of the Rat River to the river's source, which was a collection of small ponds in a mountain meadow. Because of the ice and a thick snow lying on the ground, Isbister was unable to distinguish the area as the head of the Rat River. Therefore, when he came to another small river less than a mile away, which we know as the Bell, Isbister assumed that he was still following the Rat. In times of high water the sources of the Rat and Bell rivers mingle, and one can pass from one river to the other without a portage. This is remarkable, because the Bell flows westward toward the Yukon River and the Bering Sea, while the Rat heads east to the Mackenzie and thence to the Arctic Ocean. Isbister had found what the Hudson's Bay Company so earnestly wanted, a water route through the mountains, but he did not know it, as it lay hidden beneath his snow shoes.[24]

John Bell enjoyed a fine year of trade at his new establishment. His storeroom was packed with over fourteen hundred beaver pelts and a thousand marten skins, "besides some other Furs of less value, forming in all 45 packs of 85 lbs. ea."[25] The articles most avidly sought by the Kutchins were beads and tobacco. The traders had large bundles of tobacco wound up like coiled rope, which they sold in sections the size of a man's fist with his thumb extended. The bigger the Indian's hand, the longer his smoking pleasure. Each of the lengths sold for one beaver pelt, three muskrats, or two weasel skins. In order to have a leader to deal with the Hudson's Bay Company traders often appointed one Indian as a "trading chief." He was usually one of the better trappers—to set an example of the behavior that the company would reward. On the Peel River the first chief was named Red Leggings.[26]

The successful trade of the Peel River Post whetted the commercial appetite of the company. The furs gathered on the Peel appeared to be mere crumbs from the rich region west of the mountains, the valley of the Colville River.

Discovery of the Pelly River

Following the rout at Dease Lake, Robert Campbell repaired to Fort Halkett, where he spent the winter of 1839–40. It had been the original intention of the Council of the Northern Department to transfer Campbell and his men to the lower Mackenzie to assist John Bell in the founding of the Peel's River Post.[27] Governor Simpson, however, felt that Campbell's talents would be best used exploring the unknown country west and north of the upper Liard. The traders at Fort Halkett had for many years heard the Indians of this region speak of a large lake, or *Toutcho* ("great water"), which lay "no

Inside a fur trader's storeroom, circa 1900. Photograph by C. W. Mathers in Outing: The Outdoor Magazine of Human Interest, July, 1904.

great distance from the Headwaters of the West Branch and from Simpson's Lake discovered by Mr. John M. McLeod in 1831."[28] In the spring of 1840, Campbell was ordered to explore this lake, make contact with the Indians of the region, and be alert for any navigable rivers "flowing in a Northerly or NorthWesterly Course."[29] It was hoped that Campbell might fall upon the headwaters of the Colville River.

At the end of May, when the ice had left the Liard, Campbell left Fort Halkett. With him were seven men, including Lapie, Kitza, and Hoole. Campbell's route took him up the river that the fur traders sometimes called the North Branch of the Liard, which was to be named the Frances River by Campbell after Lady Frances Simpson, the governor's wife. It was a fine, clear river that wound its way through mountainous country, not unlike the Dease River in its striking beauty. Beaver were abundant along its banks, and the explorers ate their fill of the valuable animal, alternating this fare with grayling and Dolly Varden trout, which could be easily caught on hooks baited with beaver kidneys or livers.

The Frances's current was moderate for the first few days of upstream travel, until the party reached Middle Canyon. There yellowed and rugged limestone cliffs shadowed the river and constrained the current in a canyon strewn with boulders and jutting ledges of rock. The canyon, about three miles long, is caused by Simpson's Mountains, which block the Frances River's passage south,[30] creating a hazard to navigation. The voyageurs had many anxious and difficult moments, scrambling along the nearly precipitous banks of the river, as they tried to pull the canoes upstream.

Middle Canyon was the prelude to two further canyons on the Frances River. The first of these, False Canyon, was an extremely picturesque place with fine black granite cliffs hemming the river. Its beauty was enhanced because the water, although constricted to a narrow 200-foot passage, ran deep and smooth, free of rapids. The voyaguers had no such luck with Upper Canyon, which was an unpleasant succession of rapids and small falls; they were forced to repeat the wearisome tactic of wading and towing the canoes. Three miles above Upper Canyon, Campbell came to the final rapids on the Frances,

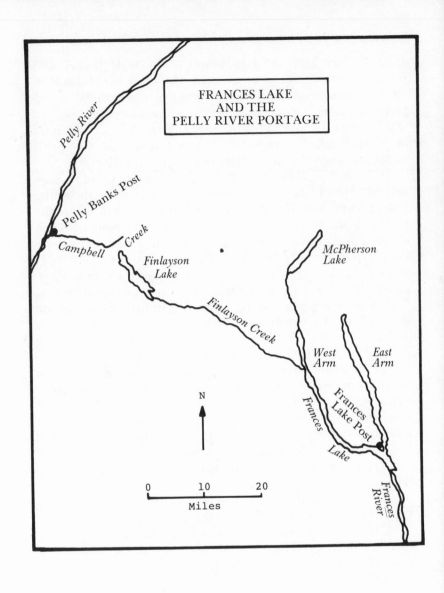

FRANCES LAKE
AND THE
PELLY RIVER PORTAGE

Pelly River

Pelly Banks Post

Campbell   Creek

Finlayson
Lake

Finlayson Creek

McPherson
Lake

West
Arm

East
Arm

Frances
Lake Post

Frances
Lake

Frances
River

N

0   10   20
Miles

Frances Lake. Photograph by the author.

a deceptive, difficult half mile of fast water.[31] In his journal Campbell makes little mention of the canyons on the Frances, which a later traveler referred to as "savage and dangerous."[32] Perhaps, after repeatedly navigating the rapids of the Liard, white water had ceased to make an impression on him.

On July 19, Campbell reached the source of the Frances, "a beautiful sheet of water" that he named Frances Lake, again in honor of Governor Simpson's wife. Frances Lake might more properly be regarded as two lakes, each about thirty miles long and averaging a mile in width. The east and west arms of the lake are separated by a detached mountain range, whose highest point is a round peak that Campbell named Simpson's Tower in honor of his superior.[33]

Campbell directed the canoes up the west arm of the lake. The deep, quiet waters of the mountain lake provided a pleasant change from the constant rushing of water that had slowed their river travel. On the explorer's left, as he proceeded up the lake, was a group of low mountains no more than five or six thousand feet above sea level. They did not attract Campbell's notice, though today they are known as the Campbell Range, one of the few geographic features that bear his name. Campbell was trying to find a route from Frances Lake to a large river that was rumored to be on the northwest. He halted his party at a small island about twenty-five miles up the west arm of the lake, where he left three of the crew "with a canoe & nets & guns to fish & hunt round there & wait our return."[34] Meanwhile, Campbell, Hoole, Kitza, Lapie, and another Indian set off overland, hoping to find a river that might guide them west.

A small, unnavigable river enters Frances Lake from the west. Campbell proceeded up its narrow valley, hoping that it would lead him to the height of land separating Frances Lake from the large river that he hoped to find. The explorers traveled light, carrying only their guns and a few blankets; for provisions they were trusting to the fortunes of the hunt. Even so they found the going rough. Their march was slowed by deep, thick carpets of moss that gave way at each step, brush thick with alder bushes, and intermittent stretches of swamp.[35] After twenty-five miles of such difficulties, which were made worse because they had not eaten for three days, the explorers came to a narrow body of water about ten miles long. Campbell named the lake and the small river that drained it after Chief Factor Duncan Finlayson.

Rather than continue overland, Campbell and his men hastily built two pine-bark canoes. They traversed Finlayson Lake and managed to shoot several beaver and a deer at its west end. Then, their energies renewed, they continued overland from the lake. Soon after they left it, they came upon several streams, all flowing westward, which alerted Campbell that he had successfully crossed the divide between the Mackenzie River system and the unknown watercourses ahead. Finally, on their sixth day of travel from Simpson's Tower, Campbell spied from a high ridge "a large river in the distance flowing Northwest."[36] Hastening to the river's bank, they drank its "pellucid water to Her Majesty & the H. B. Co."[37] Campbell named his discovery the Pelly River after

John Henry Pelly, the London governor of the Hudson's Bay Company and a former director of the Bank of England.

Campbell searched the riverbank for a large pine tree from which to construct a canoe, but was unsuccessful. He contented himself with throwing together a rude little raft and drifting a short distance down the Pelly. He also floated a sealed tin can, which contained a record of his discovery, and sent it downstream. The company men then hoisted the Hudson's Bay Company flag and carved the company's claim to the area on the bark of a tree. Then, "highly delighted" with their success, and justly so, they headed back to Frances Lake.[38] The return trip was much easier than the outward march because Campbell was able to use the canoes that he had constructed on Finlayson Lake to float down the Finlayson River to within ten miles of Frances Lake. Yet he remained unsatisfied that that route was the best possible access to the Pelly River. He hoped that one of the other streams feeding Frances Lake might reach closer to the Pelly and therefore require a shorter portage. Back at Glenlyon House, as his men pretentiously called the tent cabin that they had built during his absence, Campbell had the voyageurs build two more pine-bark canoes.[39]

After exploring further the area around the cabin, Campbell and his party canoed down the west arm to the base of Frances Lake, where they discovered the entrance to the east arm. The lower reaches of the east arm give every appearance of being a river; its waters enter the main body of the lake with a strong current through a narrow channel, and for the first few miles the winding lake shores look very much like riverbanks. Then after ten miles of this deception the lake dramatically changes its appearance. Expanding to a mile in width, its waters are deep and clear and reflect like a gigantic mirror the snow-covered mountains that rise from the lake's long, sandy beaches. Campbell led his men through some of the most beautiful scenery in the Northwest to the head of the east arm. There he discovered another river feeding Frances Lake, which he named the Thomas River after Thomas Simpson, the arctic explorer. It was a small, swift-flowing stream which proved impractical as a route to the Pelly River.

Although Campbell was unsuccessful in finding an alternate route to the Pelly River, his exploration of all of Frances Lake enabled him to assess the resources of the country. He thought it rich in beaver and that the lake would provide enough fish to keep starvation at bay. Satisfied that he had carried out his orders, he set off down the Frances River and arrived back at Fort Halkett in mid-September.[40]

Shortly after he arrived back at his base on the Liard River, Campbell was greeted with good news. Murdock McPherson, whom Campbell blamed for the Dease Lake disaster in 1838–39, had been replaced as commander of the Mackenzie District by a robust, forty-nine-year-old Englishman, named John Lee Lewes. Born in 1791, the son of a popular actor, Charles Lee Lewes, John Lewes had entered the Hudson's Bay Company's service in 1807. He rose to chief trader in 1821 and was chief factor in 1830. George Simpson, although he respected Lewes's integrity, sneered that he was "Deficient in point of Education."[41] Lewes's correspondence, however, reveals a knowledgeable man with a lively pen. In November, 1840, he closed a letter to James Hargrave with the plea:

If you do not send me something to read by the P. L. L. [Portage La Loche] Boats I shall sett you down as a thirsty book worm, wishing to keep all the good things' to yourself, anything I care not what it is I am miserable for want of something to drive away the dull hours', so Charity, it is one of the Cardinal Virtues, and you should extend it even to the far distant clime of MK. R. [Mackenzie River].[42]

Governor Simpson would have to agree that Lewes was a man of energy, one who could get things done. He was dispatched to put into effect Simpson's plans to extend the company's operations to the Colville River.[43]

In a summary journal of his experiences in the Hudson's Bay Company before 1853, Robert Campbell states that during his journey he failed to encounter any Indians. Yet in his contemporary report to Chief Factor Lewes he mentions a good deal of secondary information about the Pelly River, which he presumably garnered from the Indians trading at Fort Halkett. These informants told the explorer that salmon ascended the Pelly River as far as the spot that he had reached, "which would indicate that there is no serious obstacle from here to the coast to impede navigation."[44] They also told him that Eskimos were known to travel the river "and even to extend their inland excusions to Frances Lake." These reports, plus the "course and magnitude" of the Pelly River, caused Campbell to inform Lewes that "I have no doubt it is identical with the Colvile."[45] Thus the discoveries of John McLeod and Robert Campbell on the Liard, of John Bell on the Peel, and of Dease and Simpson on the coast were all joined together. The Hudson's Bay men were closing in on the geographic mysteries of the Far Northwest.

While Campbell was flushed with the success of his summer's journey and beginning to lay plans for the expansion of his trading operations to the Pelly River, fortune again intervened for the worse, as the explorer and the company's affairs in the Mackenzie District were beset by a new series of disappointments and disasters. When Campbell had returned to Fort Halkett in September, 1840, he had sent John Mowat, who had minded the post throughout the summer, back to Fort Simpson with eight voyageurs in a new North canoe. The party had left Fort Halkett early in the morning and, after putting in a hard day on the Liard, they succeeded in crossing Devil's Portage and shooting down the dangerous Grand Canyon of the Liard. Before them lay one more rapid, after which they planned to make camp for the night. The early evening is one of the best times to run a rapid, because during the day the glare of the sun may hide a rock, a standing wave, or some other hazard. Although the voyageurs had run this particular rapid several times without incident, the Liard is always treacherous; the slightest fluctuation in water level will create an entirely new collection of obstacles.[46] After the veteran canoemen had guided the craft through the boiling onrush of water and safely maneuvered it to the end of the rapid, they began, with a great sense of relief, to congratulate one another; "all cause for dread was past." Then the canoe's progress was suddenly arrested, and it spun around, as the Liard without warning opened into a giant whirlpool. Before the stunned voyageurs could react, the body of the twenty-five-foot

craft was drawn into the yawning black mouth. John John-
stone, Jean Baptiste Bruce, and another voyageur were able to
spring from the stern of the canoe just as it broke in two. The
shattered canoe and the six remaining men, including John
Mowat, were sucked into the vortex; the rushing waters of the
Liard muted their cries and enveloped their bodies.[47]

The three men who had leapt from the canoe, though they
were carried far downstream by the current, managed to reach
shore safely. They studied the river vainly, hoping for a sign
of their companions. They saw only the bleak and desolate
face of the Liard; the river did not give up its dead. The sur-
vivors then began a desperate march overland to Fort Halkett,
which they reached after much "hard toil and misery" three
days later.[48] Campbell was stunned by this reverse. He later
wrote in his journal that the news "was inexpressibly sad to
me, I knew them all so well."[49]

The disaster cost the Mackenzie District, which was always
short of men, the services of six veteran servants. Furthermore,
the accident made many of the district's voyageurs leery of
taking assignments on the Liard. John Lee Lewes wrote that
the Liard had "long been the dread of people in McKenze's
River, and the sad catastrophe of last Autumn has now rendered it doubly so, the very best and first-rate men are required for navigating that dangerous stream."[50] Hence plans
to extend the fur trade to Frances Lake and the Pelly River
had to be postponed for a year.

In the spring of 1841, Campbell descended the Liard to
Fort Simpson. At the depot he met Alexander Isbister, who
had just returned from Peel River and was retiring from the
service of the company. In their short time together they became good friends, and Campbell later was a frequent guest
at Isbister's house when he later visited London. Campbell
also met Chief Factor John Lewes for the first time. Unlike
his predecessor, Lewes promised "cordial support" for Campbell's exploratory efforts.[51]

Campbell also had some farewells to make, though he might
have said good riddance. Alexander R. McLeod, Jr., his second-in-command at Dease Lake and Fort Halkett, was being
removed from the district. The wayward young man had cast

his eye upon the wife of Campbell's interpreter, Hoole, and she had been by no means an unwilling lover. Although she had been married to Hoole for some years and had borne him several children, she had boldly begun to live with A. R. Mc-Leod, Jr., as his wife. Campbell, who tried to keep things calm in the crowded little community of Fort Halkett, had been unsuccessful in trying to separate the lovers. McLeod had greeted Campbell's efforts with scorn; John Lee Leewes wrote, "McLeod's behavior to that Gent^m. as his Junior was most shameful, not content with constently disobeying all orders, insolence, the most barefaced and unbecoming was added, and instead of being a support to Mr. Campbell was greater the reverse."[52] Such behavior had gotten young McLeod recalled to Fort Simpson, where John Lee Lewes took an interest in the affair, no doubt out of respect for the young man's father, Chief Factor Alexander Roderick McLeod, who had died only months before. McLeod told him to mind his own business and thus earned himself a discharge. The woman decided to remain with her husband.[53]

Campbell remained at Fort Simpson for the rest of the summer. He was in charge of the headquarters while Chief Factor Lewes journeyed to Portage la Loche for the next year's supply of trade goods. When the boats returned from the portage, Campbell again made his way up the Liard to his winter quarters at Fort Halkett. With him he carried a letter from Governor Simpson, who had recently been knighted for his role in sponsoring the Dease-Simpson Arctic Survey. Sir George was well pleased with Campbell's discovery of the Pelly River, but was not at first confident that the Pelly was part of the Colville. Instead he thought that it flowed to the Pacific. He was anxious for Campbell to extend the company's operations to Frances Lake during the following summer.[54]

Robert Campbell was able to carry out the governor's wishes in the summer of 1842. At Fort Simpson the explorer received orders from Chief Factor Lewes to establish a post on Frances Lake and during the following spring to explore the Pelly River to its mouth, which was presumed to be on the Pacific. Campbell left Fort Halkett on July 27 with two York boats. After a "tedious, toilsome, and laborious voyage" he reached Frances Lake.[55] Camp was made at the foot of Simpson's Tower near Glenlyon House, the rough shanty that his men had built in 1840. The site provided easy access to the mouth of the east arm, where fast water made a promising fishing ground.

The explorers' first concern upon reaching their wintering grounds had to be the erection of suitable quarters; the bitter and brief autumn was already upon them. Construction was begun immediately on Frances Lake Post. It was to be much like any other post in Rupert's Land. There were only two buildings: a store thirty by twenty feet and a dwelling house thirty by sixteen feet. These structures were probably of the old provincial French style that had been dominant on the northern frontier since the French regime. Posts were erected on the sill logs in the corners and formed the supports for the squared horizontal logs that made up the walls.[56] Both the house and the store were enclosed in a stockade of wooden pickets with a bastion in each corner. The Company flag flew overhead. Inside the dwelling house partitions were sometimes erected to provide a little privacy for the post's inhabitants. Campbell had his own room, which he furnished by his own hand with a table, chair, and bedstead. Much of his time, however, was spent either out of doors or in the main room, where there was a large fireplace made of mud and stone.[57] The fireplace was the sole source not only of heat but also of light. Campbell did not even have the luxury of a candle. Unfortunately, this kind of heating system usually proved incredibly smoky, so that except in the severest blizzards residents of the post spent as much time in the fresh air as possible.

While the post was under construction, Campbell became concerned that the food resources of the Frances Lake area were not as promising as he had originally expected. In his first few weeks on the lake the fishnets consistently yielded fifty to sixty fish a day, but, as was often the case, the fish moved to different locations after the lake froze over. To alleviate the strain on the post's larder, Campbell elected to send three men back to Fort Simpson for the winter.[58]

At this time he received a letter from Sir George Simpson. The governor had always had a personal as well as a profes-

Fort McPherson, or Peel River Post, circa 1900. Photograph by C. W. Mathers in Outing: The Outdoor Magazine of Human Interest, *July, 1904.*

sional interest in Campbell's career. He often took the time
to drop the young man a line of encouragement and tell him
some of the news of Rupert's Land. On this occasion he wrote
Campbell:

I heard of your friend the Nahany chiefess, who assisted you in
your distress in the Mountains 3 year ago. She was then upon a
visit to the Coast, where she is much respected. I understand she
spoke of you in terms of high commendation. . . . Truely concerned to see that you are "still haunted" at Fort Halkett, by your
old enemy starvation; a smell even of the flesh pots of Red River,
would I have no doubt, be a treat to you, and braxy [rotten sheep
meat] a perfect banquet.[59]

Circumstances at Frances Lake were hardly better when
Campbell read the governor's letter, but at least he could be
assured that Simpson, who had spent the past winter touring
California and the Hawaiian Islands, appreciated his efforts.

The food situation at Frances Lake was made worse because
one of Campbell's best hunters, Hoole, was inactive. The hap-
less interpreter seems to have gone from one misfortune to the
next. Having only recently gotten his wife back from A. R.
McLeod, Jr., he had now cut his foot while chopping wood
and was disabled for much of the winter. There was no call
for optimism at the post that year. Even the great Scottish
festival of Saint Andrew's Day found Campbell grimly tending the fishnets, freezing his hands and hoping for just a few
fish for supper.

In February, 1843, Chief Factor Lewes sent Campbell instructions concerning the further exploration of the Pelly
River. Since the discovery of the Pelly in 1840, the fur traders
had rethought their original supposition that the river was
actually a headwater of the Colville. The true identity of the
Pelly, which was really the upper Yukon River, was to be a
subject of constant speculation during the ten years between
its discovery and exploration. It is clear from the orders that
Lewes and Simpson sent to Campbell in 1843 that they expected the Pelly River to flow westward to the Pacific Ocean.
They thought that Campbell would be able to descend the
river to the sea and return to Frances Lake by the end of the

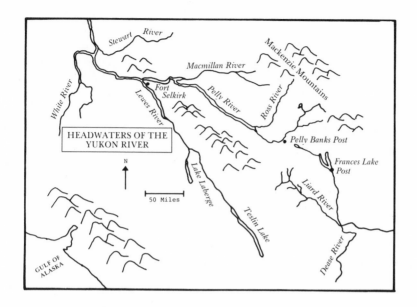

summer. Campbell himself had changed his opinion that the
Pelly might be a headwater of the Colville. He explained to
Governor Simpson that the only reason that he had been so
mistaken "arose from having no map, nor anything to correct
my judgement but the very faint idea I had in memory of how
the country lay."[60] Now Campbell felt that the Pelly River
would turn out to be either the "Comptrollers River (perhaps the modern Copper River) or the apocryphal Cook
River. Here again the concept of Captain Cook's River was
determining an explorer's thinking. Like Peter Pond, Sir Alexander Mackenzie, and Samuel Black, Robert Campbell felt
that the river might hold the key to the geography of the interior. What the map makers were then calling Cook River
was in all probability the Susitna, which is an important river
in the Cook Inlet region of Alaska but not a major route to
the interior.[61]

Part of Campbell's uncertainty about the probable course
of the Pelly River stemmed from his inability to make accurate readings of longitude and latitude. In May, 1843, just before his expedition on the Pelly, he had made a thinly veiled
plea to Governor Simpson for the proper equipment:

I regret much that I have not Instruments with the necessary
Books, and a few lessons for taking altitudes, to enable me to ascertain the geographical position of the more prominent points of
the country through which I have, and may yet likely pass, it is
most desirable that they be accurately known and the task would
be to me a pleasent one, It is a science for which I ever had an
ardent desire to cultivate practically but fortune has so far denied
me the chance.[62]

Governor Simpson did not acknowledge Campbell's request
for mapping instruments, although the instruments would
have greatly aided the resolution of the perplexing geographical questions of the upper Yukon by letting the company
know the exact location of Campbell's post. It is possible that
the governor wished to keep the company's western explorations obscured by geographical uncertainties. He must have
suspected that, as Campbell pushed northwestward, he was
approaching the 141st meridian, which since 1825 had been
the agreed-upon boundary between Russian and British North
America. With no precise information concerning the location of its posts and explorations the company was less vulnerable to charges of trespassing.

In this regard the company's exploring effort in the Yukon
valley was selective. Robert Campbell, John Bell, and later
Alexander H. Murray were dealing with a real geographic
problem: the nature of the Yukon River valley. It was a mystery as perplexing as the source of the Nile, which other British explorers were seeking at the same time. Yet the Hudson's
Bay Company did not attach great importance to expansion of
scientific knowledge in the Northwest. Rather the company
continued as usual to focus on the commercial prospects of the
region. For its purposes the exploration of the Pelly River
would be complete when it had located and exploited the fur
resources along the Pelly's banks. It would not greatly cloud
the company's perception of the area if the Pelly's source and
ultimate destination were unknown.

That is not to say that purely geographic questions were ignored during the company's expansion into the Yukon. A man
such as Robert Campbell felt the same urge to explore the unknown, to aid the advance of knowledge, as the celebrated ex-

plorers of Africa in the mid- and late nineteenth century. His "ardent desire" to contribute to geography was only partially inhibited by the company's selective goals.[63] Although only fur-trade objectives were sponsored, the explorers remained interested in purely geographic questions as well.

Early in June, 1843, Campbell left the Frances Lake Post and headed for the Pelly River to continue his explorations. During the winter he had dispatched Hoole to the Pelly River to build a house there and make things ready for the summer journey. The house was appropriately called Pelly Banks. When Campbell arrived there on June 6, he found a large canoe that had been made with birchbark from Fort Liard. It was built, gummed, and ready for service.

Campbell's exploration party consisted of Hoole, Lapie, Kitza, two French Canadians, and an Indian hunter named Gauche. It was traditional among some of the northern Indian tribes that before a journey of any kind a shaman or some individual gifted in conjuring should foretell the future. Thus the party might be warned of possible ambushes and alerted concerning the hunting conditions ahead.[64] On the evening before they set off down the Pelly, Kitza, Lapie, Gauche, and perhaps the Canadians gathered together without Campbell's knowledge. In the firelight the men turned their attention to Gauche, whose name referred to his left-handedness and who was known for his uncanny psychic powers. In his mind's eye he saw the party proceeding downriver and after a certain time meeting with two Indians on the right bank. Later they were to meet an Indian family and eat with them. He saw the expedition traveling through mountainous country in which the hunters would kill plenty of small game but no big game animals. Finally the expedition would reach the junction of two large rivers and fall in with a large group of Indians. After that Gauche's vision of the future began to blur, and he could see no further. Since he failed to detect any sign of blood, he felt safe in assuring his listeners that they would not quarrel with any of the Pelly Indians.[65]

The men were satisfied that the coming voyage would be a safe one. They slipped into their blankets and went to sleep. Campbell was unaware of the clandestine voyage into the fu-

ture until the real Pelly trip was nearly over, but on many
occasions, after one incident or another, he was to hear his
men mumbling, "That's what Gauche said."[66]

On June 10 the explorers embarked on the Pelly River. It
was flanked by high hills on both sides of its course, and the
Pelly Range on the south dominated the scenery. After going
downstream about thirty miles, Campbell came to a deep,
swift river about fifty feet wide, which he named in honor of
his interpreter, Hoole. Below the mouth of the Hoole they
came to a dangerous rapid, known as Hoole's Rapid, which
drops the waters of the Pelly six feet in about two hundred
yards of white water. The rapid is navigable when the water
is low but, traveling in June, when the spring runoff was still
entering the Pelly, Campbell was forced to make a short portage along the north bank. After Hoole's Rapid the Pelly's
current increased, and the river was between three and four
hundred feet wide. The scenery varied from scarped banks of
grey and white silt to open, grassy meadows interspersed with
thick cottonwood groves and scrubby stands of spruce.[67]

As Campbell canoed downriver, he named the geography
for his personal friends and companions. This was a refreshing
change from the government expeditions, such as Franklin's,
whose leaders placed names of London gentry on some of the
most beautiful and foreboding features on the continent. The
Ross River, a major waterway draining the Mackenzie Mountains to the southwest, was named by Campbell for Chief Factor Donald Ross, who had befriended Campbell during his
journey to Rupert's Land thirteen years before. The Kitza
River, a small mountain freshet, he named after his Indian
hunter Kitza. The Macmillan River he named in honor of his
cousin, Chief Factor James McMillan, who had been responsible for his joining the company. A modern map of the Pelly
also reveals Lapie River. This stream, however, was named by
George M. Dawson of the Canadian Geological Survey, who
was a friend of Campbell's later in life. Dawson felt that, if
Kitza had a river named after him, Lapie deserved equal consideration.[68]

The farther the voyage progressed the more the voyageurs
were impressed with the accuracy of Gauche's predictions.

Indian camp on the Mackenzie River, circa 1900. Photograph by C. W. Mathers in Outing: The Outdoor Magazine of Human Interest, *July, 1904.*

During their second day on the river they encountered two
Indians, with whom Campbell held a brief interview. On the
following day, as they rounded a sharp turn, they surprised an
Indian family, who were camped on the river. The Indians
fled into the forest, but soon returned when they saw that the
Hudson's Bay men's intentions were peaceful. Then, exactly
as Gauche had predicted, the fur traders had a peaceful smoke
and dinner with the family before proceeding downstream.[69]

On the sixth day of the voyage the party arrived at the junction of the Pelly and another large river. This swiftly flowing
waterway Campbell named the Lewes River for Chief Factor
John Lee Lewes. Just downstream from the fork of the Lewes
and the Pelly the explorers encountered a large group of natives, whom Campbell called "wood Indians." Actually they
were Northern Tutchones. They were taken completely by
surprise by the first white men that they had ever seen.[70]
Campbell directed his voyageurs to land the canoe near the
Indians' camp so that he could establish trade relations with
them.

After a moment of shock the Tutchones recovered their
composure, and two of their leading men stepped forward to
greet Campbell. Thlin-ikik-thling and his son K'anan were
both "tall, stalwart, good-looking men, clad from head to foot
in dressed deer skins, ornamented with beads & porcupine
quills of all colors."[71] They shared the "pipe of peace" with
the explorers. Since the Tutchones were friendly, Campbell
moved freely among them, distributing tobacco and other
gifts, but, when he made known his intention of continuing
downriver, "they all raised their voices against it." Through
sign language and a smattering of the Tutchone tongue that
his interpreter knew, Campbell was informed that the tribes
of the lower river were a warlike people with whom no parley
was possible; not only would they kill the Hudson's Bay men,
they would also eat them. Campbell thanked the Tutchones
for their concern, but he was unaffected by their warnings,
perhaps thinking that neighbors are often the worst character
witnesses.[72]

The explorers set up camp for the night across the river
from the Tutchones. Campbell was surprised to find that his

men were very much frightened by their warnings. After discussion among themselves the crew refused to go farther downstream. Campbell was enraged and used every threat and argument at his disposal, but was unable to shake their resolve.

Thus Campbell's exploration came to an end. He had traveled over 320 miles down the Pelly, but his hopes of following the river to its mouth were dashed. Before the journey he had written to Governor Simpson that he hoped to follow the Pelly to the sea, open up a new trade route, and then retire to a nice country farm. Now those plans had to be postponed, as the geographic mystery of the Pelly remained unsolved. In fact, the mystery was increased by the discovery of the Lewes River. The Indians of Frances Lake and the Northern Tutchones had told him much about this river, which they said flowed from a large lake in the mountains. The lake was so wide that from its "center the land is hardly discernible on either side, and of several days march in length." This was Lake Laberge. Southeast of the lake the Indians of the interior rendezvoused with the native traders of the coast at a place known as "the point of peace." Campbell had hoped to investigate this area. The timidity of his men prevented him.[73]

In retrospect, it was probably better that Campbell did turn back at that time. He was not prepared for a long voyage, and, although the Pelly and the Lewes together form the Yukon River, which flows to the Pacific Ocean, the journey is about fourteen hundred miles—not the short float down to the coast that the Hudson's Bay men expected. Campbell, however, was very dejected and lost in the gloom of disappointment. He admitted, "I was perfectly heedless of what was passing."[74]

Campbell remained in his despair through the first two days of his party's voyage back up the Pelly River. During the third day of travel Campbell noticed fires burning on top of the hills on both sides of the river. His men were at a loss to explain what they were, but Campbell "conjectured that as in Scottland in the older times, these were signals to gather the tribes so that they might surround and intercept us." This roused the explorer "to the sense of our situation." They were still in basically unknown country with limited native contacts. The small Hudson's Bay party might easily be overcome,

and their meager possessions have been a treasure to the poor
tribes of the Pelly. The voyageurs doubled their efforts with
their paddles and the tracking line, trying to get upstream as
fast as possible.[75]

On the next morning they met a party of Indians gathered
on the opposite bank of the river. The Indians beckoned
Campbell to cross, which he did. The strange tribe proved to
be anything but friendly. They stood stone-faced on the high
bank of the river with their bows drawn in a menacing fashion. Moving confidently yet slowly, so that his actions would
not be misinterpreted and bring a host of arrows down upon
them, Campbell removed some tobacco from his pack and had
one of his hunters present it as a gift. The Indians did not
seem very grateful; "they would scarcely remove their hands
from their bows to receive it." Campbell "then ascended the
bank to them, as they would not come down to us, and our
bold and at the same time Conciliatory demeanor had the effect of cooling them down. We had an amicable interview
with them carried on with words and signs. It required some
finessing however to get away from them." As soon as the explorers were seated in their canoe, they quickly pushed off.
The voyageurs paddled out of arrow range, while Campbell
with gun ready stared down the Indians.[76]

The party traveled as fast as they could all day, working
against the current with all their strength. Campbell had
hoped that by nightfall they would reach a rough section of
the river that he had named Desrivieres' Rapid, but, as twilight closed in, they were far short of the spot. As he ordered
his men to make camp, he knew that there was still a possibility of Indian trouble, and he wanted a watch kept. Since
his voyageurs after a hard day's work were dead to the world,
Campbell had them sleep in his tent while he stood guard.[77]
The camp had been set up at the base of a steep bank with
large trees on its slope. Campbell climbed into the branches
of one of the trees and sat there with his rifle in his lap, reading James H. Hervey's *Meditations* in the twilight of the midnight sun.[78]

The explorer was ready for trouble, but felt that the hostile
band was most likely left behind. In fact, at that very moment

the Indians were closing in around the camp. They had followed the Hudson's Bay men throughout the day, carefully
remaining out of sight but always on their trail. The Indians'
plan was to rush the white men's camp, steal their goods, and
perhaps capture the white men themselves, but only if they
could be taken by surprise. The Indians did not want to risk
losing one of their own men to the strangers' guns. Therefore,
while Campbell stood guard, reading snatches of religious
prose, those who had plotted the ambush edged closer, waiting
for him perhaps to doze off. The Scotsman meanwhile fought
off the urge to sleep and climbed down from the tree. He
walked along the riverbank and found that "all was still."
The Indians, carefully hidden, remained true to their purpose, patiently waiting. It was to be their signal to attack if
the white man took a drink of water from the river. He would
then have to kneel down and, with his back turned, would be
at their mercy. Campbell, however, allowed them no such
opening. He used a horn cup to drink from, and, "after filling
it, turning quickly round & glancing up & down the river &
towards the hill while in the act of drinking," he showed that
he was ever alert. As dawn came, the Indians gave up their
ambush and withdrew from the camp. Two years later, when
Campbell was on good terms with the Indians of Pelly River,
he learned how close he had come to ambush that night:
"They confessed that had I knelt down to drink, they would
have rushed me & the sleeping inmates of the tent."[79]
    The explorers continued their homeward journey the next
day without realizing how close they had come to death. Traveling overland, they crossed the divide and returned to Frances Lake at the end of July.[80] Campbell found his post much
as he had left it, with its inhabitants in want of food. Even
his dogs, debilitated with hunger, ambled up to their master
hardly able to bark. Campbell's post was "still haunted" by
his "old enemy starvation." As the season changed, that specter loomed larger and was not the only threat as a host of new
trials descended upon the settlement.
    Campbell's exploration of the Pelly River to its junction
with the Lewes had brought the Hudson's Bay Company into
the heart of the Yukon valley. This was the region that un-

knowingly it had been moving toward since the Contract of
1839. The company wanted a large section of undeveloped
country to exploit. The drive to reach the Colville River had
been motivated by the desire to increase the Mackenzie District's fur returns.[81] Although Governor Simpson was unaware
that it was actually the Yukon River valley that his men were
exploring, Campbell's account of the Pelly River's fur-trade
potential told him all he wanted to hear. He advised Campbell that the fork of the Pelly and Lewes rivers sounded like
an excellent site for a trading post and directed him to establish one there as soon as was practical.[82]

Unfortunately, supply problems both at Frances Lake and
in the Mackenzie District as a whole made such an ambitious
move impractical for a number of years. The starvation that
Campbell faced at Frances Lake was also plaguing the entire
Mackenzie District. In the winter of 1841–42, John Lee Lewes
wrote, "All the Gents' in charge of the several Posts, one and
all singing the same song, scarcity of food."[83] The chief factor
himself suffered "from hand to mouth the whole winter."[84] In
the worst situation of all was Chief Trader Alexander Fisher
at Fort Good Hope. Throughout the winter he exercised the
greatest possible economy over his meager provisions. Even so,
in February Fisher and staff found themselves so weakened by
the growing numbness of starvation that they were "nearly on
all fours."[85] With his men subsisting on beaver skins, Fisher
knew help was needed. Accompanied by an Orkneyman, who
was the only other member of the post capable of making the
journey, Fisher set out for Fort Norman, which was normally
an eight-day march to the south. For thirteen days they stag-
gered through the snow before reaching the neighboring post.
Aid was quickly dispatched, and the fur traders were saved.
Upon returning to his charge, Fisher found:

52 Indians, men, women & children had perished by famine and
the surviving living on the dead carcasses of their Relations all
within 200 yards of the Fort during my absence, my man and his
family living on Moose Skins, Pack Cords, Bear Skins, Leather
Sled Trappings etc. These poor Indians seldom could get sleep,
they both men and women kept axe in hand for self preservation

& if any found knapping instantly was knocked on the head and as soon devoured by their nearest relatives.[86]

Although in that horrible winter of 1841–42 the fur traders were not reduced to the sad extremity of many of their aboriginal neighbors, they did not escape the season unscathed. The winter mail-packet drivers, a Scotsman and an Orkneyman, were murdered on the trail between Fort Good Hope and the Peel River post. One night a party of starving Indians slipped into their camp, slew the Hudson's Bay men, and ate their provisions. That meager amount of food hardly dented their hunger, and the two white men were then butchered and eaten by the Indian women. News of this atrocity shocked the district, but it did not cause the company's officers to lose their sense of perspective. Sir George Simpson advised Chief Factor Lewes not to punish the Indians involved. The governor noted that cannibalism was not unknown even among civilized peoples during periods of extreme want, and that the Indians had already suffered enough.[87]

Simpson's understanding attitude stemmed in part from the realization that the company's fortunes in the Mackenzie depended on the same meager subsistence base that was the Indians' livelihood. Separated from the nearest centers of production and political power by over three thousand miles of trail, frozen in for over half the year, the Mackenzie District fur traders were denied the use of the agricultural surpluses upon which their culture was based. In 1834, in an effort to reduce costs, the Council of the Northern Department prohibited the importation of flour into the area. The district was to supply its own.[88]

The experimental growing of wheat was not very successful at Fort Simpson. At Fort Liard wheat was able to ripen in good years, and it was ground into flour for use by the traders. Barley was successfully grown at Forts Simpson, Liard, and Norman, as well as potatoes, turnips, cabbage, and even beets.[89] The garden returns were meager, but more often than not they made the difference between starvation and survival.

The bulk of the fur traders' diet, however, was composed of fish and game. Each fall the Hudson's Bay men prepared

Fur traders preparing a meal on the trail. Illustration by Frederic Remington for Caspar Whitney, On Snow-Shoes to the Barren Grounds (London, 1896).

for the fishing season. Nets were repaired, and the fishermen, who were often engaged especially for the task, were dispatched to a nearby lake. A good fishery could supply its mother post with as many as ten thousand fish, but all too often except for Big Island Fishery on Great Slave Lake the Mackenzie District fisheries fell woefully short of that figure.[90] The fish were trapped in gill nets, which were lowered through the ice. Preservation was not a problem, as they froze solid within minutes of being caught. Fish was the sole diet of the company's sled dogs throughout the winter.

Snowshoe rabbits constituted a major portion of the diet of the posts' inmates. They were snared by the women and children, by the local Indians, and by hunters who were specifically employed for the purpose. When the rabbit cycle climaxed, and their population dramatically fell off, a winter of privation was assured for both whites and Indians. There was a direct relationship between the lynx and rabbit populations. When there were fewer lynx, there was less predator pressure on the rabbits, which then became abundant for both the lynx and the hunters. Subsequently the lynx would increase and decimate the rabbits, causing the lynx once again to die off and the hunters to starve, until the hares recovered. Rabbit hunting was all the more important along the Mackenzie River because big-game hunting was generally poor there.

Moose and caribou hunting went on all year long, though the most productive season was the late winter, after the new year and before the spring thaw. At that time the drifts were deep, and the snow had frozen with a thick, crusty surface. Aided by breezy weather, which would cover their noise and blow their scent downwind, skilled hunters could bring in an incredible amount of meat. In one three-month period during the winter of 1826–27 nearly eleven thousand pounds of meat, mostly moose and caribou, were collected for Fort Simpson.[91]

Most of this hunting was done by Indians, who were either official "fort hunters" paid in powder and shot, or members of the independent local bands known as the "home guard." The provisions trade was the easiest way for the Indians to acquire European goods. Unlike setting up traplines, moose and rabbit hunting could be done without disturbing the traditional

Moose hunting in the Yukon River. Illustration by Frederick Whymper in his Travel and Adventure in the Territory of Alaska *(1868).*

winter hunting-band structure. Perhaps because of this, the Indians seemed to have been more consistent in supplying the trading posts with food than in trapping furs. Captain John Henry Lefroy, who visited Fort Simpson in 1844, was surprised to see a group of Indians drag a sled of dried caribou meat all the way from the Coppermine River. The Indians refused to touch the meat that they meant for trade, even though they had been without food themselves for days. After they had reached the fort and traded the meat to the company, one said, "I am starving, give me something to eat."[92]

Thus trade goods were vital to the provisioning of a Hudson's Bay Company post, although in time of famine, when the Indians were starving, no amount of goods could keep the traders from doing likewise. The Hudson's Bay men's physical welfare under normal conditions was dependent upon the supply of trade goods at hand, since the goods served a double function, in the provisions trade and the fur trade. The barter

Rabbit hunters' camp. Illustration by Frederic Remington for Caspar Whitney, On Snow-Shoes to the Barren Grounds (London, 1896).

system of supplying the posts had both advantages and disadvantages for the Hudson's Bay Company. The biggest plus,
though the traders did not know it, was that the fresh meat
provided by the Indians rendered scurvy an unknown disease
in the Mackenzie District. The British Empire's naval explorers were still plagued by scurvy in the twentieth century.[93]
The main disadvantage of the system was that trade goods, the
medium of exchange, had to be imported at great expense and
over great distances into the district.

If mistakes or miscalculations were made in ordering the
district's trade outfit, disaster could result. This occurred at
Dease Lake in the winter of 1838–39. Campbell had been ordered by Governor Simpson to expand the district's frontiers,
but, when he petitioned Chief Trader McPherson for additional supplies, he was refused; the chief trader pleaded that
he had none to give.[94] The result was a winter of starvation
for Campbell and his men.

Of course, the opposite situation was bad for the company
as well. If more trade goods were imported into the Mackenzie District than could be sold, transport costs increased without any corresponding return in profits. The great distance
between the Mackenzie District and the London fur market
aggravated the situation. Goods purchased in London could
not be turned into a profit for five years. If the company purchased an outfit of goods for the Mackenzie District in 1840,
it would reach York Factory on Hudson's Bay by the end of
that summer. In 1841 the outfit would be shipped to the inland depot of Norway House on Lake Winnipeg, and only in
1842 would the goods reach Fort Simpson. The furs purchased
with those goods would be sent out from Fort Simpson in
1843. In 1844 they would be forwarded from Norway House
to York Factory. Not until 1845 would the furs be sold in
London, completing the cycle.[95] When the company expanded
into the Yukon drainage system, an additional two years was
required from investment to profit. In today's climate of high
inflation few business firms could weather a five-to-seven-year
delay in profits. Even by nineteenth-century standards the
Hudson's Bay Company was assuming quite a risk in the Mackenzie District. Governor Simpson tried to lessen the risk by

Trade goods being unloaded at Fort Resolution, Great Slave Lake, circa 1900. Photograph by C. W. Mather in Outing: The Outdoor Magazine of Human Interest, July, 1904.

demanding the strictest economy from his Mackenzie traders.

Murdock McPherson, however, in his term as district commander adhered too closely to Governor Simpson's law of "Oeconomy." As Robert Campbell found out, McPherson had forgotten the rationale behind the dictum. In 1840, McPherson dispatched John Bell to establish the new post at Peel River, but did not ask York Factory to supply Fort Simpson with the necessary increase in trade goods for the district. When John Lee Lewes assumed command at Fort Simpson, he found the district's supply system in chaos and immediately set about reforming it. Looking at McPherson's ledgers, Lewes remarked that he must have been "possessed of some secret, whereby to make Amm^n [ammunition] & Tob^o [tobacco] go further."[96] If there were any more economy of McPherson's sort, the company "had better shut up shop or abandon some of our Posts."[97]

Lewes was not pleased with his assignment to command at Fort Simpson. He referred to the sparse Mackenzie Valley as "this Land of Nod" and confided to a friend, "I want to be off as soon as I can with safety to my old ways."[98] The best way to achieve that end was to reorganize the district as quickly as possible. Lewes nearly doubled the amounts of gunpowder, shot, and tobacco imported into the Mackenzie.[99] These goods were the most valuable because there was a constant demand for them among the Indians. Gun powder and tobacco were especially important in opening up new regions, where the Indians were capable of living without white goods because they were not available. As soon as the company had a good supply of trade goods on hand at a new post, it could quickly reduce the Indians into a state of dependence, at least for such basics as gunpowder. Both John Bell at Peel River and Robert Campbell on the upper Liard had been hindered by McPherson's failure to realize this basic law of the fur trade.

Chief Factor Lewes applied himself to solving another problem that plagued the district's supply system: a distressing amount of damaged or spoiled merchandise. The culprits were the voyageurs who transported the trade goods from Norway House to the long portage:

The portage La Loche Boys' are a sett of rough & terrible fellows' caring little for the contents of packages. All their *aim is* to get through the voyage as quick as possible their cry is the *D—l take the hindermost* helter skelter, bing, bang, the pieces containing the most brittle ware are as tenderly dashed on the rocks' as two or three pieces of bar iron.[100]

Those who packed the "pieces," or bales, of trade goods were inclined to be negligent about how the goods were arranged in the bundles when they left York Factory. In 1840, when Lewes was on his first trip from Portage la Loche to Fort Simpson, he and his boat crew stopped for a short snack on an island in Great Slave Lake. Lewes had promised his men some cheese he had ordered from England. An expectant group of hungry voyageurs gathered around the chief factor as he opened his personal cassette of food. All thought of a treat left their heads as their normally "strong noses & Stomachs" were greeted by the pungent odor of rotten cheese. Worse yet, the cheese had been packed with Lewes's yearly allowance of tea and sugar, articles that would be sorely missed throughout the winter. This problem Lewes tried to solve (at least to the satisfaction of his temper) by writing a long letter to the York Factory office describing the proper way to load fragile and perishable items.

In short, Lewes was an energetic force in reorganizing the logistics of the Mackenzie District. In spite of severe problems like the famine of 1841–42 he was able to build a solid base from which the expansion of the district could proceed with greater dispatch. Because of his experience and intimate knowledge of the administration of all of Rupert's Land, Lewes was able to convince Simpson to approve his requests. That was something that the less-experienced and less-trusted Murdock McPherson might not have been able to do, even if he had been inclined. When Lewes wrote, "Let those who's business it is supply me with officers Men and other means', and by the powers' of St. George, I will not leave a stone unturned to ferret out the gold of the North (Beaver),"[101] Simpson knew that Lewes meant what he said.

CHAPTER 8

What Is the Colville River?

ON May 26, 1842, John Bell and his staff were driven from the Peel River Post by a flood. The breaking ice of the river had jammed and formed a natural dam, forcing the water to overflow its banks. Though the water spilled through the fort and into the dwelling house, Bell did not panic. He had been through this miserable situation before in 1836, when the ice on the Mackenzie River had jammed and a flood had destroyed Fort Good Hope. Coolly Bell helped his men remove the fort's valuables to a high hill behind the post. When they had checked that all was in order, the fur traders themselves retreated to the elevated point, taking with them a large wooden boat just in case things got worse.[1]

In this wet and dangerous way spring came to the Peel River and put an end to the winter of 1841–42. The season had been as difficult on the Peel as at the other posts in the district. As at Fort Good Hope the inhabitants of the Peel River Post had been reduced to eating rather than trading beaver skins.[2] Bell wrote that one Indian family, who had been reduced to a diet of beaver skins, "looked more like McBeath's Ghost than human beings!" In spite of such extremities he had enjoyed a good trade, though he was somewhat short of beaver skins. The hardship of the season was only somewhat mitigated by the news that he had been promoted to the rank of chief trader.

The majority of the furs brought into the Peel River Post

came from the west, across a range in the Mackenzie Mountains known as the Richardson Mountains. The Indians who
traded at the post were Kutchins, or Loucheux. The Kutchins
were among the most numerous of the Athapascan Indian
tribes in northwestern America. The eastern Kutchins, who
lived along the Peel River and in the Mackenzie delta, had
been in steady contact with white traders since the establishment of Fort Good Hope in 1804. With easy access to Fort
Good Hope and later to the Peel River Post, they had become
middlemen between the Hudson's Bay Company and the large
numbers of Indians west of the Richardson Mountains. Most
of the western Indians were also members of the Kutchin
tribe, but they were known to the traders as the Gens du
Large, the Gens de Rat, and the Vanta Kootchin.[4] There was
also a small tribe of Han Indians along the Yukon River, who
were called the Gens de Fou.[5] The transmountain Indians
were able to visit the Peel River Post only rarely or in some
cases not at all, though they in fact produced a large portion
of the furs that were traded there. The Hudson's Bay Company was therefore eager to penetrate west of the Richardson
Mountains, where they expected to find not only a great many
furs but also the valley of the Colville River. Thus John Bell
wrote on August 24, 1841:

I had a visit from the Indians beyond the Western Rocky Mountains by the last Ice of May. They brought valuable hunts consist-
ing of fine Beaver. . . . These Indians are in the habit of making
annual excursions to the lands of another tribe more remote than
theirs, where they generally pass the Winter in hunting and trading. . . . Could I once succeed in inducing these strangers to visit
the Fort, I have not the least doubt but a very profitable trade
would be the result.[6]

Bell was unsuccessful in inducing any of the western tribes to
visit the Peel River Post, but he did manage to convince a Rat
Indian to conduct him through the mountains and into the
rich fur lands beyond the divide.

   Two additional factors, besides furs and the search for the
Colville, motivated Bell to explore the Richardson Mountains.
First was the large amount of caribou meat that was hunted

in the mountains and traded by the Indians at the Peel River Post. Bell was eager to secure a direct route to the hunting grounds and hoped to find a good location for an outpost there.[7] The auxiliary post would serve as a provisions center and also would encourage the transmountain Indians to trade. The second factor motivating Bell's explorations was the pressure that Sir George Simpson had brought to bear on Chief Factor Lewes to expand his operations in the direction of the Colville.[8] Bell was anxious to win Simpson's approval because he had recently petitioned the governor for a transfer to one of the more southerly and less severe districts.[9]

On June 23, a gray and overcast Thursday, Bell set off on a "trip of Discovery across the Mountains" with two voyageurs, named Wilson and Boucher, the Rat Indian who was to serve as a guide, and an Indian interpreter.[10] The party was ferried across the Peel River to a point about a mile downstream from the fort, where they landed on the west bank. There the overland journey began. The Hudson's Bay men were traveling light, with little in the way of provisions or trade goods. Bell did attempt to transport a small canoe, which he hoped could be portaged across the mountains and used to reach the Colville.

In the first few miles they traversed a thick forest of spruce. The overhanging branches of the trees made it difficult to carry the canoe. When they emerged from the forest, they ascended a steep terrace about 150 feet high, which led them to a broad, flat plain. Any relief that the absence of thick forest may have engendered was quickly dispelled as they proceeded across the plain.[11] What looked at a distance like a fine grassy prairie interspersed with patches of willow bushes turned out to be a swampy lowland. Four miles of difficult marching brought them across the plain to the base of a second, higher terrace. When they reached the summit of the second terrace, Bell and his party had already climbed more than 1,200 feet above the level of the Peel River Post.[12]

Unfortunately, the second slope led to another swampy plain, which, because of the elevation, was devoid even of shrubbery. The barren horizon was broken only by the peaks of the Richardson Mountains and a few stunted larches. Walk-

ing across the plain was difficult because of large tufts of grass
that the voyageurs indelicately called *têtes des femmes*. R. G.
McConnell, who crossed the mountains in 1888, accurately described the problems that the tufts caused the explorers:

These project a foot or more above the clayey soil, and are the
cause of constant stumbling which becomes somewhat exasperat-
ing when one is weighted down with a pack. An attempt to walk
on top of the mounds soon becomes excessively fatiguing on account of the irregular length of strides, and a slight miscalculation
as to distance precipitates the unlucky traveller down into the
muddy depths between. When down, the resolve is usually made,
and adhered to for awhile, to keep to the lower levels, but the
effort required to step over the intervening hillocks presents obvious disadvantages of a different kind.[13]

This sort of terrain forced Bell to abandon his canoe during
the second day of the journey.[14]

As Bell and his men approached the mountains, the swampy
ground was left behind. The mountains about them were unlike any other in the long succession of peaks that make up
the Rockies. They were rounded and somewhat uniform in
shape, an appearance fostered by a covering carpet of moss
and rock that seemed to smooth off any rough edges. The only
variation between the dull greenish gray of the mountains and
the color of the sky was in patches of snow that lay protected
in the shadows of the mountains' folds. What is unique about
the geography of the Richardson Mountains is that the summits of the peaks scarcely top 4,000 feet; the mountains are
among the lowest in the entire Rocky Mountain chain. Most
of the terrain traversed by John Bell was less than 2,500 feet
above sea level.[15]

After "four days of hard labourious traveling" the Hudson's
Bay men had crossed over the Richardson Mountains, which
constitute the divide between the Yukon and Mackenzie rivers.[16] Their overland journey came to an end at the banks of
a meandering mountain stream. Their guide told them that
this river led to another larger river, which flowed through
the territory of the Indians from whom the eastern Lou-
cheaux, or Kutchins, acquired many valuable furs. Bell and
his men searched the banks of the small river, among stands

of aspen and spruce, for wood suitable for building a raft.
The small canoe that they had been forced to leave behind
was bitterly missed when they finally embarked in their less-
than-satisfactory craft. The small river is known today as the
Bell River. The fur traders called it the Rat River, which is
confusing because only a few miles away on the east there was
another river known as the Rat flowing into the Peel River.[17]

The Bell River is a sluggish stream between forty and fifty
yards wide with little current.[18] It was hardly an ideal river
for rafting, and Bell and his men made slow progress. After
three frustrating days the explorers came upon three small Indian hunting canoes. Without hesitation Bell abandoned the
raft and approached the canoes.[19] Unfortunately, they were
small and unstable, and Bell was forced to lash two of them
together with rope to give them the stability required to support two men in each. The third canoe with one man preceded the double canoe. It was hoped that he would be able
to surprise any game along the river and provide some supper
for the men. Bell noted that with the Indians' canoes they
"proceeded more expeditously," but that the "least wind and
waves would sink them to the bottom."[20]

Shortly after finding the canoes, the explorers came to the
junction of the Bell with a larger river flowing from the northwest. John Bell assumed that this was just a branch of the Bell
River, but in reality it was the Porcupine River, a major river
in its own right, over five hundred miles long, and an important tributary of the Yukon River. The explorers proceeded
cautiously down the Porcupine until the Rat Indian guide
called a halt near an abandoned encampment of his band.
There the guide proposed that the explorers stop for the day,
as he wished to travel inland and visit his relatives. He said
that he would procure some dried fish for the Hudson's Bay
men. As Bell was out of provisions, he agreed to let the man
go. On the next morning the Indian did not return as promised, but did send a replacement to continue to guide the
traders west. Initially Bell was "highly pleased with his sub-
stitute, [since he was] an experienced man and seemed acquainted with the River to which we were bound." Then, on
the day after he began to guide the party, Bell was "much

surprised in hearing him declare he would proceed no further with us, alleging the distance to reach the large River I so anxiously wished to see, to be so great that we should be overtaken by the cold before we could be able to come back in the Fall, and that for want of clothing he was not prepared for such a long journey." Bell tried to sway the Indian's mind but "remonstrated with him in vain on the impropruity of his conduct."[21]

Without a guide and short of provisions Bell was hesitant to advance. He did not know how far he was from the large river on the west. At this point he was in the vicinity of the present-day border between Alaska and the Yukon Territory. Although his guide had described a long journey, he was, in fact, less than 150 miles away from the Yukon River with no rapids or portages in between. If Bell had gambled that the Indian lied, he could have pushed on to the Yukon. Instead he elected to return safely with the information that he had already garnered. A further consideration was his concern for his duties as a fur trader. He was apprehensive because "had I perservered in reaching the object of my search without a Guide, I might probably return too late to forward the [Peel River fur] Returns to Fort Good Hope."[22] He returned to the Peel River Post on July 24 after a journey a month and a day long.

Chief Trader Bell was not pleased with the results of his exploration. Though he believed that the land west of the mountains was "rich in Beaver and large animals," he did not think it could be profitably exploited.[23] He wrote to James Hargrave at York Factory, "I fear we cannot succeed in transporting our Goods for the trade through such an abominable track where I could hardly travel with My Gun on My shoulder, scrambling up and down Mountains & deep vallies where goats and Deer could hardly get footing!!"[24] His disappointment was all the more acute because he believed that the large river that he had come close to reaching was the long-sought Colville. In fact, he believed that the Porcupine River, which he had discovered, together with another large river coming up from the south (which we know as the Yukon River), formed the Colville River.[25]

John Bell could not know that all that separated him from
the Yukon River, which he thought was the Colville River
drainage, was one of the lowest mountain ranges in the Rocky
Mountain chain. He failed to grasp the advantage that geography offered because his judgment was blinded by immediate
problems, both real and imagined. Most important was the
bias, reinforced by the entire history of the fur trade, that
caused him to look for a water route through the mountains.
His frustration was real when he wrote, "What a pity it is that
a water communication does not exist to enable us to form an
Establishment in that apparently rich Country."[26] Every post
in Rupert's Land was built on some navigable waterway, and
nearly all were supplied by water. It is easy to see why Bell
looked for a water route west. It was not only generally
cheaper to ship by water but also was standard company policy. As early as 1839, when he had explored the eastern Rat
River and found it too difficult, Bell had sought a water route
west. His 1842 journey represented an attempt to see how
much of a portage was necessary to reach western waters. That
he regarded it as a portage is demonstrated by his attempt to
carry a canoe across the mountains. The portage trail that he
found was not easy—it was sixty miles long over some difficult
terrain—but it was shorter than the company's route through
the Canadian rockies at Athabasca Pass, which was over eighty
miles long.[27] Bell was driven to discount his discoveries by his
lack of means to exploit them in 1842. Since he did not have
enough men to pack a complete outfit of trade goods sixty
miles across the Rocky Mountains, he disregarded the route
that would require such an effort and concentrated on finding
a route that he could exploit.

A year later, in June, 1843, he dispatched James Purden, a
young post master, with two veteran voyageurs, Lewis and
Boucher, to make a second journey over the mountains. Another Rat Indian, named Tarshee, claimed to know a new
route westward, "in which were many Lakes in the Portage
for easy transport of the canoe across the Mountains."[28] The
exact route that was followed by Purden and his party is
difficult to determine. Since Tarshee had spoken of "many
Lakes" and later of "the Portage beyond the Rat River," it

seems that he knew of no new pass westward, but merely led the Hudson's Bay men up the eastern Rat River through Mc-Dougall Pass. That was the route west that John Bell and Alexander Kennedy Isbister had taken in 1839.

Leaving the Peel River post, Purden canoed down the Peel River to its mouth and into the Huskie Channel of the Mackenzie River delta. After a few miles the channel led them to the mouth of the Rat River.[29] Then Purden and his men battled their way up the Rat River, eventually reaching the riverhead and a chain of five small lakes that led across the Mackenzie-Yukon Divide. Upon reaching the lakes, the guide told Purden to abandon the canoe, as he had another hidden at the end of the portage. There was something about Tarshee's behavior that made Purden suspect his honesty, and the young trader decided to continue on with the canoe. This suspicion was confirmed on the next day, when Tarshee refused to lead them farther across the mountains and deserted the company's service. Without a guide Purden was forced to turn back, and he arrived at the Peel River Post less than a week after his departure.[30]

This second failure in two years did nothing to dispell Bell's pessimism about extending the trade to the Colville River. He recorded in the Peel River Post journal, "The unexpected failure of this second attempt in discovering a practicable overland track by which we might be able to transport goods for carrying on the trade beyond the western Mountains, has blighted my fond hopes."[31] Like Bell a year earlier, Purden had been stopped by the desertion of his Indian guide.

The eastern Kutchin Indians were in a very advantageous position. They enjoyed a profitable role as middlemen between the Hudson's Bay men and the western Kutchins and Han Indians across the Richardson Mountains and some Eskimo hunting bands on the north. The Kutchins' commercial sense was as highly developed as the Hudson's Bay Company's. Though they were thankful that the white men had established the Peel River Post in their territory, they were not anxious to see the company expand its operations to any of the tribes on the west. Through intimidation and often open hostilities they kept the Eskimos from trading at the Peel

River Post.[32] It is no wonder then that the Hudson's Bay Company had difficulty finding eastern Kutchins willing to guide them west. Both Bell and Purden had a Rat Indian (a Crow River Kutchin) as a guide, and it is significant that they both served the explorers well until they reached Rat Indian territory. Since the Indians did not want the white men to expand their trade past their own territory, they deserted there.

Another tactic adopted by the Mackenzie District Indians to slow the Hudson's Bay Company's western expansion was to attribute warlike designs to their neighbors. Robert Campbell was a victim of such a slander campaign in 1843 when the northern Tutchones convinced his voyageurs that it would mean certain death to advance past the fork of the Lewes and Pelly rivers. The Peel River Kutchins often warned the fur traders of impending Eskimo attacks or near ambushes.[33] This left the impression that the Eskimos were the ones who opposed free trade rather than the Kutchins. Sir George Simpson, if he had not been the victim of their deception, would have appreciated the Kutchins' acumen.

Exploration of the Keele River

By the summer of 1843 the Hudson's Bay Company had probed the flanks of the Mackenzie Mountains. On the southwest Robert Campbell had circumvented the mountains and had reached one of the sources of the Yukon River, the upper Pelly River, but his progress was slow because of his tenuous supply line up the deadly Liard. On the northwest John Bell had blazed a trail through the Richardson Mountains and had managed to reach the Porcupine River, a major tributary of the Yukon River, but again the route that Bell discovered was a long and difficult one. The Hudson's Bay Company was closing in on the Yukon River (which it still thought of as the Colville), but it had not yet found a satisfactory route by which it could exploit that river's fur trade. In order to discover such a route, John Lee Lewes launched a third exploratory survey in the Mackenzie District.

Whereas Campbell and Bell had explored the extremes of the Mackenzie Mountains, Lewes planned to send a third party into the very heart of the range. The man selected for the task was Adam McBeath, a native of Rupert's Land, who had joined the company's service in 1829.[34] McBeath was promoted to the rank of post master in 1836 and was assigned first to Fort Simpson and later to Fort Norman.[35] It was from the latter establishment that he embarked upon his exploratory survey. His purpose was to ascend the Keele River, a Mackenzie River tributary (then known as the Gravel River) that enters the Mackenzie from the mountains on the west. He hoped to reach a large lake that the Indians reported to be the Keele River's source.[36] It was hoped that the Keele would provide better access to the headwaters of the Colville than Bell and Campbell had found.

McBeath left Fort Norman on July 3. In his North canoe were four Indians, who were to serve as guides and hunters, and an *engagé*, named La Rocque, from the fort. They followed the Mackenzie River up to the mouth of the Keele, which they reached late on the first day. Like most rivers falling from the mountains, the Keele is swift and shallow. McBeath was hindered not only by the fast current but also by strong headwinds blowing in from the west. He kept his canoe in the smaller channels, protected from the wind, but was confounded by snags of driftwood that so blocked his path that the Indians had to march ahead with axes to make the way clear for the canoe. To make matters worse, the river was rising, and its strength kept increasing. After three days of slow progress McBeath called a halt, to allow the Keele to drop in volume and to allow his hunters to increase the supply of provisions.[37]

After two days of waiting the Keele's current did not abate. McBeath elected to abandon his canoe and proceed on foot. He was now at the base of the Mackenzie Mountains, which had been only faintly visible when he had entered the Keele. His journey, which had not been easy, now became positively brutal. Tormented by mosquitoes and flies, the party scrambled up and down steep mountain ridges. McBeath reported that, while crossing "one of the Deep chasms of the Mountains, one of the indians got his arm much injured by a fall, myself and others got severe bruses."[38] This accident convinced McBeath that it was "too difficult to climb Mountains with any weight [being] carried," and the explorers erected a cache to store their unnecessary equipment.[39]

Proceeding with lighter loads, the Indians led McBeath up the deep valley of the Keele River. The wild, rugged scenery about them threatened the success of the expedition, yet Mc-Beath was still struck by its beauty. On June 12 he wrote, "I have something strange to record it appears the same everywhere we are now deep in the mountain & can see little but sky above us, to look so it might appear terrific yet it is a picturesque sight & worth the beholders eyes."[40]

On the next day they left the Keele River and proceeded up a small tributary that the Indians called the Deer River. Because the Keele took "a windy direction at this place," it was possible to make better progress marching along the Deer, which they followed until about ten o'clock at night. At that point they were again ascending the mountains, to rejoin the Keele. The late subarctic sunset overtook them "on the summit of the highest [mountain] without anything to pass the night but the hard stone, neither wood nor moss to cook our supper with." The explorers had the choice of dining on the raw flesh of a mountain goat or huddling in the rocks hungry.[41]

As they continued the march the next morning, the Indian hunters spotted a herd of almost thirty mountain goats. The explorers gave chase, but were unsuccessful in procuring any for their larder. They descended to the Keele River for part of the day, finding it still flowing swiftly between banks that were about 150 yards wide. On June 15 they were again in the high country; they camped that evening on the edge of the timberline amid snow-covered mountains.[42]

That was as far as McBeath was able to proceed. On the morning of June 16 he awoke to find "to my great chagrin and disappointment that two of my Indians had deserted during the night." The loss was especially important because "those were the very two I solely depended upon as one was Guide & the other my principal Hunter." The Indians were tired of "the laborious duty of climbing the mountains."[43] It must have seemed pointless to them to keep plodding along through such difficult terrain. Indeed, they were correct, for it was painfully clear that the Keele River was not going to yield a trade route west. Unfortunately, the desertion left McBeath without a guide and short of provisions in rugged, mapless country. With a touch of understatement McBeath described his plight as "a situation very difficult for me to extract myself."[44]

On the following morning, "with a sorrowful heart," McBeath, La Rocque, and the remaining two Indians began the march home. Unsure of their position, they decided to strike straight across the mountains. If worse came to worst, they could head east until they hit the Mackenzie River. As it turned out, during the day they encountered a river that McBeath thought might lead them back to the Keele. For the remainder of the day they followed it and at nightfall camped on its bank, "still ignorant of where we were."[45]

The river turned out to be the Deer River, and they had no trouble following it to the Keele. Their departed guide had led them on a more difficult route during their outward march. By a fortunate accident McBeath had found an easier line of march home. It would never be of importance to the fur trade, but it saved his party's lives. When they reached the Keele, they were out of food, and McBeath was forced to stop and try to catch fish. After a supper of trout and a night's rest McBeath was ready to continue the march back to the Mackenzie. His two remaining Indians, however, had other ideas. They were through with walking and wanted to build pine-bark canoes and float down the Keele. McBeath, who for a fur trader seems to have been surprisingly inept at handling Indians, disregarded their suggestion and continued the march with only La Rocque following. Two days of travel through a swamp of knee-deep muck and thick forests brought McBeath and La Rocque to the place where they had cached the canoe. The site was hard to recognize because a forest fire had swept through the area, burning to within a few yards of the overturned canoe, which suffered only minor damage.[46]

On the next morning the two Indians drifted down the Keele and presented the fur traders with some reindeer steaks for breakfast. They had been bothered by none of the swamps and thickets that had harassed McBeath, and they arrived quite fresh. Together the party returned to Fort Norman. The trip took a mere six hours, while on their outward journey six days had been required to cover the same distance.[47]

Adam McBeath gave a discouraging report to Chief Factor Lewes. The country through which he had traveled supported only a small fur-bearing population.[48] The Keele River was too shallow and swift to be of practical use in penetrating the interior, and the Mackenzie Mountains were too formidable to be breached by a frontal assault. If the Honorable Company was going to reach the Yukon River, it would have to go by the routes blazed by John Bell and Robert Campbell.

Sir George Simpson was even more disappointed with the results of McBeath's exploration than Chief Factor Lewes was. Simpson saw it as not only a failure but also a waste of resources. He dashed off a note of disapproval to the district commander: "You seem to be carrying your Explorations farther than I contemplated or you were authorized to do so, in forwarding Mr. A. McBeath up the Gravel [Keele] River. Two surveying parties, say those of MRS. Bell and Campbell I consider to be quite sufficient at one time."[49] Governor Simpson was back to his old inconsistent policy of economy and exploration; he wanted expansion, but not its risks or costs.

Difficulties at the Frances Lake Post

The winter began for Robert Campbell in much the same way as the summer had ended, with the inmates of the Frances Lake Post short of food. The provisions situation was aggravated in early October when the boats from Fort Simpson finally arrived with the year's trade outfit. The boats also brought Campbell reenforcements of men, whom Campbell was forced to send back for want of means to feed them. Remaining at Frances Lake, however, was William Lucas Hardisty, a clerk who was to be Campbell's new assistant. Hardisty was the métis son of Chief Trader Richard Hardisty. He was an intelligent and inquisitive young man, who would later make important contributions to the early natural history of the Mackenzie Valley. In addition, he later wrote an important piece of pioneer ethnology, "The Loucheux Indians," which appeared in the Smithsonian Institution's *Annual Report for 1866*.[50] Simpson trusted Campbell with Hardisty's education as a fur trader. The first lesson was to be austerity.

As the ice closed over Frances Lake, the number of fish caught in the gill nets fell off. To counteract this, Campbell dispatched his fishermen to several of the small lakes in the vicinity of the post. Unfortunately, the results were "indifferent" at best.[51] Campbell's food gathering was further hampered by a new problem: feuding among the Indians. Shortly after his return from the fork of the Lewes and Pelly rivers, a Tutchone woman, who had recently come with her three sons to the Frances Lake region, was slain. Campbell swore to have the murderer "hung to a tree" if he caught him. Then in October he received a report that several Indians who traded at his post and provided him with provisions and furs had also been killed.[52]

Campbell was originally inclined to blame the deaths on traditional blood feuds. A few weeks later, however, he received a report that "our old enemies the Nahannies in concert with the Tribe or tribes south of the Pelly river towards the Lake of the head of the Lewes River are [trying] to cut off ourselves and establishments and dependent upon us, in the early part of this winter."[53] As soon as his trading partners heard this, Campbell could not "get an Indian to remain."[54]

The Hudson's Bay Company post at Frances Lake, which Campbell and Simpson had assumed was established in virgin fur territory, was actually located on the fringe of a rival commercial network. The Tlingit Indians on the Pacific Coast, particularly the Chilkat tribe of the Lynn Canal region, had been in contact with white maritime traders since the late eighteenth century. The Chilkats had traded furs first with the Boston men, as the American traders were called, and later with the Russian merchants. After the Contract of 1839 they dealt with Hudson's Bay Company ships. The trade goods thus acquired they packed into leather bundles of one hundred or more pounds. Each spring the Chilkat traders with numerous slave auxiliaries would transport these bun-

dles through Chilkat Pass and over the Coastal Mountains. In
the cordillera region the Chilkats traded their goods with the
Tagishes, the inland Tlingits, and the southern Tutchones.
On more far-ranging ventures the Chilkats even floated down
the Lewes River to the Pelly, where they traded with the
northern Tutchones, with whom Campbell had established
contact in the summer of 1843. What is more, the Chilkats
were not alone in conducting far-ranging trade expeditions.
The Tagishes, the inland Tlingits, and the southern Tutchones, after dealing with the Chilkats, themselves entered into
a lucrative barter with the Indians of the Pelly River.[55]

The structure of the native trade system in the southern
Yukon was the same as that of the Stikine River area, which
Campbell had known in 1838. The coastal Tlingits lorded it
over the interior tribes, but those Indians who were nearest to
them—in the southern Yukon, the Tagishes, and in the Stikine
region, the Tahltans—although forced to endure the Tlingits'
insults, were in an advantageous position to exploit the tribes
farther inland. In 1838 and 1839, Robert Campbell's presence
at Dease Lake had disrupted the trade of the Tahltans, or, as
he called them, the Nahannis. The resulting harassments
eventually drove him from the area. In 1843 his establishment
at Frances Lake was in a similar position. The Indians whom
he described as "our old enemies the Nahannies" were probably the Tagishes, whose trade as middlemen he had broken.
The fighting among the Indians who traded at Frances Lake
was caused probably not so much by a blood feud as by a commercial realignment.

Campbell's position was less precarious at Frances Lake
than it had been at the Dease Lake, because the region seems
to have been a no-man's land. It was an unclaimed borderland
between the Kascas of the Liard River, the northern Tutchones of the Pelly River, and the Tagishes and Tlingits on the
south. During the winter of 1843 Campbell began to acknowledge at least the existence of an aboriginal trade system. In
May, 1844, he wrote Governor Simpson, telling him that the
majority of the furs that he collected at Frances Lake would
otherwise make their way to the Pacific Coast and be bought
by the company at higher cost there.[56] What Campbell did

not realize and what he would not know until 1852 was the strength of the aboriginal trade network.

After the New Year, as the threat of "Nahanny" (Tagish) attacks subsided, native visits to Frances Lake began to increase. Campbell recorded meeting "strange Indians many of whom had never seen a white man before." As the fur trade improved, so did his food situation. Caribou began to frequent the area, and the post hunters were able to bring in large quantities of fresh meat.[57] In March the snow on Frances Lake began to melt, and from under the as-yet-thick ice came the loud, deep clap, like rolling thunder, of the shifting ice sheet.[58] Just before the last of the snow had melted, dispatches from Fort Simpson arrived. Campbell was ordered to bring his post's fur returns down to the depot and take command of Fort Simpson for the summer.

Campbell's trip down the Liard to Fort Simpson was a miserable journey. Upon arriving at Fort Halkett, he found that Alexander Christe, the clerk commanding the post, had been forced to eat the pemmican that had been reserved for the voyaguers from Frances Lake. The same occurred at Fort Liard. Campbell and his men were therefore forced to provide for themselves as they made their way downriver, and they had an unwelcome opportunity to practice the all-too-familiar exercise of fasting.[59]

When Campbell arrived at Fort Simpson, he was warmly greeted by Chief Factor Lewes. Lewes was preparing unexpectedly to leave the Mackenzie District. The fifty-three-year-old fur trader had not been fond of his posting in the austere Mackenzie District, but he had planned to stay to see the completion of the company's expansion toward the Colville River. Unfortunately, in November, 1843, he had suffered a nearly fatal accident. In a moment of carelessness he had accidentally discharged his shotgun, blowing off his right hand and a considerable portion of his forearm. He could hardly have been farther from surgical care at Fort Simpson, and a man of a less hardy constitution would have died. Luckily, a young clerk, August Peers, was able to dress the bleeding stump. He meticulously tied up every artery and vein exposed and then washed the wound thoroughly. For many weeks Lewes was gaunt and weakened, but he gradually recovered his strength. In time, only the cold bothered his mutilated arm, and he remedied that by designing a thick fur sleeve. At the same time, although he had suffered severely in the past from neuralgia, he shook off that condition completely.[60]

Also at Fort Simpson that spring was Captain John Henry Lefroy of the British Army. Lefroy had been sent to Rupert's Land with the backing of the Royal Society to take magnetic readings in northern British America. After leaving Toronto in April, 1843, and touring much of the Hudson's Bay Company's territory, he had reached Fort Simpson in March, 1844. An affable man, he got along very well with the little society at the fort. Robert Campbell, when he arrived that spring, particularly enjoyed Lefroy's company. Ever eager to improve himself, Campbell had Lefroy give him a crash course in astronomy and its practical uses.[61] Lefroy also expressed an interest in Campbell's explorations in the direction of the Pelly River, which he feared would lead to conflict with the Russians. Campbell's acquaintance with Lefroy was short, because Lefroy remained only a few months in the Mackenzie District, but he and Campbell corresponded frequently over the years, forming a friendship of which Campbell wrote that he "derived much pleasure and benefit."[62]

Also at Fort Simpson that spring was Chief Trader John McLean. The forty-five-year-old trader had joined the Hudson's Bay Company in 1821 and had seen service in New Caledonia and Ungava (northern Quebec). In the latter district he had distinguished himself by his steady management of the company's posts and by two arduous journeys across the Labrador Peninsula. During the second journey he had discovered the Great Falls of Labrador on the Churchill River.[63] From Governor Simpson's correspondence both McLean and Lewes were led to believe that, when Lewes left the district that summer, McLean would assume control of its affairs. Campbell was sorry to see Lewes depart. The chief factor had done much to encourage Campbell's explorations, and he had improved the flow of trade goods into the Mackenzie Valley. On the other hand, Campbell was pleased with the apparent selection of McLean to succeed Lewes in charge of Fort Simpson.

He felt that McLean "was a very active enterprising officer."[64]
Because he was an explorer himself, McLean was familiar
with the problems of opening up a new area to commerce.
Campbell shared another trait with McLean: "Wherever we
were stationed near water, we invariably took our morning
dip outside until the ice got too thick to break a hole
through."[65]

Campbell remained at Fort Simpson for the rest of the sum-
mer, supervising operations there while McLean went to Portage La Loche to receive the district's supplies. Upon Mc-
Lean's return Campbell made his way up the Liard to Frances
Lake. Instead of voyageurs, most of Campbell's boatmen were
Indians, whom the company hired at lower wages than white
men and could dismiss after the completion of the voyage.
This was an unsatisfactory arrangement, as the Indians had
neither the experience nor the discipline of the voyageurs.
They deserted in ones and twos with the increasing difficulties
of the Liard River. Finally, at Devil's Portage the remaining
Indians deserted en masse. Campbell and the few remaining
men managed to cross the portage only with great difficulty
and with some help from the *engagés* of Fort Halkett. Campbell was not, however, able to proceed with his entire outfit to
Frances Lake. John McLean had fortunately given him permission to deposit half of his supplies at Fort Halkett if circumstances required, and Campbell took advantage of that
freedom and proceeded to Frances Lake with a reduced outfit.[66]

Campbell's difficulty with the Indian boatmen was not an
isolated incident in the summer of 1844. The grim famines
that had plagued the Mackenzie valley in the early 1840s had
taken close to three hundred Indian lives out of a population
that probably had not exceeded four thousand people.[67] Many
Indians blamed the traders for that fearful sweep of death
through their ranks. At Fort Good Hope one group of Indians
plotted to redress their grievances. Nine hunters, with their
bodies blackened and armed with both daggers and guns,
burst into the post's trading room. George F. Deschambeault,
the clerk commanding the post, offered the men the pieces of
tobacco that were usually given as a pretrade gratuity. The In-

dians refused and accused the Hudson's Bay Company of being responsible for all of the Indian deaths during the past few years. At the end of the harangue the leader urged his followers to revenge themselves on the whites and at the same time began a personal attack on Deschambeault. The clerk, however, was equal to the situation:

> M. Deschambeault, *dicto citius*, instantly sprung upon him, and twisting his arm into his long hair laid him at his feet; and pointing his dagger at his throat, dared him to utter another word. So sudden and unexpected was this intrepid act, that the rest of the party looked on in silent astonishment, without power to assist their fallen chief, or revenge his disgrace.[68]

Deschambeault's quick action probably saved the post from plunder, if not destruction. At Fort Liard the Indians took a less violent but more effective form of action by not supplying the traders with food or furs.

John McLean was not free to respond to these challenges. In August he had received a letter from Sir George Simpson which stated that "another gentleman was appointed to the charge of McKenzie's River District."[69] Furthermore, Simpson chided McLean for thinking that he would be given such a valuable charge. The high-strung McLean was touched to the quick. He dashed off an emotional letter to the governor, in which he listed his meritorious past services to the company. McLean also told the governor that John Lee Lewes and other officers who had read the district correspondence book all had interpreted Simpson's letters as giving the command of the Mackenzie District to him. The outcome of this dispute was that Murdock McPherson was brought back to Fort Simpson to assume command of the district, while McLean was given charge of a trading post on Great Slave Lake. A year later McLean quit the company's service. In his retirement he wrote a detailed narrative of his life in Rupert's Land, *Notes of a Twenty-five Years' Service in the Hudson's Bay Territory*, which is one of the best eyewitness accounts of life in the company, marred only by McLean's bitterness over his dispute with Governor Simpson.

John McLean was not the only one upset by the return of

Murdock McPherson. For Robert Campbell it was an unexpected reversal. He blamed McPherson for his winter of harassment and starvation at Dease Lake. Had McPherson been more generous in supporting Campbell, two of Campbell's men might not have died of famine in 1839. Also, McPherson was not a believer in the exploration westward. During his sojourn in Canada, McPherson had written to a friend:

I was happy to learn that Peel's River is likely to realize expectations; others thought only of the magnificent Colville River which is to make all our fortunes. Under the able and judicious management of my friend Bell I knew there would be "no mistake" about Peel River.[70]

McPherson thought only of the account books in front of him. His concern was not future profits but present expenses, and exploration constituted one of the larger expense items. Campbell knew McPherson's tendencies and wrote that his reappointment "tended to the disadvantage of the District & the discomfort of the junior officers."[71]

What Campbell did not know was that it was McPherson's tightfistedness that endeared him to Simpson. The governor had wanted Chief Factor Lewes, an active enterprising man, to expand the Mackenzie District toward the Colville River. before his accident Lewes had begun to do this, going so far as to launch three exploratory probes at the same time. Meanwhile, Lewes had demanded and received from the depot at York Factory across-the-board increases in trade goods to support his operations, new and old. The resulting increase in costs was an insult to everything that Governor Simpson held dear. The Mackenzie District was exporting furs that were worth on the average, £12,000 to £15,000 annually.[72] Since the maintenance of the district cost no more than 10 to 20 percent of that figure, it would seem that a slight increase in overhead would be easily allowed by the profits accrued. Unfortunately, Governor Simpson was forced to view the Mackenzie fur trade from the perspective of all of Rupert's Land and not just the district. The company needed large profits from the Mackenzie District to support other areas where the fur trade operated at a loss because of competition or depletion of the fur-bearing animals. Thus Simpson was very much alarmed when under Lewes the amounts of trade goods sent into the Mackenzie Valley increased nearly to the size of the Columbia District requisition.[73] The governor felt that some "curtailments" were in order and that Murdock McPherson, who in the past had kept the district undersupplied if anything, was the man to do the pruning.

John Bell on the Yukon River

While Governor Simpson was making his personnel changes, John Bell at the Peel River Post, the northernmost establishment in North America, continued to grapple with the problem of the Colville River. In December, 1844, he wrote to his old friend Murdock McPherson that it was his intention "to make another excursion across the mountains, early [this] ensuing June, with the view of reaching, if possible, the large river supposed to be the Colville."[74] As Governor Simpson was still as interested in exploration as he was in economy, Murdock McPherson gave his approval of John Bell's plan.

Bell left the Peel River Post on May 27, 1844. Two *engagés* were with him, and two Indians who were to serve as guide and interpreter. So slim were the means that McPherson afforded Bell that, when two of the men at Peel River were taken ill in April, Bell was nearly forced to postpone the proposed journey.[75] The line of march that he was to follow was the same that he had taken in 1842. He did not attempt to find a water route across the mountains; the experience of the intervening three years had taught him that no such route existed. He resigned himself to the "harassing walk of five days" that was required to cross the mountains. By June 1 the Hudson's Bay men had reached the westward-flowing waters of the Little Bell River,[76] the stream that flows from the portage to join the Bell River.

For the next week Bell and his party camped along that mountain stream. The Indians hunted in the brush of the surrounding country, trying to build up a stock of provisions. Under John Bell's supervision the two *engagés* worked on a canoe, which they constructed out of birchbark that they had carried over the barren mountains. When they had completed the canoe, the explorers set off down the Little Bell River. The stream was swift with the runoff of melted snow from the Richardson Mountains, and the canoe made fast progress in spite of the many twists and turns in the river's course. In only a few days' time they reached the Porcupine River and continued westward upon its current. Passing the spot where he had turned back in 1842, Bell noticed that the banks of the Porcupine gradually rose up and formed rocky defiles and ramparts of weathered rock on both sides of the river. In this section the Porcupine contracts so that it is a mere seventy-five yards wide, and the constrained water increases its flow, occasionally breaking into small riffles. Yet no significant obstacle to navigation was encountered by the explorers.[77]

On June 16, Bell reached the mouth of the Porcupine River. Before him was another large river nearly two miles across and filled with small, wooded islands. The brown waters of the Porcupine River spilled into the pale gray flow of the larger stream. Were it not for the river's strong, swift current, the grand waterway might easily have been mistaken for a large lake. Pleased with their success, the explorers eased their canoe into the midst of the river. The country about it was "flat but extremely dry, and free from swamps"; it formed no restricting valley, but instead lay prostrate before the river. On the bank of the river Bell noticed two Indians, an old woman and a boy. From them he learned the name of the great river. It was the *Youcon*, meaning "white water" or "swift-flowing river."[78]

Bell remained a week on the Yukon River, exploring its junction with the Porcupine River and trying to make contact with the natives of the area. Except for the old Indian woman and the young boy, from whom he was able to glean little information, Bell was unsuccessful in making contact with the Indians. Most of them were away from their hunting grounds on a trading expedition down the great river.[79] On June 22, Bell left the Yukon and headed back up the Porcupine River. During his return voyage he was fortunate enough to meet with three western Kutchin Indians, who lived on the Yukon River.

According to their accounts the country is rich in Beaver, Martens, Bears, and Moose deer, and the River abounds with Salmon, the latter part of the Summer being the season they are most plentifull, when they dry enough for winter consumption. The Salmon ascends the River a great distance but disappear in the fall.[80]

The Indians assured Bell that there was little trading in the area and that the manufactured goods that they possessed had come from white men. These traders had been "seen by Natives further down the river with boats from the sea coast on trading excursions, they describe them as being very liberal with their goods. The Esquimaux from the Westward ascend the 'Youcon' and carry on trade with the distant Musquash Indians who annually visit Peel's River."[81] Most of the trade goods found in the various Indian encampments along the Porcupine River were of Russian manufacture.

John Bell and his party returned to the Peel River Post on June 9, having successfully reached the Yukon, the fourth longest river in North America. The Yukon was the river that, the Kutchin Indians had told Sir Alexander Mackenzie in 1789, flowed from the Rocky Mountains to the Pacific Ocean. It was the great western river that, Sir George Simpson had hoped since 1822, would provide a new field for commercial expansion as profitable as the Mackenzie River. Hudson's Bay men had now breached the Yukon valley in two places: Robert Campbell had found the Pelly River, the Yukon's upper branch; and John Bell had reached the main river itself. Yet Governor Simpson and his explorers were farther than ever from understanding the geography of the transmountain region. Their minds were still cluttered with apocryphal concepts that twisted their interpretation of the course of the Yukon.

The most significant factor influencing Sir George Simpson, John Bell, and Robert Campbell, was the Colville River. That river, since Peter Warren Dease and Thomas Simpson had discovered its mouth in 1837, had been the basis of the supposed geography of the Far Northwest. All subsequent information was related to it, often at the expense of logic. John Bell believed that the Yukon River was the same as the Colville River of Dease and Simpson.[82] The Yukon flows north-

westward where Bell fell upon it, and Bell assumed that the
river kept this direction until it flowed into the Arctic Sea.
Bell had also been in communication with Robert Campbell,
and the two explorers agreed that the Pelly and Yukon rivers
were one and the same and that they both were the Colville.[83]
The Pelly River and the Yukon River are, of course, the
same river. Although it would be some years before Bell and
Campbell would prove their point, they were at least right in
their assumption. Where they were mistaken was in thinking
that those two rivers were identical with the Colville River.
Two clues garnered during his 1845 journey should have prevented Bell from making such a mistake. The Indians had
told him that white men traveled up the lower reaches of the
Yukon on trading excursions. The mouth of the Colville
River was well east of Point Barrow in the midst of seas that
were dangerous even for exploring expeditions. From Thomas
Simpson's own published account of the Colville River, it
should have been clear that no commerce was possible from
that direction. Thus, if the Indian report was to be relied
upon, and Bell had seen supporting evidence in the form of
Russian trade goods, the Yukon could not empty into the Arctic Ocean like the Colville, but instead must have its mouth at
a more accessible location on the Bering Sea or North Pacific.
The second clue that Bell ignored was the presence of salmon
on the Yukon River. Murdock McPherson realized the importance of this in a letter to Governor Simpson: "Whether it
[the Yukon] falls into the sea east of Point Barrow or into one
of the deep inlets to the west I will not say. We have not heard
of Salmon on this side of Point Barrow."[84] In the western fur
trade a river with salmon invariably meant a river flowing
into the Pacific Ocean.

Bell and Campbell were at least correct on one account,
the like identity of the Pelly River and the Yukon River. Sir
George Simpson, who was supposed to be directing their operations, was even more confused. He "scarcely" thought it possible that the Pelly River and the Yukon River were one. The
mouth of the Pelly, the governor was certain, was somewhere
on the Pacific coast. He had suggested many possible locations
for the Pelly's estuary, but reserved his fondest hopes for

"Comptroller's Inlet" near the mouth of the modern Copper River.[85]

What made the Hudson's Bay Company's task in sorting out the Yukon drainage all the more difficult was the remarkable character of the waterway. The ultimate sources of the Yukon River are the innumerable streams and freshets that spill down from the Coastal Mountains. Some of these rivulets reach to within fifteen miles of the Pacific Ocean, but because of the mountains they spill eastward toward the Yukon lakes. As the Lewes River and, farther downstream, as the Yukon River proper this water is carried northwestward, away from the Pacific Ocean. Then, after it passes the mouth of the Porcupine River, the very spot where John Bell reached the Yukon, the great river radically changes its direction and flows southwestward toward Norton Sound and the same Pacific Ocean that witnessed its birth.[86] With such a contradictory arching course it is no wonder that the fur traders were confounded when they attempted to reconcile the Yukon's geographic realities.

The Russians on the Yukon River

The Hudson's Bay Company was not alone in its efforts to exploit the fur trade of the Yukon River valley. Since the Anglo-Russian Convention of 1825 the Russian American Company had been directing its operations increasingly toward the unexplored interior of mainland Alaska. The Contract of 1839, by which Russia removed itself from active involvement in the fur trade of the Northwest Coast, reflected that change of emphasis. In 1832 Baron von Wrangel, as governor of the Russian American Company, dispatched Fedor Kolmakov to establish a trading post on the Kuskokwim River. The company's interest in the Bering Sea region was also demonstrated by the naval expedition of A. K. Etolin and Mikhal Tebenkov, who explored Norton Sound and verified the mouth of the Yukon River. A year later, in 1833, Tebenkov returned to the area and erected Fort Saint Michael on Norton Sound.[87]

The Russians' trade prospered at Fort Saint Michael and

soon began to expand into the interior. In 1835, Andrey Glazunov, a Creole native of Russian America, who had previously explored the Yukon delta, traveled overland from Saint
Michael to the Yukon River. Glazunov explored the lower
river and found an excellent location for a trading post at the
present-day village of Russian Mission. A year later, in 1836,
Glazunov established the Ikogmyut post, the first Russian post
on the Yukon River.[88] Also in 1836, Vasily Malakhov, another
adventurous Alaskan Creole, journeyed even farther up the
Yukon; he and his companions made their way almost 450
miles upriver to the Koyukuk River. It was then March, 1836,
and the snow and ice had become soft, making travel dangerous and laborious. Malakhov halted to await the spring break-
up. When the Yukon was clear of ice, Malakhov purchased
umiaks, native skin boats, for his party and drifted back down
the river to Norton Sound. In his report to his superiors Malakhov noted a good location for a trading post at Nulato, a
short distance from his farthest point of progress.[89]

The most important Russian explorer on the Yukon River
was Lavrentiy Alekseyevich Zagoskin, a lieutenant in the Imperial Russian Navy. In December, 1838, Zagoskin, looking
for more active service than he had found in the Baltic Fleet,
transferred to the Russian American Company. For two years
he captained company supply ships. Then, in 1840, he sent a
proposal to Baron von Wrangel for the exploration of the
Alaskan interior. In 1842 the Russian American Company finally moved on the suggestion, and Zagoskin's expedition was
approved. It is interesting to note that the company specifically requested that Zagoskin investigate the trade routes by
which furs made their way west from the interior of Alaska
to the coast and through aboriginal traders to Siberia. They
were interested in Indian trade rivals and gave no thought to
the possible activities of the British traders on the east.[90]

After four months of preparation Zagoskin and four companions left Fort Saint Michael on December 4, 1842. With
five sleds of supplies and twenty-seven dogs they made their
way up the Yukon River to Nulato. There they found an officer of the Russian American Company, named Deryabin, with
five men constructing a trading post. Zagoskin and his men

The Yukon in Spring: break-up of the ice. Illustration by Frederick Whymper in his Travel and Adventure in the Territory of Alaska *(1868).*

Auroral light seen from Nulato on the Yukon River, December 27, 1866. Illustration by Frederick Whymper in his Travel and Adventure in the Territory of Alaska *(1868).*

helped with the work, and the fort, or redoubt, as the Russians referred to their post, was completed before spring. The
winter was hard at Nulato, and the fish traps set under the ice
yielded insufficient food for all the men at the post. It was not
until mid-April, when the geese began to make their way
north, that the Russians were again able to enjoy three meals
a day.[91]

On June 4, 1843, Zagoskin noted in his journal, "We prayed
to God and took leave of our Nulato comrades."[92] With a
large skin boat and six companions the young naval lieutenant set off to explore the Yukon River to its source. Zagoskin
had read Sir Alexander Mackenzie's *Voyages from Montreal
. . . to the Frozen and Pacific Ocean,* and the Scotsman's narrative had greatly influenced his exploration plans:

We ourselves did not know where we were going, but we entertained hopes of reaching the ridge that divides the British possessions from ours. I proposed that we undertake to prove Mackenzie's supposition about the true direction of the "Great River"
that flows westward from the Rocky Chain. I have no doubt that
what he was told concerned the Yukon.[93]

Taking advantage of the midnight sun, the Russians pushed
off at ten in the evening.

Where Zagoskin began his journey, the Yukon River was
almost a mile and a half wide and frequently filled with
wooded islands. The local Indians called the river the *yuk-
khan,* meaning "big river."[94] The explorers, as they struggled
upstream against the strong current, would have agreed with
the Kutchins' name, *youcon,* or "swift water." The skin boat
that they were forced to use was awkward. They were inexpe-
rienced at handling such a craft, and with the relentless push
of the river there was little opportunity to learn how. Much
of the time they pulled the boat upstream from the shore,
mostly by a line, but sometimes by its very gunnels. Furthermore, the boat had been inadequately greased, so that after
any length of time in the water the skin began to leak, and it
had to be dried in the sun. Zagoskin bitterly regretted his inability to get a canoe for the trip.[95]

Their difficulties with the boat were, of course, incidental

The frozen Yukon River. Illustration by Frederick Whymper in his Travel and Adventure in the Territory of Alaska *(1868).*

to the ordinary hazards of wilderness travel, obstacles to navigation, procuring food supplies, and enduring the nuisances of the trail, such as mosquitoes. Of the last Zagoskin wrote, "To say nothing about the midges and mosquitoes would be to remain silent about the most acute suffering we had to bear on this trip, a suffering to which one becomes accustomed, as to an inevitable evil from which there is no escape."[96]

The expedition's progress was often slowed by the necessity to stop and hunt for food. The rations of hard biscuit, which made up the bulk of their stores, did little more than take the edge off the appetites of men who battled the Yukon for fourteen hours a day. The most frustrating delays, however, were when the changing shoreline forced them to cross the river to gain an adequate tracking beach. Even with the boatmen straining at their oars to cross the wide river, the explorers were inevitably pushed downstream, losing hard-won ground.[97]

Zagoskin had proceeded about 150 miles up the Yukon when on June 30 his progress came to a halt near the present-day town of Ruby, Alaska. There the Yukon flows through a series of rapid, rocky shallows that are normally no great hazard to navigation. In the spring of 1842, however, frequent rains had redoubled the strength of the current, and that, combined with the inadequacies of the *umiak*, halted the Russians. Zagoskin tried different tactics to overcome the riffles, but each one failed, whether it involved pole, paddle, or line.[98]

Near his point of farthest progress Zagoskin was able to inquire among the Indians about the source of the Yukon. The natives told him that he was about three hundred miles from the headwaters, which were at a place where the river forms a large lake "so broad that one bank cannot be seen from the other."[99] The location described by the Indians resembles the section of the river known as Yukon Flats. John Bell would reach it two years later. The actual sources of the Yukon were more than a thousand miles farther south.

Lieutenant Zagoskin and his party returned to Nulato on July 7 after a journey of more than a month. During the next year the naval officer continued his exploratory survey, but traveled to the southwest along the Kuskokwim River. He never again approached the upper Yukon. His expedition represented the peak of the Russian American Company's expansionist energies. Roving promyshlenniks made their way upriver, hunting and trading furs, but for Russia the upper Yukon remained officially unexplored. In his report Zagoskin remarked: "The Yukon is our only fairly easy route to the heart of the interior. . . . Judging from the vegetation and wealth of fur-bearing animals in the part we surveyed, one can hope that further explorations will be rewarding."[100] Zagoskin was correct, but it was the British who would undertake and benefit from further explorations.

Zagoskin's journal reveals that the Russian American Company had little interest in the upper Yukon River and that they did not expect the British to impinge upon their territory from that direction. The British meanwhile were naturally wary of being caught where they had no right to be and therefore apprehensive of Russian activities west of the Rocky Mountains. John Bell's 1845 exploratory probe to the Yukon River brought him across the 141st meridian, which according to the Anglo-Russian Convention of 1825 formed the boundary between British and Russian America. Murdock McPherson informed Governor Simpson that "The 'Youcon' where Bell saw it was unquestionably on Russian Territory." Sir George Simpson, however, held the view that violations of boundaries and other niceties of international law exist only when the victimized party is aware of the interloper's activities. In a June, 1844, letter to Robert Campbell, he wrote:

You seem to have been anxious to have proceeded down to the sea, that, however, I think at present unnecessary, & would be impolitic, as it would bring us into competition with our Russian neighbours, with whom we are desirous of maintaining a good understanding.[101]

The Hudson's Bay Company had no qualms about exploiting Russian territory, but it did so discreetly, restraining its operations to keep the Russians unaware.

The company's strategy in exploiting the upper Yukon was in many ways similar to its earlier policy in the western United States. In the Oregon country the British shared joint occupancy with the United States, but the Hudson's Bay Company, with its depot at Fort Vancouver, dominated the region. In order to maintain this status quo, and insulate the company's Columbia District, Governor Simpson dispatched bands of roving trappers to the regions south and east of the Columbia to clear the country of fur-bearing animals. These forays served two valuable functions. They created a barren no-man's-land that discouraged American mountain men from working their way into the district, while at the same time the company quickly withdrew large quantities of furs from a territory over which it had no superior rights and that it had no guarantee of maintaining within its grasp.[102] In the Yukon the Hudson's Bay Company had no legal rights whatsoever except that the Contract of 1839 indicated the Russians' willingness to compromise. John Lee Lewes reflected the English attitude toward the Yukon frontier in an 1840 letter: "Our Lease with the Russians sevens' Years' more will be expired and who can tell if they will be willing again to renew it with us. We should therefore in the meantime with spirit and activity work up the Country bordering on their terretory, plenty of Beaver is in that part of the Country."[103] The company meant to exploit the Yukon River valley, to reap what furs it could from the area, until such a time as the Russians were able or disposed to police their own territory.

In the decade of the 1840s, particularly during the later years, the Mackenzie District's expansion into the Yukon became increasingly important to the Hudson's Bay Company. In spite of the success of the company's frontier policy American agricultural settlement of the Oregon country was eroding British control of the Columbia valley. In 1845 the company shifted its district headquarters from Fort Vancouver, north of the 49th parallel, to Fort Victoria on Vancouver Island. A year later a formal treaty between the United States and Great Britain gave to the Americans control of what had formerly been the Honorable Company's most profitable district. In other areas of Rupert's Land and Canada the fur trade was weakening, as missionaries and, in some areas, even farmers began to expand their operations. Old fur traders like Chief Factor Lewes could only shake their heads: "To the south our trade is on the wane, retrograding before Priests and I *wot* not *wot*, bidding fair at no very distant period to a total exterpation, the North is now our only strong hold, and in it McKenzie's River, is not the place of the least importune."[104] The Yukon valley was the last frontier left on the North American continent except for the Arctic Archipelago. At a time when the Hudson's Bay Company's strongholds were under siege, the Yukon held the promise of expansion.

CHAPTER 9

On the Yukon River
Forts Selkirk and Yukon

IT WAS with feelings little short of disgust that Robert Campbell studied his outfit of trade goods for the winter of 1845–46. Even the two articles most important in opening a new area, tobacco and gunpowder, were lacking. He had hoped for more substantial supplies, but with Murdock McPherson again at the helm of the district he was not surprised at the meager amount he had received. Frustrated and angry, Campbell dashed off a quick letter to Governor Simpson:

> I cannot conceive what can be the object of extending trade to these parts, when, though we have opposition to contend with, we are without the staple artifacts in chief demand for trade. Than such proceedings nothing can be more absurd, and impolitic, and which can only end in involving us in trouble with these Savages.[1]

Campbell was prepared to use his influence with Simpson to get the trade goods he needed. He did not care what effect going behind Murdock McPherson's back might have on his relations with the district commander. The battle lines between them had already been drawn.

During that winter the Frances Lake Post enjoyed as good a trade as its supply of goods allowed. Young William Hardisty commanded the post, while Campbell spent much of the winter at Pelly Banks. Campbell had carefully extended his operations toward the Pelly River, which he thought would be best exploited from a trading post at the junction of that

Hudson's Bay Company sledge. Illustration by Frederick Whymper in his Travel and Adventure in the Territory of Alaska.

river with the Lewes. During each summer since 1844 he had sent Kitza, Lapie, and his other Indian retainers to hunt along the Pelly. Campbell wrote in his autobiographical journal, "This paved the way for opening trade relations" with the Indians of the Pelly, "who were only too glad to get serviceable articles of which they were utterly destitute."[2] In the summer of 1846 he sent some men from Frances Lake across the divide to Pelly Banks to build a permanent post there.

The Pelly Banks post was a well-built fort with a stockade, store, and dwelling house, but it was a difficult post to maintain. After the year's outfit had been brought by boat along the Liard and Frances rivers to the Frances Lake Post, it had to be cached until winter, when it was hauled on dog sleds to Pelly Banks.[3] Robert Campbell introduced the Yukon to the dog sled, which became a popular symbol of the area in the tales and ballads of Jack London and Robert Service.

Campbell spent the winters of 1845–46 and 1846–47 in poor spirits at Pelly Banks. Since 1837, for almost ten years, he had been involved in the arduous service of pioneering new country for the company. His rewards had been meager. In 1838 he had been made a clerk in the company, and on several occasions he had received Governor Simpson's personal approbation. His efforts at Dease Lake had resulted in no appreciable gain for the fur trade, while at Frances Lake the limited success that he enjoyed had been earned through years of hardship and hunger. Campbell regarded Murdock McPherson's tight-fisted management as personal harassment. During the solitude of the long winter it is little wonder that Campbell, assaulted by such thoughts, slipped into melancholy. In March, 1846, he wrote Simpson that he wished to "have once an opportunity of exercising my address elsewhere, here every-

thing about my name is become stale and constant difficulty
have all but overcome my ardour."[4] A few weeks later Campbell tendered his resignation from the company, effective in
the spring of 1847.[5]

Sir George Simpson, however, had no intention of letting his
best frontier officer withdraw from the field. Annoyed by the
bickering between Campbell and McPherson, he had already
acted to give Campbell the freedom of action and supplies he
needed. In June, 1845, Simpson advised McPherson:

Mr. Campbell's extraordinary exertions in the cause of Discovery
in that quarter are beyond all praise, and as no one can so well
understand the difficulties he has to contend with, I have to beg
that, all his views and wishes in reference to the mode and means
necessary for carrying our intentions into effect be met, as far as
the resources at your disposal may admit.[6]

This order, which seemed to give Campbell carte blanche at
the district depot, had one snag in it. The final phrase said
that Campbell could have all that he wanted "as far as the resources at your disposal may admit." McPherson still remained the judge of what could or could not be spared.

Simpson meanwhile assumed that he had taken away Campbell's cause for complaint in the summer of 1845. He was
therefore quite irritated when he received Campbell's letters
of despair in 1846 and his proposal of retirement.[7] Campbell
was not at fault; he seems not to have received Simpson's orders. This was quite unusual, because Campbell was usually
kept posted concerning the company's wishes both by personal
letters from the governor and by official dispatches from the
district commander. McPherson had kept mum about Campbell's expanded authority, and the explorer did not receive a
personal notice from Simpson. Campbell was aware that all
correspondence, private and otherwise, had to be channeled
through Fort Simpson. He suspected that McPherson was
tampering with his mail, but was wise enough not to act upon
mere suspicion.[8]

Instead, in the summer of 1847, Campbell made the 630-
mile journey to Fort Simpson to supervise personally the allotment of his outfit. It was a risky trip on the ever-dangerous

Liard, especially in the small canoe that he and Lapie were forced to use. Still Campbell had better luck with the rapids and whirlpools of the Liard than he did with Murdock Mc-Pherson. The Mackenzie District commander refused to honor any of Campbell's requisitions. All of the posts received small outfits of trade goods from McPherson, but Campbell thought that his was the smallest, a circumstance that he found particularly unnerving because he claimed that he saw trade goods "lying idle in the Depot."[9]

Robert Campbell's need for a larger outfit was particularly pressing in the summer of 1847 because he planned to expand the company's business to the banks of the Yukon River itself. He had obtained Simpson's permission to build a new trading post at the fork of the Lewes and Pelly in the summer of 1848. Campbell thus needed supplies for three posts, Pelly Banks, Frances Lake, and the proposed post on the Yukon. When Mc-Pherson refused all his requests, Campbell wrote to the governor:

I have done all, but gone upon my knees to Mr. McPherson, begging a small addition to the very small outfit he has given me. But my entreaties backed as they are by your instructions avail nothing. . . . The carte blanche you kindly granted me for carrying the Company's business through, though it procures me nothing here, would any else where be the ne plus ultrea. But in plain private truth I belive, that, jealous of your kindness, and favors to me, has turned some of my best friends to be my subtle enemies—should this be the case, I regret and forgive it most sincerly.[10]

That, however, was a somewhat futile gesture, since the governor would not receive the letter for months. There was nothing for Campbell to do but restrain his anger, return to Pelly Banks, and make do with what he had.

Accompanying Campbell, as he journeyed up the Liard, was James Green Stewart, a young clerk assigned to aid in the move to the fork of the Pelly and Lewes rivers. Stewart's service was especially needed, because William Hardisty, Campbell's assistant at Frances Lake, was ill and had to be sent back to Fort Simpson. If Hardisty recovered in time, McPherson promised to return him to Campbell in the spring. Campbell himself was in poor health. He was suffering from breathing problems and severe coughing. Far from medical attention, his only recourse short of retiring from the district was to write to the company's surgeon at York Factory and describe his symptoms. The surgeon informed Campbell early in 1849 that his illness was probably not as serious as he feared. Rather than consumption or some other potentially fatal disease, Campbell probably suffered from a mild asthma.[11]

Physically failing and mentally worn from his dispute with McPherson and the worry of preparing to expand to the Yukon, Campbell retired to his winter quarters at Pelly Banks. Winter for Campbell was usually a struggle for survival, a time of grim austerity. Happily, this second winter that Campbell spent at Pelly Banks was a marked contrast to those that he had known at Dease and Frances lakes. The hunting was better along the Pelly River than at Frances Lake, and so was the fishing. Campbell had discovered that Finlayson Lake was an especially good fishing ground with large numbers of plump whitefish. Because Pelly Banks was located on the river, Campbell was able to continue his morning baths:

This practice I kept up until the ice got too thick. As the season advanced our cook would knock at my door to tell me the hole was made in the ice ready for me. I would then run down with a blanket round me, dip into the hole, out again, & back to the house, my hair frozen stiff before I got there. . . . After a good rub down I would dress, & no one who has not tried it can have any idea of the exhilarating glow produced on the whole system by this hydropathic treatment.[12]

It is no wonder that Campbell complained of coughing.

Campbell kept his men busy during the winter. He had brought with him in the autumn a boat builder from Fort Simpson. He was put to work with the *engagés* on the craft that Campbell would need for the spring journey. By the beginning of May they had completed a York boat, a skiff, and some canoes.[13]

In March reinforcements arrived with the mail packet from Fort Simpson. Among them was Pierre Chyrsologue Pamburn, Jr., the half-blood son of Chief Trader P. C. Pamburn of the Hudson's Bay Company. Pamburn had been assigned by Mc-

Pherson to assume command at Frances Lake and Pelly Banks. Campbell had hoped that Hardisty would be well enough to manage those posts, but he had yet to recover from his infirmity. Campbell was critical of the selection of Pamburn. He had seen the latter's management of Fort Halkett and described him as "well-known to possess neither the judgement nor the foresight nor the energy requisite at a remote & isolated charge like that, where everything so much depended upon his own efforts."[14] McPherson, on the other hand, regarded Pamburn as one of the best clerks in the district.[15] Campbell sought to offset Pamburn's managerial deficiencies by giving him detailed instructions on how to provision the Frances Lake and Pelly Banks posts.

As soon as the ice left the Pelly River, Campbell embarked for the Lewes River. His little flotilla included James Stewart, eight *engagés*, and a contingent of Indian hunters, including Kitza and Lapie—all aboard a crazy collection of crafts: a York boat, a skiff, and canoes, dragging in tow a raft of cut planks for the construction of the new trading post. The journey was uneventful until they were within fifty miles of the forks of the Pelly. They then began to encounter large groups of Indians, who gathered to greet the fur traders.[16]

When Campbell was near the spot where a hostile Indian party had threatened him in 1843, he noticed another band of Indians. The Hudson's Bay men stopped and began to distribute tribute tobacco among the Indians, a customary gratuity and a symbol of peace. One of the Indians stepped forward with a large bundle of furs and presented them to Campbell. The hunter explained that five years before he was among the Indians who had planned to ambush Campbell's camp. Since that time, because of the explorer's great "medicine," he had been rendered lame in one leg. Now the Indian "was sorry for what he had done in ignorance of our intentions & that he wished me to restore the use of his leg. I declined to take the furs without payment, & postponed the 'cure' for the present."[17] Campbell continued his journey and without further incident reached the forks of the Pelly, the beginning of the Yukon River proper, on June 1, 1848.

Waiting there for the traders were the northern Tutchones,

or, as Campbell called them, the Gens de Bois. Work was immediately begun on the new post, which was to be named Fort Selkirk. The site selected was on a narrow tongue of land with the Pelly River on one side and the Lewes River on the other. Campbell remarked that the site reminded him of Prairie du Chien in Wisconsin. The Tutchones, who knew only skin tents and brush lean-tos, were impressed by how swiftly the Hudson's Bay men, armed with iron nails and stout mallets, erected the permanent log structures. Campbell made a further impression when the lame Pelly River Indian again asked to have his leg cured. This time the Indian was accompanied by his hopeful-eyed wife, children, mother, and father. Campbell, with nothing to lose but a little time, and with the redoubled respect of the surrounding Indians to gain, took out his little medicine chest and attempted the cure. Whatever he did proved successful. The Indian was returned to his former agility, and Campbell was reknowned as a great healer.[18]

During the summer of 1848, as work proceeded on the fort, Campbell began to solidify his position with the Tutchones. The traders were impressed by the friendliness and strict honesty of the Indians. Bundles of trade goods and tools were left unguarded about the post, and nothing was found missing. In fact, when an article was lost, the Tutchones would travel, often for miles, to return it. The only thing that prevented Campbell from cementing his position with the Indians was the "paltry" outfit of trade goods that he had with him. He was forced to trade very tightly, taking only certain furs and then only those of the best quality. The gifts that the company customarily used to establish good relations also had to be curtailed.[19] Still, when he considered the means that he had at his disposal, Campbell must have been pleased with his summer's work: Fort Selkirk was established.

Early one August evening, when the day's work was winding down at Fort Selkirk, the fur traders heard the sound of singing and chanting drifting down from the Lewes River. The English were a bit bewildered, but the Tutchones knew immediately what was afoot. They warned Campbell that a Chilkat trading brigade was approaching the fort. They advised him to hide all the company's tools, trade goods, and anything else that was not nailed down, because the Chilkats were notorious thieves.[20]

The Chilkats were a Tlingit people. As the robber barons of the aboriginal trade network, they were not at all pleased to find Campbell and his men so comfortably situated at the site of their traditional rendezvous with the northern Tutchones and other tribes. As Campbell noted, however, the Chilkats' motto was "Might Is Right," and, with the fur traders at full strength and supported by the interior tribes, the Chilkats knew that the time was not ripe to show their anger. They merely went on with their trade. Campbell's pathetic outfit had been all but used up, and the Tutchones had plenty of furs left to barter. Campbell was also willing under the circumstances to agree to free trade, and he took the opportunity to study his opponents.

Ironically, the Chilkats had acquired their trade goods from the Hudson's Bay Company steamer, *Beaver*. That ship, the first steamer on the Pacific, operated out of the Columbia Department and traded furs along the entire Northwest Coast. The goods that the Chilkats brought inland were not to be compared with the quality of Campbell's outfit. Many articles were broken; others had been badly worn from use by the Chilkats. Yet even secondhand articles were valuable to the interior tribes, who normally had no other source of supply. After a few days of trading the Chilkats, rich with profits, pressed their furs into heavy leather packs weighing between one hundred and two hundred pounds and set off on the long march back to the coast.[21]

Campbell may have underestimated the Chilkats because they behaved relatively peacefully during his first encounter with them. They had contented themselves with merely stealing a few items from the fort. He did not apprehend much danger from them in the future and, in fact, took advantage of their visit to Fort Selkirk to open up a correspondence with Captain Charles Dodd of the *Beaver*. The Chilkats expressed "awe" at the "mysterious form of speaking" embodied in a letter and for a small fee faithfully carried it to the intended party.[22] Campbell even entertained hopes that the Chilkats would show him their trail through the Coastal Mountains to the sea—a route that he hoped might someday be used to supply the Yukon River fur trade.[23] In his official correspondence Campbell emphasized only the hopeful prospects of his new post. Perhaps he simply did not realize the strength of the Chilkats' trade network or their determination to maintain their ascendancy. The visit of the Chilkat traders foreshadowed the strife and frustration that lay ahead for him.

With the founding of Fort Selkirk the Hudson's Bay Company was firmly established in the heart of the Yukon River valley. The trade of the fourth largest river in North America was within the company's grasp. Unfortunately, Campbell was not given the support and freedom of action necessary to exploit the area to full advantage. Fort Selkirk and its two support posts at Frances Lake and Pelly Banks should have been given the status of a district separate from the Mackenzie, and Campbell's needs should have been supplied directly from the main depot at York Factory. Instead all of Campbell's supplies had first to be approved by Murdock McPherson, whose opposition to Campbell was only thinly veiled. This administrative flaw retarded the development of the Yukon trade.

The Founding of Fort Yukon

Robert Campbell's success on the upper Yukon River was mirrored by the progress of the northern division of the Hudson's Bay Company's westward pincer movement. On June 27, 1847, Fort Yukon was founded at the forks of the Porcupine and Yukon rivers. Alexander Hunter Murray, a senior clerk in the Honorable Company, commanded the operation.

Born in 1818 at Kilmun, Argyllshire, Scotland, Murray had chosen the fur trade as his passport to wealth in America. Unlike most of the Hudson's Bay Company officers, he took his internship in the business in the United States, not in Canada or Rupert's Land. He served with the American Fur Company for some years on the Missouri River before joining the English company in 1845.[24] He was an educated man and a skilled observer and during his short tenure in the Mackenzie District made some sketches depicting the habits and dress of the Kutchin Indians. Sir John Richardson thought so much

Alexander Hunter Murray. Courtesy of the Hudson's Bay Company.

of the drawings that he included them in his two-volume work, *Arctic Searching Expeditions: A Journal of a Boat-Voyage through Rupert's Land and the Arctic Sea.* Murray also gave Richardson many details concerning the natural history of the Yukon area.[25] Murray's one drawback was his undiplomatic attitude toward his subordinates. It is not clear whether he had an authoritarian nature or merely a hot temper, but Dr. John Rae of the Honorable Company observed, "Mr. Murray is evidently an excellent manager and a very interested person, but unfortunately his men will not stay any length of time with him. This is a sad drawback at so distant a post, it being requisite to keep two or three additional men in the District for the purpose of changing."[26] That same resolute character made Murray valuable in opening up new territory.

Governor Simpson personally selected Murray for the Yukon assignment, probably because of his previous fur-trade experience in the United States. Murray left for Fort Simpson in the summer of 1845. For the first part of his journey he took passage with the company's famed Athabasca Brigade, a flotilla of York boats that annually traveled from Norway House near Lake Winnipeg to Portage la Loche. Among Murray's fellow travelers were Chief Trader Colin Campbell, the commander of the Athabasca District, and his two daughters, both of whom were of marriageable age.[27] While many passengers found the trip to Portage la Loche rather dull because the low relief of the Canadian Shield presents scenery of monotonous similarity, Murray enjoyed himself and found the northern vistas engrossing. The natural beauty that particularly held his attention was that of seventeen-year-old Anne Campbell. When Murray noticed her attempting a landscape sketch, he offered the benefit of his own drawing experience. Murray and Miss Campbell spent the rest of the journey in each other's company, sketching and talking about the scenery and each other. Murray's thinly disguised romance did not escape the attention of Bernard Rogan Ross, the editor of a short-lived fur-trade gossip sheet entitled *Athabasca Journal and English River Inquirer.* The *Inquirer* sarcastically noted:

Signoir Murray takes this opportunity of returning his sincere thanks to the Nobility, Gentries and Public for the support he has received since he commenced to give lessons in Landscape drawing. He begs leave here to state that he still continues to teach that valuable branch of education and will attend any hour for the purpose of sketching from nature. Fees, as formerly, Gentlemen, 10/6 pr. lesson; Ladies, gratis.[28]

The *Inquirer* was wrong on one point: Alexander Hunter Murray would not be giving any more lessons in landscape sketching. Anne Campbell had decided to engage his services permanently; before they reached Fort Chipewyan, she and Murray became engaged.[29]

Murray and his fiancé were married when they reached Fort Simpson. There was neither a minister nor a justice of the peace at that far-removed locale. In such circumstances at sea the captain of a vessel may perform the marriage ceremony. In Rupert's Land a similar custom prevailed, but, in keeping with the company's commercial nature, a contract between the two parties was signed before Murdock McPherson, as commander at Fort Simpson, who then pronounced the couple man and wife.[30]

The newlyweds' honeymoon was spent descending the Mackenzie River. The purpose of the voyage was not romantic. Murray was being sent to the Peel River Post to follow up on John Bell's 1844 journey to the Yukon River by establishing a trading post on the Yukon. John Bell had already laid the groundwork for this extension of the trade by constructing an outpost at the end of the portage across the Richardson Mountains. This post, known as Lapierre House, served a dual purpose. It was located in fine caribou hunting country and could provide meat and leather for the Peel River Post. It also served as a halfway house for the goods shipped across the mountains from Peel River that were destined for the Yukon.[31]

The Murrays wintered at the Peel River Post. Early in the spring Murray took Anne to Lapierre House over the ice by dogsled. This spared her the rigors of the march across the mountains. One wonders why he did not use the same method to haul all the supplies meant for the Yukon. Later this became standard procedure. When Robert Kennicott visited Lapierre House in 1861, all transport was conducted during the winter.[32] Perhaps John Bell did not have enough dogs and sleds on hand to attempt such a large operation.

It was June, 1845, when Murray again set out for Lapierre House, this time with the trade outfit meant for the Yukon. Soon after he exchanged the "customary adieus" with John Bell and the population of the Peel River Post, Murray realized what a difficult route the portage trail was during the summer. The *engagés* familiar with the trail told him that the name of the first stage of his journey was the "slough of dispond." The knee-deep muck and the mosquitoes convinced Murray that the appellation was approppriate.

After three hours on the trail Murray left the majority of the party under the supervision of Alexander Mackenzie, a company clerk. Murray and two other men—a voyageur known as Manuel and Tarshee, an Indian hunter—continued ahead with lighter burdens than the portage crew. Murray recorded in his journal that he wanted to reach Lapierre House ahead of his men "so as to have my letters answered and things in order, so that the voyage might not be delayed on that account."[33] His bride of only a few months, waiting at the outpost, may have been a greater encouragement to rush ahead.

Manuel, Tarshee, and Murray continued on the trail until ten in the evening. Since they could find no high ground to sleep on, they each picked out one of the tufts of grass and moss that rose above the tundra and made it their bed. Morning found them sleeping in pools of swampy water, as their grass beds had gradually sunk during the night. They marched until noon, reaching the firmer rocky ground of the mountains. With the heat of day upon them Murray elected to call a halt, take a short nap, and proceed on the march during the night—taking advantage of the midnight sun. In this manner the party made good progress, and Murray expected to reach Lapierre House by the end of the next day. A short distance from the post, however, the portage trail crossed the Little Bell River. Normally the river was easily forded, but that spring the water was rather high, and the current was stronger.

Murray could not use a raft to cross the river because of the large blocks of ice still drifting downstream. Manuel volunteered to attempt a crossing. Armed with a wooden staff to aid his footing, he waded into the river. Two-thirds of the way across the current became too much for his legs, which were numbed by the cold. He was swept off his feet, but, swimming for his life, he made the far shore safely.[34]

One of the party was now across the Little Bell, but at the expense of his gun and toque and nearly his life. Murray profited from Manuel's effort by throwing a rope across the river, which Manuel used to pull Murray across safely. Tarshee, the Indian, watched the proceedings disapprovingly; to him it was obvious that the river was not meant to be forded there. He marched a short distance upstream, found a broader, shallower crossing, and reached the west bank with considerably less trouble.[35]

Delayed by this adventure, Murray did not reach Lapierre House and his waiting wife until the next day. Murray had been eager to rejoin his wife for more than romantic reasons. He had not received word from the outpost for some time, and the Rat Indians (or Crow River Kutchins), particularly their leader, Grand Blanc, had threatened to prevent the company from extending its trade to their rivals on the west.[36] Murray found the post safe, but the Indians had refused to deliver messages to the Peel River Post or help collect provisions for the journey to the Yukon.

Murray remained four days at Lapierre House, preparing his expedition. On June 18 the Hudson's Bay men shoved off "with three cheers for the Youcon." The majority of Murray's men and all of his supplies were jammed into the *Pioneer*, a large wooden boat that had been built at Lapierre House especially for the journey. Murray's entire crew were armed with rifles and ammunition, "in case of meeting with hostile Indians etc." It was for that reason that Anne Murray, pregnant with her first child, was left at the little outpost in the care of a Kutchin woman. She would not see her husband again for over a year.[37]

Murray was anxious not only about the potentially hostile eastern Kutchin middlemen but also the Russians. He knew that the Yukon River was in Russian territory and had even had a warning while at Lapierre House that the Indians of the Yukon had been visited by the Russians the summer before. As he drifted down the Porcupine River, he kept watch for a potential site for a post on the English side of the boundary, "should it so happen, that we are compelled to retreat upon our own territory."[38]

After a journey of a week Murray reached the Yukon River. As the boatmen rowed the *Pioneer* out of the slack waters of the Porcupine River, they were impressed by the strength of the Yukon's current. Using all of their strength, the voyageurs pulled the boat two miles up the river before coming to the entrance of a small lake that seemed to offer a fine campsite.

Murray was particularly unimpressed by his first glimpses of the Yukon. He wrote in his journal, "I never saw an uglier river, every where low banks, apparently lately overflowed, with lakes and swamps behind, the trees too small for building, the water abominably dirty and the current furious."[39] The myriad of mosquitoes that filled the air made the scenery even more unappealing. Although Murray was a veteran of the mosquito country of the Mississippi valley, he was unprepared for what he encountered on the Yukon: "We could neither speak nor breathe without our mouths being filled with them, close your eyes, and you had fast half a dozen, fires were lit all around but to no avail. Rather than be devoured, the men fatigued as they were, preferred stemming the current a little longer, to reach a dry spot a little further on."[40] Thus the fur traders fled to their boat, routed from their first camp on the Yukon.

On the next morning, June 26, Murray located a suitable site for a post about three miles up the Yukon River from the mouth of the Porcupine. The traders set to work at once, constructing temporary bark shelters and cutting timber for a permanent fort. Trade also began immediately. Murray suffered from the same problem that haunted Robert Campbell, a lack of trade goods. To stretch his supplies, he accepted only beaver, marten, and fox pelts—the most valuable furs.[41]

The local Indians, the Yukon Flats Kutchins, were not at all adverse to that policy. They had long been exploited by

A summer Indian encampment on the Yukon River. Illustration by Frederick Whymper in his Travel and Adventure in the Territory of Alaska *(1868).*

Indian middlemen and were thankful at last to have direct access to the trade goods. Since the opening of Fort Good Hope and, more importantly, the Peel River Post, the eastern Kutchins had done extensive trading with the Yukon Flats band. On the south the Han Indians were supplied by Tutchone and Tagish middlemen, and by occasional visits to the Peel River Post they also enjoyed commercial superiority over the Yukon Flats people. The Yukon Flats Kutchins were also exploited by the tribes lower down the Yukon River, who received their goods from the Russians at Nulato or across the Bering Sea from Siberia.

In addition to those trade contacts, the Yukon Flats Kutchins told Murray that they recently had made contact with other white men from lower down the river. These whites, whom Murray naturally assumed were Russians, were described to him as follows:

Being all well armed with pistols, their boat was about the same size as ours, but, as he thought, made of sheet iron, but carrying more people. They had a great quantity of beads, kettles, guns, powder, knives and pipes, and traded all the furs from the bands, principally for beads and knives, after which they traded dogs, but the Indians were unwilling to part with their dogs, and the Russians rather than go without gave a gun for each, as they required many to bring their goods across the portage to the river they descended. The Indians expected to see the Russians here soon, as they promised to come up with two boats, not only to trade but to explore the river to its source.[42]

Although Murray did not realize it, this Indian report should not have been taken at face value. Historical documentation affords no supporting evidence of Russian penetration of the Yukon as far east as the Porcupine River in the 1840s. Even Lieutenant Zagoskin did not come within three hundred miles of the junction of the Porcupine and the Yukon rivers. Perhaps because of some confusion in interpreting the Kutchin language, Murray heard a secondhand account either of Zagoskin's voyage on the lower Yukon or of Robert Campbell's 1843 journey down the Pelly River. Nonetheless, he believed the report to be correct and during his first year on the Yukon was always apprehensive that the Russians might make a sudden appearance.

Murray also did not trust the Han Indians. They inhabited the Yukon River above Murray's post and were not pleased to see the Yukon Flats Kutchins trading most of their furs to the Hudson's Bay Company. They were accustomed to having their way with the less numerous Yukon Flats band and acted as if they expected the same deference from the fur traders.[43] They inspected Murray's encampment, going where they pleased and asking first for one thing then another. Murray lost his rather short temper when two of the Hans started browsing through his tent. He "shoved one of them out by the shoulders, and the other followed of his own accord in double quick time."[44] The Indians responded with a thinly veiled threat. The Russians, they said, "were once the same, they would not give them what they wanted, but they (the Indians) killed a number of their people and pillaged one of their Forts on the coast, and ever since that they had been refused nothing."[45] Murray was unshaken. He reminded the Hans, "We were a different people from the Russians and not so

easily frightened, we were always prepared aginst enemies."
He also instructed them in a basic tenet of Hudson's Bay
Company's policy: "We did not mean to give away our goods
for nothing."[46]

On July 1 construction began on the permanent post, which
Murray had been ordered to name Fort Yukon. Since he was
fearful of Russian and Indian hostilities—a fear that may have
been accentuated by Murray's previous experiences among the
warlike Plains tribes on the Missouri River's turbulent frontier—he elected to build a true fortification. Many Hudson's
Bay Company posts, though called forts, bore little resemblance to military structures. Fort Yukon was an elaborate
affair. Formal bastions were placed at each corner and united
by a fourteen-foot wall of squared timber. Even the dwelling
houses were bulletproof and fitted with loopholes for com-
bat.[47]

The work went slowly at first. Murray's men, though hard-
working fellows, were hardly accomplished woodsmen. Many
had been recently engaged from the Orkney Islands off Scotland and were "green hands" with axes and mauls. For a
while they succeeded in doing as much damage to themselves
as to the trees. Each day a cut or temporarily lamed *engagé*
graduated from the school of hard knocks, a bruised but wiser
carpenter. When their work was finally completed, they had a
fort that Murray thought was the "best and strongest (not ex-
cepting Fort Simpson) between Red River and the polar sea."
Behind Fort Yukon's battlements the fur traders were confident "the Russians may advance when they please."[48]

Although Murray was relatively new to the Mackenzie District, he was well aware of the interest that had been aroused
by the identification of the Yukon River. While at Fort Simpson he had studied some of Robert Campbell's journals, and
he tried to piece together what Campbell had discovered with
what the Indians at Fort Yukon had told him and what the
company thought it knew about the Colville River. In a plot
of sand that Murray kept especially for the purpose, the Yukon Indians traced the Yukon's course westward, which they
themselves knew only from other tribes. Initially Murray was
unable to accept this information because he believed too

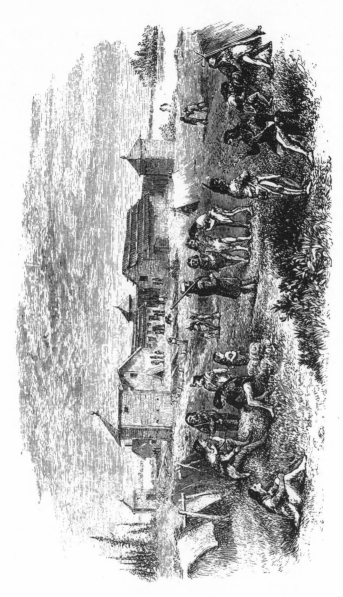

Fort Yukon. Illustration by Frederick Whymper in his Travel and Adventure in the Territory of Alaska *(1868).*

firmly that the Yukon was the Colville River; he wrote, "Had I not known where the Colville was, and gone by their account, I should have placed the mouth of the Youcon much farther west."[49] Only later, after continued conversations with the Indians, did Murray accept that the Yukon was separate from the Colville and that it flowed to the Pacific Ocean.

Murray was less confused by the geography of the upper Yukon. He hypothesized that the Yukon and Lewes rivers were one and the same, but he mistakenly failed to assign the Pelly River a large role in the river system.[50] With only a compass and a homemade astrolabe he attempted to correlate his information into a new map of the Northwest. The map has been lost to posterity, but was given to Sir John Richardson, who used it to make his own map of Arctic America. The Richardson map shows neither the Lewes nor the Pelly joined with the Yukon and correctly shows the Yukon flowing into Norton Sound, not on the course of the Colville. Whether the changes were Murray's or Richardson's is not clear.[51]

The Search for Franklin

Dr. John Richardson, who had served as Sir John Franklin's second-in-command during the latter's two Arctic Coast explorations, was again in the Mackenzie District in the summer of 1848. Richardson had been drawn back to the Far Northwest by one of the most futile and romantic ventures in arctic exploration, the search for the lost Franklin Expedition. Sir John Franklin had set out on his final exploration in May, 1845. His two ships, the *Erebus* and the *Terror*, had been ordered to attempt the elusive Northwest Passage. The expedition was last seen in July, 1845, sailing west toward Lancaster Sound. What befell the expedition after that is unclear. It is known that the ships were beset by ice in the fall of 1846 and that they remained imprisoned until the starving and scurvied crew abandoned them in 1848. The seamen then began a doomed march down the Arctic Coast toward the Back River, and the entire expedition perished.[52]

Though the first evidence of the expedition's fate was not discovered until 1853, concern for Franklin began late in

1846. When no dispatches had arrived by the fall of 1847, the British Admiralty sent out three expeditions to ascertain his fate. Dr. John Richardson was given command of a boat expedition that was to proceed through the interior of Rupert's Land to the Mackenzie River and then search the coast between the mouth of that river and the mouth of the Coppermine.

The Hudson's Bay Company played an important role in Richardson's expedition and the other Franklin searches that were to follow. The arctic manhunt, though unsuccessful in retrieving the *Erebus* and *Terror*, was a boon to geographic knowledge, as each search expedition expanded the map of arctic America. Yet the searches did nothing to aid the Hudson's Bay Company's program of westward expansion and exploration, because the extraction of men and supplies from the Mackenzie District retarded the efforts of the fur-trade explorers.

Richardson and his exploration crew arrived in the district in July, 1848. It was his plan to proceed immediately down the Mackenzie River to the sea. Richardson felt that he would be able to search his assigned territory in one field season, and in this he was correct. The coastal journey from the Mackenzie River's mouth to the Coppermine River was efficiently conducted. No sign of Franklin's expedition was encountered. Nor was any new coastline added to the map, because the area had been previously charted in 1826 by Richardson himself. The doctor's expedition was aided by John Rae, a physician and explorer of the Hudson's Bay Company, and John Bell, who handled most of the logistical work.[53]

Having completed his assignment in the summer of 1848, Richardson wintered at Great Bear Lake and left Rupert's Land in 1849. In that same summer the Mackenzie District traders were asked to aid another exploring expedition, Lieutenant J. S. Pullen's Royal Navy search team. Pullen was an officer on H.M.S. *Plover*, which was to search the Arctic's Coast from the Bering Sea to Wainwright Inlet. At the latter point the *Plover* launched a boat expedition, led by Pullen, to search the coast as far as the Mackenzie River. The Royal

Navy assumed that the boat crews could winter in the Mackenzie District and return to Britain through Rupert's Land
in the spring. Unfortunately the Hudson's Bay Company was
not notified, and the Mackenzie District was unprepared to
offer any assistance.[54]

Lieutenant Pullen and his crew found no clues concerning
Franklin's fate, but performed their difficult assignment admirably. Then, when the two whale boats of seamen arrived
at the Peel River Post, the fur traders were at a loss what to
do. The post commander, August R. Peers, was away from the
post, and his subordinates did their best to make the explorers
comfortable. It was obvious even to Pullen that the meager
food resources of the post, which so often faced famine even
under normal conditions, could not support the Royal Navy
men for very long. He relieved the situation somewhat by embarking in one of the boats for Fort Simpson, where he spent
the winter. Mate William H. Hooper and four other sailors
remained at the post for a short time longer. When Peers returned to the Peel River Post, he persuaded Hooper to remove the remaining explorers to old Fort Franklin on Great
Bear Lake.[55]

Relations between the Royal Navy men and the fur traders
appear not to have been warm. The naval explorers do not
seem to have appreciated the limited resources of the Mackenzie District, and they were not pleased that the fourteen sailors
had to be distributed among several different posts that were
over eight hundred miles apart. Chief Factor John Rae, who
commanded at Fort Simpson in the winter of 1849–1850,
wrote to Sir George Simpson, "Both Pullen and Hooper are
vastly civil to me, yet for some cause or other which I cannot
divine, and which they themselves would probably be at a loss
to explain, they have an evident dislike for the Company or
those connected with them."[56] Rae's response was angry. He
observed with some justice:

These selfsufficient donkeys come into this country see the Indians
sometimes miserably clad and half starved, the causes which they
never think of inquiring into, but place it all to the credit of the
Company quite forgetting that 10 times as much misery occurred

in Ireland during the last few years, at the very door of the most civilized countries in the world, than has happened in the Hudsons Bay Cos. Territories during the last ¼ century.[57]

But, in spite of what Rae suspected, neither Pullen nor Hooper were impolitic enough to publish any of their criticisms upon their return to England.

Their return was delayed. In June, 1850, the Royal Navy men were on their way to York Factory when they received new orders from the Admiralty. Pullen was directed to retrace Dr. John Richardson's route and search again the Arctic Coast east of the Mackenzie River. The Admiralty suspected that, if the Franklin Expedition had abandoned its ships, the men might try to follow the coast to the Mackenzie River and its trading posts. Pullen accepted the unexpected assignment and set out with two boats for the coast. This second boat journey of his cleared out the Mackenzie District's supply house. Rae gave the explorers close to 4,500 pounds of provisions and "a carte blanche on all our other resources."[58] This occurred at a time when Forts Yukon and Selkirk were short of the supplies needed to establish the company's presence in the Yukon, and when other posts in the district were also short of supplies. In fact, while Pullen and Hooper were criticizing the company, fur traders were starving to death at Pelly Banks.[59]

Pullen's second coastal search yielded no evidence of the lost expedition, and at the end of the summer he was back at Fort Simpson. Finally, after another uneasy winter with the fur traders, the Royal Navy men returned to England. The Hudson's Bay Company continued in the search for Franklin, but in a more independent fashion. Chief Factor John Rae, who had already led two previous arctic exploring expeditions, and who had assisted Richardson in 1848, commanded the company's 1851 and 1853–54 search teams. Rae represented a new breed of arctic traveler, not unlike Thomas Simpson or, for that matter, Robert Campbell. He traveled light and therefore swiftly, calling upon the resources of the country to supply his wants. The hardy determination, skill, and efficiency that he had acquired as a fur trader and physician in the company's service made him what Franklin, Back, and Pullen could not aspire to be; he was a professional arctic traveler. Rae's traditions later produced such men as Nansen, Cook, Peary, and Amundsen. The details of Rae's explorations, directed as they were toward the eastern Arctic, are beyond the scope of this book. Suffice it to say that Rae uncovered the first evidence of the fate of Franklin's expedition.

One other aspect of the Franklin search may have affected the Hudson's Bay Company's westward expansion. In the winter of 1850–51, Lieutenant John James Barnard, who was temporarily attached to H.M.S. *Plover* in the Bering Sea, visited the Russian American Company post of Fort Saint Michael. The Russian officers at the post were eager to aid, in any way that they could, the search for Franklin, and they had received from their Indian trappers reports of a party of white men in the interior of Alaska. On the faint chance that this might be a reference to the Franklin party, Barnard journeyed to the source of the reports, Nulato, which was the Russians' advance base on the Yukon River. The white men of whom the Indians had spoken were Alexander Hunter Murray's traders at Fort Yukon. Lieutenant Barnard was not aware of that; though he was in a position to unite the British-explored upper Yukon with the Russian-explored lower river, he never had a chance to journey farther upriver. Before spring arrived, the Nulato post was attacked by hostile Indians, and Barnard was killed.[60]

The net effect of the search for the lost Franklin Expedition on the Hudson's Bay Company's exploration of the Yukon was to sidetrack the Mackenzie District's limited resources from the newly established frontier posts. The first years after the establishment of a post were critical in determining its success or failure. The local Indians had to be assured of the reliability of the trader to supply their needs. The Indians also had to be convinced to spend more time in actual trapping than they were accustomed to do. This was impossible if the posts were short of trade goods and supplies. For the Yukon posts, particularly Fort Selkirk and Pelly Banks, the Franklin search was most inopportune and caused a good deal of hardship.

Fur Trade on the Yukon, 1849–50

In the spring of 1849, Chief Factor Murdock McPherson and Robert Campbell were on anything but cordial terms. The feud over McPherson's frugal outfitting of frontier posts had degenerated into a personal struggle between the two. Campbell was angered by McPherson's subtle jabs at his abilities as a trader. He wrote to Governor Simpson, "I am glad to learn that Mr. McPherson though he regrets my hard luck, has been making favorable mention of my perserverance, as I was given to understand, that of late, his favorable mention of me was in like style as Antony did of Brutus."⁶¹ As for McPherson, he was no doubt tired of having all of his decisions regarding Campbell reported by the latter to Governor Simpson. McPherson's hand was not strengthened by the diminishing returns in furs that the district was producing under his administration.⁶² It was in the best interests of both McPherson and the district that the chief factor retire from the area, where he had spent twenty-four years of his life. Dr. John Rae was given charge of the Mackenzie District.

It was some time before Campbell and his men heard of the change of command. They were dependent upon the Pelly Banks and Frances Lake posts to relay supplies and communications. Campbell had no faith in either Pierre Pamburn, Jr., or John O'Brien, the clerks responsible for those posts. His opinion was confirmed in September, 1848, when Campbell sent James Stewart to Frances Lake for the winter's trade outfit. Stewart found both Frances Lake and Pelly Banks in a state of confusion. The supply boats from Fort Simpson had been late, and the men had suffered from hunger. By the time things were straightened out, ice was beginning to form on the Pelly River, and Stewart was unable to forward his trade goods to Fort Selkirk.⁶³

The winter at Fort Selkirk, considering the dearth of supplies and the trader's lack of familiarity with the region, might have been disastrous. But Robert Campbell was by now a master of living off the country and making ends meet. The men on the Yukon enjoyed a season of relative abundance as the fishery and the hunters produced more than enough provisions. The same could not be said for Pamburn's men at Pelly Banks and Frances Lake. They made insufficient use of the fishing lakes discovered by Campbell and were not careful in rationing their supplies. Nor was Pamburn able to advance the Fort Selkirk outfit, which, like the Pelly Banks outfit, had to be carried across the divide from Frances Lake each winter by dog sled. Worse than not even attempting that task, Pamburn made a complete mess of it. He hauled a small quantity of goods across to the Pelly River, but the majority were spread out over the trail or left at Frances Lake. When Campbell's men arrived in April to pick up their supplies, they were able to salvage only a small part of what had been allotted them.[64]

These inefficiencies set the stage for the tragedy that later occurred in the winter of 1849–50. Late in the summer of 1849, Campbell sent his assistant James Stewart and a group of *engagés* to Pelly Banks to try to retrieve some of the supplies that had been mishandled the winter before. When the salvage operation was completed, the men returned to Fort Selkirk except for Stewart and another man, Andrew Flett. Stewart and Flett had decided to wait for the annual supply boats from Fort Simpson in order to collect any letters or dispatches meant for their post. Unfortunately, John O'Brien, who had left Frances Lake to bring up the supply boats, failed to make his appearance. Stewart and Flett waited well into the winter season before they concluded that the supply boats would not arrive. The two men then began the long march back to Fort Selkirk. They stopped at Pelly Banks Post on their way west. P. C. Pamburn and his two assistants were short of provisions, but they had plenty of gunpowder and fishing equipment. They rejected Stewart's advice that they should all retire to Fort Selkirk.[65]

Stewart and Flett, with no provisions for their journey, hoped that their guns would keep them in food until they reached Campbell. Hunting while on the march is a difficult task, and the two traders spent many nights hungry. When they were at the end of their strength, they noticed a cache along the frozen Pelly River. Breaking it open, they found a small supply of fish. The cache was one of several that Campbell had ordered made when Stewart had failed to return before winter. Only this expedient permitted Flett and Stewart to reach Fort Selkirk alive; they looked like "mere skeletons" to their comrades.[66]

Campbell was forced to spend a second consecutive winter at Fort Selkirk short of provisions and trade goods, but, though he and his men missed their tobacco, tea, and flour allowances, they did not suffer the pangs of famine. The traders at Pelly Banks did not fare as well. Their situation had been critical when Stewart visited them. It degenerated further in late November, when through some act of carelessness the post caught fire and burned. Eight hundred pounds of furs were destroyed, along with most of the supply of gunpowder.[67] Pamburn gave his two *engagés* (a French Canadian named Dubois and an Orkneyman named Forbisher) the remaining furs as provisions and then removed himself to one of the fishing lakes. Between his nets and his gun Pamburn was able to scrape together enough food to keep up his strength. The two *engagés* did not fare so well. In March, 1850, Dubois perished from hunger and exposure, and Forbisher was reduced to cannibalism to try to keep himself alive. When Pamburn returned to the site of the post after a two-month absence, he was shocked to find Dubois dead. Before long he suspected Forbisher of eating his companion, but, instead of taking pity upon the wretched man, who was too weak even to cut wood for a fire, Pamburn again abandoned his subordinate to fend for himself.[68] Within a few days Forbisher also died. Pamburn probably would have followed him if James Stewart had not returned to Pelly Banks in April, 1850.

Robert Campbell had dispatched Stewart (whom he described as "always ready for any enterprise") on the long journey to Fort Simpson.[69] Fort Selkirk had not received any news or supplies since October, 1848. Even Campbell could not remain safely on the Yukon without more supplies. If Stewart did not return with supplies for the Yukon by September, 1850, Campbell had decided he would have to abandon Fort Selkirk. Since it would be too late at that time of year to journey to Fort Simpson, he had a contingency plan to float down the Yukon to its mouth, presumably in Russian America, and throw himself at the mercy of his rivals. Thus the future of the Hudson's Bay Company's operations on the upper Yukon rested upon James Green Stewart.[70]

P. C. Pamburn joined Stewart on his march. The most difficult section of their route was between Frances Lake and Fort Halkett. The spring sun made the deep snow heavy and wet, rendering each step, even with snowshoes, all the more difficult. Nor did they have any rations for the trail. Stewart was often forced to stop the march to hunt. By the time when they reached Fort Halkett, the Liard had lost its ice and was open for navigation. When they reached Fort Simpson, Stewart explained the urgency of Campbell's situation to Chief Factor John Rae. The district commander immediately stripped the depot of all available supplies and quickly sent Stewart back up the Liard with the promise of yet more trade goods in the autumn.[71]

Stewart had already journeyed nearly one thousand miles to reach the district headquarters, but, upon obtaining the supplies, he immediately set out on the return journey. The young clerk knew that he needed every available day to push up the Liard, which was running fast with the spring flood, in time to head off the abandonment of Fort Selkirk. He arrived at Frances Lake in mid-August and sent an Indian runner ahead to inform Campbell that relief had arrived. Campbell received the good news on August 23, just over a week ahead of the date that he had set for quitting the Yukon.[72]

Campbell gathered his men together and set out for Frances Lake to aid Stewart in transporting the much-needed supplies. During the journey he suffered an accident that nearly cost him his life. At Pelly Banks, Campbell and his men abandoned their boats and began hiking across the Arctic-Pacific Divide. Halfway across the portage trail they reached Finlayson Lake, a shallow body of water about a mile wide. Since the trail continued on the far side of the lake, Campbell and his men embarked in a collection of abandoned rafts and canoes. In their haste Campbell and a French-Canadian guide, Marcette, selected a canoe with scores of leaks from bow to stern. The wind was up, and the water choppy on the lake. Before they were halfway across, the water coming into the canoe from the holes and over the gunnels from the waves had succeeded in swamping the craft.[73]

Campbell and Marcette clung to the overturned canoe, at the same time kicking with their legs for shore. The lake, which in a few weeks would be frozen, was desperately cold, and Campbell's muscles began to stiffen. The men in the rafts were trying to reach the far shore, while those who were waiting to cross helplessly watched their leader struggle. Kitza, Campbell's loyal Indian hunter, climbed to a hill above the lake for a better view. He kept his eyes on the red wool toque that Campbell was wearing, and, every time that he saw it, he would shout to the other men, "See the Chief's head yet above water." Only when Campbell's strength was nearly exhausted, did he feel the lake bottom beneath his feet and stagger ashore. The men who had crossed on the raft "hugged us with joy, took off their warm shirts, put them on us & got a blazing fire kindled. . . . Poor Marcette who was the better swimmer, said that if I had gone down, he would never have come ashore alone."[74] Warmed by such sentiments, as well as by the fire, Campbell rested only a short while before continuing to Frances Lake for his supplies.

Consolidation of Operations on the Yukon

The years that Robert Campbell spent at Fort Selkirk from 1848 to 1852, though they were often trying, were among the most satisfying that he spent in the fur trade. His time at Fort Selkirk offered a contrast to his years at Frances Lake and Pelly Banks, where there had been constant food shortages and unpleasant disputes with Murdock McPherson. In those earlier years he had often written Governor Simpson about quitting the company's service. One of the things that had troubled him most was his sparse personal life. When Campbell had left York Factory in 1834, Simpson's last words to him had been, "Now, Campbell, don't you get married as we want you for active service."[75] Campbell seems to have abided by this precept and to have resisted taking even a temporary Indian wife—à la facon du pays. In 1847 he wrote Governor Simpson that he had made overtures (through the mail) to a young Scottish girl. As no further mention of this girl occurs in his correspondence, it seems that Campbell was unsuccessful as a suitor. Shortly after that, Fort Selkirk was founded, Murdock McPherson retired, and Campbell's spirits began to rise.

According to oral tradition among the southern Tutchones, Campbell was given a girl of that tribe for a wife.[76] His journals, which are generally frank and factually accurate, are mute on the point. Campbell's autobiographical journal was written while the trader was in retirement and the respected father of several children by his Scottish wife. He naturally might have been reticent about his past affairs out of respect for his family. Nor can we reach a firm conclusion on this subject because his official writings for the company mention no Indian wife. Simpson's advice on marriage might not have applied to an Indian woman, but Campbell, after fifteen years' service in the company, was no doubt anxious to do nothing to hinder his chances for promotion. Besides, Simpson, who coolly deserted his own Indian wife, referred to other traders' Indian wives as "his bit of brown" or "his bit of circulating copper," hardly signifying approval.[77] Unless new documents come to light, there will be no way to settle this question conclusively, but Campbell did enjoy good relations, which were perhaps intimate as well as commercial, with the Indians of the Yukon.

The Yukon natives held Campbell somewhat in awe. Since he had cured the lame Indian when he first arrived at Fort Selkirk, the Indians attributed great Shamanistic powers to the trader, and Campbell did nothing to discourage their belief. The most impressive display of his supposed powers occurred in the spring of 1851. While Campbell was at Pelly Banks, supervising the loading of his trade goods, he heard an Indian woman scream. Looking to the river, he saw the leather shirt of her son barely above the water. The boy's body was "submerged & apparently lifeless." Campbell pulled him ashore and stripped off his wet clothes. He rubbed the boy's body vigorously with a dry blanket and "breathed hard into his mouth." It is impossible to say how acquainted Campbell was with modern first-aid procedures, but his instincts were sound, and the boy began to breathe again. The boy's mother "was full of gratitude and wonder," as were all those present. They credited Campbell with having "brought him back to life."[78]

To Campbell the exploration of the Yukon River below Fort Selkirk was by far his most satisfying achievement during his residence in the Yukon. As early as the spring of 1843 he had wished to complete the exploration of the Pelly and then retire from the district.[79] Governor Simpson always withheld his permission for such a venture out of fear of colliding with the Russian traders, but by 1850, Sir George had received enough information both from Robert Campbell and from Alexander Hunter Murray to trust Campbell's original supposition that the Pelly River and the "Youcon" River were identical. Only then did the governor authorize Campbell to continue his explorations of the Yukon River to prove that his theory was correct.[80]

Robert Campbell's 1851 exploration of the upper Yukon was in many ways the climax of the fur traders' struggle over more than half a century to breach the northern Rocky Mountains and exploit the fur trade of the Yukon. It is therefore ironic that the final exploratory journey was an easy, rather matter-of-fact affair. There were none of the terrible canyons and rapids that John McLeod had endured on the Liard or the hostile Indians that Campbell had faced in his early days. It was a just a peaceful float down a great river.

The explorer waited until the Yukon cleared of ice and in early June, 1851, started downriver. Early summer in the Far North is a season of almost perpetual light. Campbell made good use of this by traveling day and night, stopping only to cook food. The river increased its size the farther north they went, as many large tributary streams flowed into it from the east and the west. The current was swift but steady, and no serious hazards to navigation slowed Campbell's progress.[81]

At first the Indians whom Campbell encountered had never before been in direct contact with white men and lacked even the most basic trade goods. Then, as Campbell neared the Arctic Circle, the Indians spoke of a fort farther downstream where there were white people like the explorers. Not long afterwards Campbell's boat came within sight of the stockaded walls of Fort Yukon.[82] It was a red-letter day for Robert Campbell; he had proven that the Pelly River, which he had discovered in 1840, and the "Youcon" River, discovered by John Bell in 1844, were the same. At the same time he had completed the exploration of the upper Yukon River and united the Hudson's Bay Company's operations at Fort Yukon with those at Fort Selkirk, Pelly Banks, and Frances Lake.

Campbell did not waste any time enjoying the union of the company's two spheres of operations west of the mountains. He remained only a single day at Fort Yukon, as a guest of his friend and former assistant William Hardisty, before embarking up the Porcupine River. Campbell had long hoped to find an alternate route to the Liard River for the purpose of supplying the upper Yukon. The trader now proposed to cross over the portage to the Peel River Post, ascend the Mackenzie River to Fort Simpson, there pick up the trade outfit for Fort Selkirk, and then return to that post by the same roundabout route.

During his first day's journey up the Porcupine River, Campbell overtook Alexander Hunter Murray and a group of *engagés* from Fort Yukon. They were taking their annual fur harvest to the Peel River Post. Murray and Campbell, the commanders of the Victorian Empire's Yukon march, traveled together across the Richardson Mountain portage to the Peel River. From there Campbell and his men headed up the Mackenzie River toward Fort Simpson. As they passed the various posts along the river, the explorers were the talk of the entire Mackenzie District. Campbell was greeted by friends whom he had not seen for years and by wide-eyed apprentice clerks who had heard only reports of his adventures on the distant Pelly River. All were shocked to see his burly frame emerge from the wilderness after so long and from such an unexpected direction as the lower Mackenzie River.[83]

Campbell eventually reached the depot at Fort Simpson. Chief Factor John Rae was not at the fort. He had been ordered to continue his search for the lost Franklin Expedition, and Chief Trader James Anderson had control of the Mackenzie. Since Anderson was not at the fort, Campbell filed his report with James Purden, the clerk in charge. He then collected his outfit of trade goods. The long journey back to Fort Selkirk was marred by bad weather, but he reached the post on October 17.[84]

Campbell had barely won his race with winter, but he felt that he had proven that Fort Selkirk was best supplied not by the dangerous Liard but by the Mackenzie-Peel-Porcupine-Yukon river route. In past years Fort Selkirk had been denied its proportion of trade goods because of inefficiencies at Frances Lake and Pelly Banks. Campbell felt that the new route would alleviate those problems and expected that "for the first time [Fort Selkirk] will have a fair chance to try what it can do in the way of Returns and I am in good hopes of a favorable issue."[85] It was on that cheery note of optimism that Campbell began the winter.

There were others who did not share Campbell's enthusiasm. Chief Trader James Anderson, upon taking command of the Mackenzie, had made a thorough study of its affairs, and he was critical of the commercial value of Fort Selkirk. He wrote to Eden Colvile,[86] Sir George Simpson's second-in-command:

We will now see what Fort Selkirk can do—I must own that not withstanding Mr. Campbell's sanguine representations, I have my doubts on the subject. I fear it is too near the Coast—only about 8 days from Lynns Canal, whence I should suppose the natives could produce goods at a cheaper rate than we could afford to sell them—Hitherto from various misfortunes Selkirk has been a

Anderson closed his letter with the observation, "I have a much higher opinion of Campbell's Zeal and Enterprise than his judgement."[87]

Anderson's objections to the company's operations in the transmountain region, unlike Murdock McPherson's, were based on facts, not prejudice. The combined outfits of Frances Lake, Pelly Banks, and Fort Selkirk for the years 1848 to 1850 resulted in a net loss of over £1,400.[88] The 1851 outfit, which Campbell was so sure would prove the worth of Fort Selkirk, amounted to £147.30 worth of trade goods. The high cost of both transport (£87.17.6) and the wages of the post's staff and

voyageurs (£ 387.0.0) increased the total expense to £ 622.
0.6.[89] When Campbell was only able to produce £ 238.10.4 in
furs in the spring of 1852, Anderson felt justified in suggest-
ing that the post be either moved or closed.[90]

Campbell's trade failed not because of his deficiencies as a
merchant but because of the commercial acumen of his Chilkat rivals. The Chilkats had again visited the Fort Selkirk area
in the summer of 1851, while Campbell was away on his exploratory journey. They were bent on trouble and probably
would have resorted to violence to evict the Hudson's Bay
men had not a band of northern Tutchones under the leadership of Thlin-ikik-Thling and his son K'anan unexpectedly
arrived. The Tutchones knew that, as long as Campbell's post
remained, they would be free of the Chilkats' dominance.
They broke up the intended attack and would have given the
Chilkats more than their share of violence had not James
Stewart intervened on the side of peace. Thwarted in their aggressive intentions, the Chilkats were still able to strike a blow
against the English before the end of the trade season. They
mobilized their commercial strength and bought up all of the
available furs, not only in the Fort Selkirk area but also for a
hundred miles down the Yukon. Thus, when Campbell returned to his post in mid-October, many of the prime pelts
were already lost to the Chilkats.[91]

There may also have been fewer Tutchone Indians able to
trap for furs. The Indians of the Fort Selkirk region had been
struck by disease, the corollary to European penetration of
frontier areas. In the spring of 1851, Campbell noted a "con-
tagious malady" among the Tutchones. He thought it was
either cholera or dysentery.[92] How many Indians perished is
unknown.

In spite of these problems Campbell stuck to his belief that
with time Fort Selkirk would prove profitable. An example of
his prevailing good spirits can be found in his May 1, 1852,
journal entry. He was awakened that morning by a magpie, a
bird rarely found in the Yukon but common in Campbell's
native Perthshire. The fur trader assumed that the bird's presence was an omen and wrote in his journal, "God grant it may
be the forerunner of good tidings."[93] Only much later, when

it was too late, did Campbell realize that the bird was the har-binger of defeat.

In May, 1852, Campbell again journeyed downriver to Fort Yukon and then to Lapierre House for his trade outfit. When he returned to Selkirk in July, he found James Stewart direct-ing the *engagés* in the construction of a new fort. The original site of the post had been subject to flooding in the spring when the ice on the Pelly River broke up. The work was fairly well advanced, and, though the stockade was not com-pleted, Campbell moved into the new fort.

While the work was progressing on the fort, the northern Tutchones remained in the vicinity of the post to help defend the traders if the Chilkats again made their appearance. In August, however, the guard was lifted, as the Indians dis-persed to conduct their summer hunts. At the same time James Stewart and a group of voyageurs were away from the fort on a trading trip downriver. Campbell was left to manage the fort with two *engagés* and two Indians.[94]

It was at this time, when the trader's strength was reduced, and the Tutchones were occupied with their hunting, that the Chilkats chose again to pay Campbell a visit. There were twenty-seven of them, as Campbell described, "bent on mis-chief." One of the Indians gave Campbell a basket and some letters from company officers on the Pacific Coast. One of the letters, from Captain C. E. Stewart of the steamer *Beaver*, warned Campbell that the Chilkats had caused trouble on the coast and that they had promised to do more at Fort Selkirk. It was, however, too late for warnings. All Campbell could do was endure their insults and maintain a conciliatory de-meanor. Thus Campbell stalled for time during the remain-der of the afternoon, hoping that some of the Tutchones might arrive.[95]

That night Campbell posted his men on guard in the store and dwelling house. They locked the doors behind them and hoped for the best. The fur trader noted in his journal, "The night passed irksome enough—some of the infernal devils were on the move the whole night trying the store doors and win-dows."[96] Campbell would have kept his men in the buildings

the next morning but for the lack of water and the fear that
the Chilkats might resort to fire in an attempt to evict them.
The new day, August 21, began as the one before had closed,
with the Chilkats harassing the Hudson's Bay men.[97]

The intimidation ended, and the plundering began, when
the Chilkats sighted a boat approaching the fort. Campbell
initially thought that it contained James Stewart and his voyageurs, but it was merely two Indian hunters. Upon seeing the
Chilkats, the hunters tried to veer away from the post, but
"the savages were yelling like fiends armed with guns and
knives and as the Boat passed along the bank they rushed into
the water and dragged it ashore."[98] They stripped the boat of
its contents and began a general sack of the post. When Campbell tried to bar the door of the dwelling house, three rifles
were leveled at his heart. One Indian boldly thrust his dagger
at Campbell. The trader was saved when one of the fort dogs
sprung to defend Campbell and stopped the blade with its
chest. The dog's blood splattered across Campbell, who was
helpless to resist. The Chilkats tore his pistol out of his belt.
It was useless to the trader anyway; he knew that, had one shot
been fired, its only result would have been to signal a one-
sided battle and "the certain destruction of our people."[99]

Campbell's men had by this time scattered for safety. He
too made his way to the riverbank, where he managed to float
a boat and drift out of reach of the Chilkats. Moving down
river, Campbell was reunited with his men. Together they
continued down the Yukon, hoping to meet Stewart's party or
a Tutchone hunting band. On the next morning they encountered a group of Tutchones, ten guns strong. The Tutchones,
angered by the attack, set off with the Hudson's Bay men "to
pay our Pillagers what we owed them."[100]

When Campbell and the Tutchones reached the remains of
Fort Selkirk, they found the site deserted. Every item of value
in the store and dwelling house was destroyed or stolen. Even
the food that the Chilkats could not carry was scattered about
the ground or otherwise despoiled. Frustrated and angry,
Campbell wanted to launch an immediate pursuit of the marauders. The Tutchones, however, were not eager to engage a

Chilkat band who outnumbered them two to one.[101] Besides, since Campbell's stock of trade goods was destroyed, the Chilkats had again become their only source of trade goods.

With his stock of trade goods stolen and his provisions ruined, Campbell had no choice but to abandon Fort Selkirk. On September 1, 1852, he divided his little command. James Stewart, who had arrived too late to render any assistance, was ordered to conduct most of the men to Fort Yukon for the winter. Campbell himself was bound for Fort Simpson, where he hoped to receive supplies to reestablish Fort Selkirk and avenge himself on the Chilkats. With two men, Baptiste Forcier and Peter Pelly, he made his way up the Pelly River toward Frances Lake. He took the shorter, but more dangerous, Liard River route to the district headquarters.[102]

Campbell was forty-six days on the trail to Fort Simpson. His fragile bark canoe was sorely tested, not only by the rapids and canyons on the river but also by large cakes of drifting ice which threatened to close the Liard. At the depot Campbell laid his case before Chief Trader Anderson. He felt that the company should reestablish Fort Selkirk because the post still held out the promise of a profitable future. He further argued:

You will not allow a party of murderous villains—who took off a moment when we were alone, to inflict such a blow—to pass unpunished, but cheerfully afford us an opportunity to return it; and wash away the stigma the Indians will cast on the Character and Bravery of the Company's officers.[103]

These arguments, however, were in vain.

James Anderson felt that the cost of the men and the supplies that would be needed to repair Selkirk's commerce and punish the Chilkats was too great. He sympathized with Campbell's frustration, but the Fort Selkirk outfit had always been on the debit side of the balance sheet. Anderson did not understand that Campbell had been in a trade war in which he had seldom had the weapons with which to fight. He felt that Campbell insisted on another try at Fort Selkirk because "his views have been so long and intensely directed to one absorbing object that they have become distorted and he can no longer see things in their true colors."[104] One color that Camp-

Chief Factor Robert Campbell. Courtesy of the Hudson's Bay Company.

bell could see was red, and in a Highlander's rage he would
not accept Anderson's decision. Even though the Council of
the Northern Department had finally promoted him to the
rank of chief trader, he was still determined to return to Fort
Selkirk.

In August, 1851, Campbell had applied for a leave of absence to visit his home in Scotland. He took advantage of that
leave and, as soon as the ice of the Mackenzie was thick
enough, set out on snowshoes for Governor Simpson's home
at Lachine, near Montreal. The journey, which occupied a
day more than four months, was an epic feat. Campbell traveled three thousand miles of it, from Fort Simpson to Crow
Wing, Minnesota, on snowshoes, setting a distance record that
would stand for many years.[105]

Although Governor Simpson was impressed with Campbell's march, he was not moved by the explorer's arguments.
Simpson agreed with Chief Trader Anderson that, if Fort Selkirk were reestablished, the company would have to supply
enough resources and men not only to trade successfully but
also to inflict some punishments on the Chilkats. That was a
burden that Simpson did not want the company to assume.
Campbell was persuaded by the tactful governor to forget the
Yukon and, now that he was so close to Europe, avail himself
of the opportunity to visit after an absence of twenty-three
years his native Scotland.

In April, 1853, Campbell booked passage on H.M.S. *Asia*,
bound for Great Britain. He would never see the Yukon country again.

CHAPTER 10

Aftermath

THE DECISION in 1853 not to reestablish Fort Selkirk was the first step in a general retreat by the Hudson's Bay Company from the upper Yukon and upper Liard rivers. Frances Lake had already been abandoned in the spring of 1851, and Pelly Banks followed soon after. In 1865, Fort Halkett was abandoned. Of the frontier posts established during Governor Simpson's thirty-year expansion program, only two endured: Fort Yukon and Peel River Post (the latter came to be known as Fort McPherson late in the nineteenth century).

Was the Hudson's Bay Company's expansion into the Yukon just an expensive failure? And, if so, what were the deciding factors that defeated the efforts of men such as John McLeod and Robert Campbell?

Governor Simpson and his explorers were correct in assuming that the upper Liard and Yukon River areas were rich in furs. After the Klondike gold rush the fur trade became an important industry in the Yukon. In the years 1927 and 1928 alone well over $600,000 in furs were traded.[1] Such profits brought the Hudson's Bay Company back to Fort Selkirk, and the post was rebuilt in 1938. The company's failure fully to exploit the area's fur resources in the mid-nineteenth century was caused by three critical factors: the supply of trade goods, the rigors of competition, and the lack of any strategic policy toward the transmountain region.

In his arguments for abandoning Fort Selkirk in 1852,

James Anderson stressed the high cost of transporting trade goods across the mountains to the Yukon River posts.[2] This was indeed a problem, but not the company's only one or, for that matter, its most pressing supply liability. The kind of goods to be brought into the Yukon was also critical. The Athapascan Indian tribes of the Yukon interior, although eager for standard European goods, particularly guns and powder, were most interested in trading for items of aesthetic, symbolic, and ritual importance. Paramount in this regard were *hyaque* and glass trade beads.

Hyaque was the Indian name for dentalia, the tooth-shaped seashells found on the shores of the Northwest Coast. White in color and tubular in shape, *hyaque* were used as a medium of exchange among most of the Indian tribes of the Pacific Slope.[3] The Hudson's Bay Company's Columbia Department had easy access to a major source of these shells on Nootka Sound. A limited number of *hyaque* were brought into the Mackenzie District, but not enough to have a large effect on the trade. James Anderson tried to rectify this situation in November, 1851. In a memorandum to Chief Factor John Ballenden of the Columbia Department, Anderson pointed out:

The HBC supply the Russian Am. Co. with large quantities [of *hyaque*] for their Northern Trade, strange to say, tho' urgent demands have been made for these shells by Mess[r] Murray & Campbell . . . we have not only been deprived of an essential article of trade for the Posts, west of the mounains, but have continued furnishing our Russian Rivals with arms to oppose us.[4]

To the Indians of the Yukon region dentalia were a symbol of status.[5] Murray claimed that a box of *hyaque* shells "would be worth over *two thousand pounds*" at Fort Yukon, and that, because the company could not supply the Indians with shells, they were withholding some of their furs.[6]

Glass beads were another item in high demand among the Yukon tribes. Like *hyaque*, the beads were not supplied in sufficient numbers during the first years of operations at Fort Selkirk, Pelly Banks, and Fort Yukon. Both *hyaque* and glass beads were compact, lightweight, cheap trade items. The company might have established itself better on the upper Yukon had these goods been available. Instead bulky, less popular cloth items, such as capotes and blankets, which the Indians balked at buying even as a last resort, were included in the trade outfits.[7]

The company's failure to anticipate the special demands of the Yukon Indians was aggravated by the presence of the intertribal trade networks. Indian traders competed with the Hudson's Bay Company pioneer posts. Not only were the Chilkats and other middlemen able to supply *hyaque,* glass beads, and other traditional goods, but they were often joined to interior tribes by commercially advantageous marriages.[8] The company, in spite of its experience at Dease Lake in 1838 and 1839, did not view the Tlingit traders as legitimate rivals. In the mid-nineteenth century it was company policy to challenge any and all competitors in its territory and to accept the expenses of a trade war for the eventual advantages of monopoly. Yet George Simpson never launched a concerted effort against the Chilkats. Campbell was not given the means to drive them from the field. Ironically enough, this was perhaps because the Chilkats were themselves customers of the Hudson's Bay Company, supplied by the steamer *Beaver* on the Pacific Coast.

This anomaly of supplying the very competitors who drove them from the Yukon reveals the overriding reason for the failure of the Hudson's Bay Company's expansion campaign. At no time during the thirty-year effort did the company executives map out a coherent plan for exploiting the fruits of the westward exploration. In 1789, Sir Alexander Mackenzie heard of a large river valley west of the Mackenzie Mountains. In the 1820s Sir George Simpson broadly directed his field officers to expand westward to reach that new territory. Seldom, however, were the means, in terms of men and trade goods, allotted to accomplish this task. Exploration had to proceed slowly, constrained by the leash of economy. It was never decided whether the company wished to find a route to the Pacific, establish a new district west of the mountains (like New Caledonia on the south), or merely expand the Mackenzie District. The explorers received little general guidance and even less support from the company.

Only the rivalry with the Russian American Company at one time gave the explorers a concrete goal, the Stikine River. That was only for the short period between 1834 and 1839, after which there was only the vague objective of reaching the elusive Colville River. Sir George Simpson and the members of the company's London Committee did not attempt to integrate the activities of Robert Campbell or John Bell into the overall operations of the Hudson's Bay Company in western America. They did not articulate, for instance, any plan to develop the Yukon valley's fur trade to compensate for the loss of the Columbia River to the United States in 1846. Rather they viewed the explorations only from the narrow perspective of the Mackenzie valley trade. The accomplishments of men like Robert Campbell were valued only in relation to the general accounts of the district. When expansion did not show a short-run profit, it was ended.

Following the sack of Fort Selkirk the Chilkats regained their commercial hegemony over the southern Yukon. Their trade with the Tutchones and Tagishes continued as it had in previous decades, as if Campbell had never seen the Yukon. As the nineteenth century progressed, their trade was again threatened by the white men, this time from the coast. The Tlingits tried to keep white men out of the Yukon interior by controlling the passes through the Coastal Mountains. This policy was successful until the Klondike gold rush in 1898, when hordes of miners swept past the Chilkats and flooded into the Yukon, destroying by force of numbers the old aboriginal trade system.

The Hudson's Bay Company, with its sole base at Fort Yukon, also tried to maintain its position in the area. Fort Yukon grew to be one of the company's most profitable posts. The post collected £6,000 worth of furs in 1868 alone.[9] Such profits did not last for long, however. In 1863 the Russians finally roused themselves enough to investigate the British post in their territory. Their spy, Simonsen Lukeen, had the honor of joining the British-explored upper Yukon with the Russian lower Yukon. Yet in spite of the proof of British trespassing that Lukeen brought back to Fort Saint Michael, the Russian American Company failed to initiate even a protest against the Hudson's Bay Company's post.

The Americans, after the Alaskan Purchase in 1867, were not quite so understanding. After diplomatic protests failed to produce a British withdrawal from Fort Yukon, the United States War Department dispatched Captain Charles W. Raymond, a military engineer, to ascertain the true location of the post. In the summer of 1869, Raymond arrived at Fort Yukon and conducted a series of observations, which established that the post was over a hundred miles inside United States territory. Raymond raised the American flag and took possession of the post. It was a much more polite eviction notice than the one that Robert Campbell had received from the Chilkats, but the result was the same. The company quit the fort and established another, called Rampart House, up the Porcupine River. In 1889 this post was also found to be within American territory, and the British again moved, this time into their own territory.[10]

Although Sir George Simpson failed to establish a rich fur district west of the Mackenzie Mountains, the process of expansion yielded rich by-products. Most important was the geographic knowledge that resulted from the fur-trade explorations. In 1853, when Robert Campbell returned to Great Britain on leave, he reported to geographers and mapmakers the findings of the Hudson's Bay Company's explorers in the Far Northwest. In particular, he met with the cartographers of the famous firm of Aaron and John Arrowsmith, whose maps chronicled the exploration of North America. Campbell's data filled in what had been a vast empty space on the map of the Northwest. The area west of the Mackenzie River had been filled with little but conjecture, and even the irrepressible, though apocryphal, concept of Cook's River found life there. Arrowsmith's 1854 map of British America, based on the company's explorations, changed that. The great rivers of the Northwest were all accurately laid out: the Peel, the Liard, the Stikine, the Porcupine, the Yukon headwaters, the Pelly, and the Lewes.

The explorations of the Hudson's Bay Company produced a blueprint of the Far Northwest which was the basis for later development of the area. Men like Robert Campbell, John Bell, and John McLeod provided the first information concerning this very resource-rich area of the continent. A generation later George Dawson and R. G. McConnell of the Canadian Geological Survey continued the Hudson's Bay men's work, inventorying the specific resources of the Yukon region. Their scientific surveys, guided by the maps and notes of the fur-trade explorers, opened the door for the gold-rush stampedes of the late nineteenth century.

Following his leave of absence in 1853, Robert Campbell returned to the Mackenzie District. He was stationed at Fort Liard from 1854 to 1855. While there, he was grieved by the deaths of many of his old companions. Kitza, who with Lapie, had been Campbell's assistant for fifteen years, died in the fur trader's arms. Gauche, the prophet during the 1843 exploration of the Pelly River, died in 1854.

In 1855, Campbell was given charge of the Athabasca District, where he proved himself an able administrator. In August, 1859, he married Ellenora C. Stirling from the village of Comire, Scotland. In the spring of 1860, Ellenora gave him a son, the first white boy born on the continent's Arctic Slope. Campbell was promoted to the rank of chief factor in 1867. Disappointment, however, continued to stalk him. His wife died of typhoid fever in 1871, while the family was visiting Europe. Upon his return to Canada two months later, Campbell was unjustly reprimanded by Chief Commissioner Donald Smith for his handling of company affairs during the Riel Rebellion. This injury, occurring so soon after his wife's death, drove the trader to tender his resignation from the company, an action that he had been considering for some months. Thus it was with some bitterness that he ended his forty-one-year career in the fur trade. He retired to a ranch near Riding Mountain National Park in the present-day province of Manitoba. In 1872 he was made a member of the Royal Geographic Society. He died in 1894 at the age of eighty-six.

John Bell, who explored the fur trade's northern approach

to the Yukon River, never achieved the prominence of Robert Campbell. Though Bell was stationed in the Mackenzie District for twenty-five years, he was never fond of the posting and always hoped to be stationed south of Portage la Loche. As early as 1837 he felt that he was "being doomed to pass my best days in this dismal and secluded part of the country, without any prospect of change."[11] He hoped that his service as assistant to Sir John Richardson's Franklin Search Expedition would be rewarded with a transfer south, but, as he was leaving the district with Richardson, he received orders sending him back north.

From 1849 to 1850, Bell was at Fort Liard. He also rendered considerable assistance to John Rae in his management of the district. Finally, in 1851, Bell received a posting in a milder climate. For two years he commanded the Cumberland District along the lower Saskatchewan River. Then, from 1853 to 1855, he was head of the Athabasca District. His tenure at Fort Chipewyan, the Athabasca District headquarters, was less than successful. When he turned over the command to an old comrade, Robert Campbell, its affairs were rather disorganized. Bell then enjoyed a year's leave before he was given charge of the company's post at Sept Iles on the Saint Lawrence River. Sept Iles was as close to large cities, such as Quebec, as Bell's former post at Peel River had been to Fort Simpson. He remained in this pleasant situation until 1860 when he retired from the company's service.

John Bell married the daughter of another fur trader-explorer, Peter Warren Dease. His wife bore him at least two daughters. Upon retirement Bell moved to Saugeen in the present province of Ontario. He died in 1868 at the age of sixty-nine.

Alexander Hunter Murray and his wife, Anne, remained at Fort Yukon until 1851. While they were there, Mrs. Murray gave birth to three daughters, the first white children born in Arctic America. Murray's concern for his family made him anxious to be transferred to a less isolated post. The company facilitated this and for the next few years Murray was stationed at various posts along the United States border. In 1856 he was promoted to the rank of chief trader. He always remained very proud of his role in the establishment of Fort Yukon, the company's most removed post. In 1861 Mrs. Murray and he supplied valuable data concerning the Indians of the Northwest to pioneer anthropologist Lewis Henry Morgan.

Murray retired from the Hudson's Bay Company in 1867. He lived for seven years on a small farm along the Red River until his death in 1874. He was only fifty-six years old.

For Sir George Simpson, overseas governor of the Hudson's Bay Company, the destruction of Fort Selkirk marked the end of a thirty-year period of company-sponsored explorations to expand the fur trade. Expeditions continued, such as Chief Trader Anderson's and Dr. John Rae's Franklin search teams; but the company no longer had a terra incognita in which Simpson could envision new and prosperous fur-trade districts. The governor himself suffered declining health, though he tried to maintain his brisk schedule and firm grasp of company affairs. His active nature is illustrated by his comment, "It is . . . strange that all my ailments vanish as soon as I seat myself in a canoe."[12] His body could not keep pace with his feisty spirit, however. In 1860, while returning from a business trip, he suffered an attack of apoplexy, and six days later he was dead.

The Little Emperor, as Simpson was called, was a complex man. Capable of extreme pettiness, he gave many examples of a harsh, callous nature. At the same time he could play the role of a friend, counselor, and mentor, as he did for Robert Campbell. Above all Simpson was a man of continental vision. He saw North America as a geographic unity whose various parts were open to his firm's commerce. Although his plans for the Yukon region did not bear fruit, and although his attitude toward exploration was inconsistent, he was still one of the great empire builders of the nineteenth century, an era that fostered men such as Simpson, Murray, Bell, and Campbell.

Notes

PREFACE

1. John S. Galbraith, *The Hudson's Bay Company as an Imperial Factor, 1821–1869*, p. 3.
2. Ibid., p. 10.
3. Ibid., p. 89.

CHAPTER 1

1. This description of one of the first meetings of the new Hudson's Bay Company is based on the eyewitness account of John Todd. Arthur S. Morton quoted at length from Todd's account in *A History of the Canadian West to 1870–71*, p. 626. Unfortunately, Morton failed to supply footnotes in that otherwise excellent history. Lewis G. Thomas, who edited the second and most recent edition of Morton's history, states (p. 984): "This document [Todd's account] was given to Morton by Mr. Wm. Smith, Deputy Archivist, Ottawa, who did not know its source. Morton believed it came from the Provincial Archives of British Columbia, where there is considerable material from Todd's pen."
2. Ibid., p. 626.
3. Ibid.
4. For a description of the organizational structure of the Hudson's Bay Company, see chapter 3, where there is a discussion of the replacement at Fort Simpson of Chief Trader Alexander McLeod by Chief Factor Edward Smith.
5. W. Stewart Wallace, ed., *Documents Relating to the North West Company*, pp. 6–7.
6. George Simpson, *Simpson's Athabaska Journal and Report, 1821–1822*, ed. E. E. Rich, p. 141.
7. "The Character Book of George Simpson, 1832," in Glyndwr Williams, ed., *Hudson's Bay Miscellany, 1670–1870*, p. 172.

8. Arthur J. Ray, "Some Conservation Schemes of the Hudson's Bay Company, 1821–1850: An Examination of the Problems of Resource Management in the Fur Trade," *Journal of Historical Geography* 1, no. 1 (1975) : 50.

9. Ibid.

10. L. R. Masson, ed., *Les bourgeois de la Compagnie du Nord-Ouest, récits de voyages, lettres et rapports inédits relatifs au nord-ouest Canadien*, 1: 114.

11. George Simpson, *Fur Trade and Empire: George Simpson's Journal, 1824–1825*, ed. Frederick Merk, p. xx.

12. Masson, ed., *Les bourgeois*, 1: 150.

13. Arthur J. Ray, *Indians in the Fur Trade: Their Role as Hunters, Trappers, and Middlemen in the Lands Southwest of Hudson Bay, 1660–1870*, pp. 198–200.

14. Simpson, *Fur Trade and Empire*, p. 204.

15. George Simpson-Governor and Committee, August 10, 1824, D. 4/3 fos. 83, Hudson's Bay Company Archives, Provincial Archives of Manitoba, Winnipeg.

16. For further information concerning the search for a freshwater Northwest Passage, see Glyndwr Williams, *The British Search for the Northwest Passage in the Eighteenth Century*; and Grace Lee Nute, "A Peter Pond Map," *Minnesota History* 16 (1933) : 81–84.

17. Alexander Mackenzie, *Voyages from Montreal on the River St. Lawrence, through the Continent of North America to the Frozen and Pacific Oceans in the Years 1789 and 1793, With a Preliminary Account of the Rise, Progress, and Present State of the Fur Trade of the Country*, p. 29.

18. Ibid., p. 54.

19. Ibid., p. 64.

20. Willard-Ferdinand Wentzel, "Notice of the Attempts to Reach the Sea by Mackenzie's River, Since the Expedition of Sir Alexander Mackenzie," *Edinburgh Philosophical Journal* 8 (1823) : 78–79.

21. John K. Stager, *Fur Trading Posts in the Mackenzie Region up to 1850*, Canadian Association of Geographers, B.C. Division, Occasional Paper no. 3, pp. 40–41.

22. Ibid., p. 40. Stager's *Fur Trading Posts in the Mackenzie Region up to 1850* is the most authoritative treatment of the subject. He argues persuasively that 1807 is the date for the founding of Fort Nelson. The fort is thought to have been named for Lord Nelson, hero of the Napoleonic Wars. Nelson's crushing defeat of the French fleet at the Battle of the Nile in 1798 might have made him sufficiently famous in the Northwest to have a fort named for him. That would coincide with the date 1800 sometimes suggested for the fort's construction. It is difficult, however, to believe that at such an early date the North West Company had pushed over two hundred miles up the dangerous Liard. After the establishment of Fort Liard a post at the Fort Nelson River would be a logical extension. Furthermore, Nelson's magnificent victory at Trafalgar in 1805 would surely have made him notable in all of British America. Allowing for a year's time lag in the spread of the news, one has 1807, Stager's date for the founding of Fort Nelson.

23. Masson, ed., *Les bourgeois*, 1: 87.

24. Ibid., p. 84.

25. Ibid., p. 78.
26. Ibid., 2: 126.
27. J. J. Honigmann, *Ethnography and Acculturation of the Fort Nelson Slave*, Yale University Publications in Anthropology, no. 33, p. 30.
28. Masson, ed., *Les bourgeois*, 2: 126.
29. Ibid., 1: 106–107.
30. Ibid., 1: 109.
31. Willard-Ferdinand Wentzel, "Account of Mackenzie River," 1821, MC 19A, p. 1, Public Archives of Canada, Ottawa.
32. Ibid.
33. Ibid.
34. Alan Cooke and Clive Holland, "Chronological List of Expeditions and Historical Events in Northern Canada," *Polar Record* 16, no. 2 (1974) : 41.
35. Robert R. James, *The Archaeology of Fort Alexander, N.W.T.: Report of Investigations of the 1974 Mackenzie River Archaeological Project*, p. 33.
36. John Franklin, *Narrative of a Journey to the Shores of the Polar Sea in the Years 1819, 20, 21, and 22*, p. 141.
37. Ibid., p. 456.
38. C. Stuart Houston, ed., *To the Arctic by Canoe: The Journal and Paintings of Robert Hood, Midshipman with Franklin*, p. xxviii.
39. Canada, *Certain Correspondence of the Foreign Office and the Hudson's Bay Company*, Pt. 1, pp. 3–6. Sir John Barrow, second secretary of the Admiralty and founder of the Royal Geographic Society, was a particularly strong advocate of exploration.

CHAPTER 2

1. James R. Gibson, *Feeding the Russian Fur Trade: Provisionment of the Okhotsk Seaboard and the Kamchatka Peninsula, 1639–1856*, p. 8.
2. Ibid., p. 23.
3. P. A. Tikhmener, *A History of the Russian-American Company*, trans. and ed. Richard A. Pierce and Alton Donnelly, p. 14.
4. The charter was very much like the charter granted to the Hudson's Bay Company, but, because the czar and other government officials were shareholders, the Russian American Company always had a closer relationship with its government than the Hudson's Bay Company had with the British government.
5. Washington Irving, *Astoria; or Anecdotes of an Enterprise Beyond the Rocky Mountains*, p. 465.
6. James R. Gibson, *Imperial Russia in Frontier America*, p. 11.
7. Tikhmener, *A History of the Russian-American Company*, pp. 65–66.
8. Hector Chevigny, *Lord of Alaska*, pp. 290–91.
9. King had assumed command of Cook's expedition following the death of the great navigator in Hawaii.
10. Samuel Eliot Morison, *The Maritime History of Massachusetts, 1783–1860*, pp. 55–57.
11. Wade C. Caruthers, "The Sea-Borne Frontier on the Northwest Coast," *Journal of the West* 10 (April, 1971) : 216.

286 FUR TRADE AND EXPLORATION

12. Irving, *Astoria*, pp. 482–85.
13. Barry W. Gough, "The 1813 Expedition to Astoria," *The Beaver*, Autumn, 1973, p. 46.
14. Caruthers, "The Sea-Borne Frontier," p. 219.
15. Tikhmener, *A History of the Russian-American Company*, pp. 151–52.
16. Nikolai Petrovich Rezanov, *The Rezanov Voyage to Nueva California in 1806*, ed. T. C. Russell, pp. 69–72.
17. Gibson, *Imperial Russia in Frontier America*, p. 159.
18. Ibid., p. 138.
19. Ibid., pp. 156–57.
20. Howard I. Kushner, *Conflict on the Northwest Coast: American-Russian Rivalry in the Pacific Northwest, 1790–1867*, pp. 15–16.
21. Ibid., p. 17.
22. U.S., Congress, Senate, "Ukase of September 4, 1821," *Proceedings of the Alaskan Boundary Tribunal*, 58th Cong., 2d sess., Document 162, 2: 26–29. Hereafter cited as *ABT*.
23. Ibid.
24. Samuel F. Bemis, *John Quincy Adams and the Foundations of American Foreign Policy*, pp. 175–79.
25. Bagot to the Marquis of Londonderry, November 17, 1821, *ABT*, 2: 101.
26. Adams to Benjamin Rush, July 22, 1823, *ABT*, 2: 52–56.
27. Hudson's Bay Company to Canning, September 25, 1822, *ABT*, 2: 109–10.
28. Count Liever to the Duke of Wellington, November 23, 1822, *ABT*, 2: 115–16.
29. Kushner, *Conflict on the Northwest Coast*, p. 59.
30. Treaty Between Russia and America, 1824, *ABT*, 2: 10–12.
31. John S. Galbraith, *The Hudson's Bay Company as an Imperial Factor*, pp. 130–31.
32. Governor and Committee to George Simpson, February 27, 1822, in R. Harvey Fleming, ed., *Minutes of Council, Northern Department of Rupert's Land, 1821–31*, p. 303.
33. Simpson to A. R. McLeod, January 2, 1823, D. 4/2 fos. 34, Hudson's Bay Company Archives, Winnipeg, Manitoba.
34. Barry M. Gough, *The Royal Navy and the Northwest Coast of America, 1810–1914*, pp. 31–32.
35. Ibid.
36. James W. Vanstone, ed., "V. S. Khromchenko's Coastal Explorations in Southwestern Alaska, 1822," *Fieldiana: Anthropology* 64 (1973): 25.
37. Galbraith, *The Hudson's Bay Company as an Imperial Factor*, p. 131.
38. Ibid., p. 127.
39. Ibid., p. 133.
40. Ibid., p. 131.
41. Canning to Bagot, July 12, 1824, *ABT*, 2: 181.
42. Middleton to Adams, August 8, 1822, *ABT*, 2: 42.
43. Irby C. Nichols, Jr., "The Russian Ukase and the Monroe Doctrine: A Re-evaluation," *Pacific Historical Review*, February, 1967, p. 24.

CHAPTER 3

1. L. R. Masson, ed., *Les bourgeois de la Compagnie du Nord-Ouest, récits de voyages, lettres et rapports inédits relatifs au nord-ouest Canadien*, 1: 69.
2. James V. F. Millar and Gloria J. Fedirchuk, *Report on Investigations: Mackenzie River Archaeological Survey*, p. 99.
3. Simpson to A. R. McLeod, January 2, 1823, D. 4/2 fos. 34, Hudson's Bay Company Archives, Winnipeg, Manitoba. Hereafter this repository will be referred to as HBCA. All quotations are transcribed exactly from the manuscript cited. Original grammatical and spelling errors are reproduced verbatim.
4. Ibid.
5. Smith was a former Nor'Wester. He commanded the Athabasca District in 1822, but was soon to be transferred to the Mackenzie River District. W. Stewart Wallace, ed., *Documents Relating to the North West Company*, p. 499.
Dease was one of four brothers who pursued the beaver into the Northwest. A nephew of Sir William Johnson, a famed Indian agent, he joined the XY Company in 1801, and he traded in the Mackenzie District in their service as well as in the service of the North West Company. After the union in 1821 he was elevated to the rank of chief trader. He worked on the Second Franklin Expedition during the 1826–27 season. His most important exploit was the 1836–39 survey of the Arctic Coast from the Mackenzie delta to Point Barrow. He died in 1863 after twenty-one years of prosperous retirement. The Dease River and Dease Lake in northern British Columbia are named after him. Wallace, ed., *Documents Relating to the Northwest Company*, p. 436.
6. Simpson to A. R. McLeod, January 2, 1823, D. 4/2 fos. 34, HBCA.
7. Ibid.
8. Ibid.
9. R. M. Patterson, "The Nahanny Lands," *The Beaver*, Summer, 1961, p. 40.
10. "The Character Book of George Simpson, 1832," in Glyndwr Williams, ed., *Hudson's Bay Miscellany 1670–1870*, p. 191.
11. Fort Simpson Journal, 1823, B. 200/a/1 fos. 31, HBCA.
12. A. R. McLeod to Simpson, April, 1823, quoted in Patterson, "The Nahanny Lands," *The Beaver*, Summer, 1961, pp. 40–47.
13. Northern Department General Accounts, 1825–26, B. 239/g/5 fos. 8, HBCA.
14. C. Stuart Houston, *To the Arctic by Canoe: The Journal and Paintings of Robert Hood, Midshipman with Franklin*, pp. 112–13.
15. Simpson to A. R. McLeod, January 2, 1823, D. 4/2 fos. 34, HBCA.
16. Bernard DeVoto, *Across the Wide Missouri*, p. 329.
17. Fort Simpson Journal, 1831, B. 200/a/14 fos. 9, HBCA.
18. Clifford Drury, *Marcus and Narcissa Whitman and the Opening of Old Oregon*, p. 325.
19. DeVoto, *Across the Wide Missouri*, p. 264.
20. Ibid., p. 264. DeVoto discusses this whole episode, and it is his rendering upon which I base my account.
21. Fort Simpson Journal, 1823, B. 200/a/2 fos. 2, HBCA.

22. Fort Simpson Journal, 1823, B. 200/a/2 fos. 11, HBCA.
23. Ibid.
24. Fort Simpson Journal, 1823, B. 200/a/2 fos. 14, HBCA.
25. Charles Camsell, *Son of the North*, pp. 18–19.
26. Simpson to London Governing Committee, Hudson's Bay Company, August 31, 1825, D. 4/7 fos. 142d, HBCA.
27. "The Character Book of George Simpson, 1832," in Glyndwr Williams, ed., *Hudson's Bay Miscellany, 1670–1870*, p. 190. In spite of what Simpson may have told Alexander McLeod, the governor does not seem to have had a high opinion of the chief trader. In 1832, in the privacy of his infamous "Character Book," Simpson described McLeod as follows: "arrogant; does not confine himself to plain matter of fact, annoys everyone near him with details of his own exploits; 'I did this,' 'I did that' and 'I did the other thing' continually in his mouth, but it unfortunately happens that he rarely does anything well." Not only did Simpson find McLeod "a most overbearing Tyrannical fellow," he also thought him "capable of little mean tricks" and suspected him of being "fond of a glass of Grog in private." In summary, Simpson stated that McLeod "would have made an excellent Guide altho' he adds little respectability to the 'Fur Trade' as a partner" (ibid., p. 191).
28. Simpson to McLeod, June 16, 1823, D. 4/2 fos. 60, HBCA.
29. Wallace, ed., *Documents Relating to the North West Company*, p. 499.
30. "The Character Book of George Simpson, 1832," in Glyndwr Williams, ed., *Hudson's Bay Miscellany, 1670–1870*, p. 175.
31. Ibid., p. 176.
32. Fort Simpson Journal, 1824, B. 200/a/2 fos. 4, HBCA.
33. Fort Simpson Journal, 1824, B. 200/a/5 fos. 22, HBCA.
34. Fort Simpson Journal, 1824, B. 200/a/5 fos. 35, HBCA.
35. R. M. Patterson, "The Nahanny Lands," *The Beaver*, Summer, 1961, p. 47.
36. Ibid.
37. Wallace, ed., *Documents Relating to the North West Company*, p. 483.
38. Mackenzie District Report, 1825, B. 200/e/4 fos. 4, HBCA.
39. Ibid.
40. Fort Simpson Journal, 1824, B. 200/a/5 fos. 25d, HBCA.
41. Ibid.
42. Ibid.
43. Alan E. Cameron, "South Nahanni River," *Canadian Geographic Journal*, May, 1930, pp. 48–55.
44. E. D. Kindle, *Geological Reconnaissance along Fort Nelson, Liard, and Beaver Rivers, Northeastern British Columbia, and Southwestern Yukon*, Canadian Geological Survey Papper 44-16, p. 1.
45. Fort Simpson Journal, 1824, B. 200/a/5 fos. 26, HBCA.
46. Ibid.
47. Fort Simpson Journal, 1824, B. 200/a/5 fos. 27, HBCA.
48. Ibid.
49. Fort Simpson Journal, 1824, B. 200/a/5 fos. 28, HBCA.
50. Fort Simpson Journal, 1824, B. 200/a/5 fos. 28, HBCA.
51. Fort Simpson Journal, 1824, B. 200/a/5 fos. 28d, HBCA.

CHAPTER 4

1. Fort Simpson Journal, 1823, B. 200/a/5 fos. 28d, Hudson's Bay Company Archives, Winnipeg, Manitoba. Hereafter this repository will be cited as HBCA. Spelling errors have not been corrected.

2. George Simpson, *Fur Trade and Empire: George Simpson's Journal, 1824–1825*, ed. Frederick Merk, p. 203.

3. Samuel Black, *Black's Rocky Mountain Journal, 1824*, ed. E. E. Rich, pp. xxvii–xxviii.

4. Ibid., p. xxxv.

5. Ibid., pp. xxxvii–xxxviii.

6. Ibid., p. xli.

7. Simpson, *Fur Trade and Empire*, p. 203.

8. George Simpson, *Simpson's Athabasca Journal*, ed. E. E. Rich, p. 278.

9. Black, *Black's 1824 Journal*, ed. E. E. Rich, p. xlv.

10. Grant was also admitted to the company at this time, though at the lower rank of clerk.

11. "The Character Book of George Simpson, 1832," in Glyndwr Williams, ed., *Hudson's Bay Miscellany, 1670–1870*, p. 193.

12. Ibid.

13. Black, *Black's 1824 Journal*, ed. E. E. Rich, p. liii.

14. Ibid., pp. 19–20.

15. The deserters, Ossin and Bouche, tried to flee Rupert's Land in a canoe. They got as far as Île-à-la-Crosse on the Churchill River. They were unsure of the route after that point, and this uncertainty probably made them inclined to reconsider their action. Surrendering to the post commander at Île-à-la-Crosse, they threw themselves on the company's mercy. They were called before the Council of the Northern Department at York Factory and ordered to ". . . be immediately Handcuffed and in that situation that they be publickly exposed during one full day on the roof of the Factory, afterwards that they be imprisoned during one week, fed on bread and water, and in winter that one of each be sent to winter among the Europeans at Churchill & Severn Forts" (ibid., p. 242). This was hardly a severe punishment, though it seems almost medieval to a modern reader.

16. R. M. Patterson, *Finlay's River*, p. 4.

17. Black, *Black's 1824 Journal*, ed. E. E. Rich, p. 21.

18. Ibid., p. 25.

19. Ibid., p. 23.

20. Patterson, *Finlay River*, pp. 197–98.

21. Black, *Black's 1824 Journal*, ed. E. E. Rich, p. 36.

22. Ibid., p. 53.

23. Ibid., p. 59.

24. Ibid., p. 66.

25. Ibid., p. 67.

26. Ibid.

27. Ibid., p. 69.

28. Ibid., p. 82.

29. Ibid., p. 85.

30. Ibid., p. 87.

31. Ibid., p. 92.
32. Ibid., pp. 108–109.
33. Ibid., p. 109.
34. Ibid., p. 110.
35. Ibid., p. 112.
36. Ibid., p. 123.
37. Ibid., p. 121.
38. Ibid., p. 136.
39. Ibid.
40. Ibid., p. 125.
41. The company was not able to take any disciplinary measures against La Prise for his desertion because he was not a contracted "servant" of the company.
42. Ibid., p. 151.
43. Ibid., p. 164.
44. Modern maps retain Black's name. In naming the river Turnagain, Black may have been making a play on words. Captain James Cook had dubbed the inlet near his supposed great western river the Turnagain. Black, who was familiar with Cook's journal of his voyage, may have named the stream at the end of his search for a great western river after the geographic feature that had inspired the search almost fifty years earlier.
45. Simpson to London Committee, April 1, 1825, D. 4/88 fos. 90d–91, HBCA.
46. Ibid.
47. Black spent the remainder of his years as a fur trader in the Columbia River and Thompson River areas. George Simpson once criticized Black for his suspicious nature: "Offensive and defensive preparation seems to be the study of his Life having Dirks Knives & loaded Pistols concealed about his person and in all directions about his Establishment even under his Table cloth at Meals and in his Bed" ("The Character Book of George Simpson, 1832," in Glyndwr Williams, ed., *Hudson's Bay Miscellany, 1670–1870*, p. 193). Simpson obviously thought Black's behavior eccentric. Black, however, knew his own turbulent nature; danger and violence were facts of his life. In the winter of 1841 he was murdered, shot in the back of the head by an Indian smarting from an imagined insult.
48. R. Harvey Fleming, ed., *Minutes of Council, Northern Department of Rupert Land, 1821–31*, p. 17.
49. Black, *Black's 1824 Journal*, ed. E. E. Rich, p. 175.
50. G. P. De T. Glazebrook, ed., *Hargrave Correspondence, 1821–1843*, p. 68.
51. Black, *Black's 1824 Journal*, ed. E. E. Rich, p. 137.
52. Fleming, ed., *Minutes of Council, Northern Department*, p. 107.
53. Black, *Black's 1824 Journal*, ed. E. E. Rich, pp. lxix–lxx.
54. W. N. Sage, "New Caledonia: The Siberia of the Fur Trade," *The Beaver*, Autumn, 1956, p. 24.
55. John S. Galbraith, *The Hudson's Bay Company as an Imperial Factor, 1821–1869*, p. 125.
56. Black, *Black's 1824 Journal*, ed. E. E. Rich, p. 175.
57. Simpson to A. R. McLeod, January 2, 1823, D. 4/2 fos. 34, HBCA.
58. Simpson, *Fur Trade and Empire*, p. 72.

59. Ibid., p. 86.
60. Simpson, "The Character Book of George Simpson, 1832," in Williams, ed., *Hudson's Bay Miscellany*, p. 199.
61. Ibid.
62. Simpson to London Committee, July 25, 1827, D. 4/14 fos. 30d–31, HBCA.
63. Simpson to William Connolly, July 5, 1826, D. 4/6 fos. 15–15d, HBCA.
64. Chief Trader William Brown, who was seriously ill, went to Europe. He died there in March, 1827. Simpson, *Simpson's Athabasca Journal*, p. 431.
65. Simpson, *Fur Trade and Empire*, p. 269.
66. Ibid.
67. McDonald, *Peace River: A Canoe Voyage from Hudson's Bay to the Pacific by the late Sir George Simpson in 1828; Journal of the Late Chief Factor, Who Accompanied Him*, ed. Malcolm McLeod, p. 117.
68. E. E. Rich, *History of the Hudson's Bay Company, 1670–1870*, p. 615.
69. Fleming, ed., *Minutes of Council, Northern Department*, p. 263.
70. Gloria Griffin Cline, *Peter Skene Ogden and the Hudson's Bay Company*, pp. 102–103.
71. Ibid., p. 104.
72. Ibid.
73. "The Character Book of George Simpson, 1832," in Glyndwr Williams, ed., *Hudson's Bay Miscellany*, p. 199.
74. Galbraith, *The Hudson's Bay Company as an Imperial Factor*, p. 143.
75. James R. Gibson, *Imperial Russia in Frontier America*, p. 167.
76. Cline, *Peter Skene Ogden and the Hudson's Bay Company*, p. 110.
77. "Report of the Governor to the Board of Directors of the Russian-American Company, May 6, 1832," *Proceedings of the Alaskan Boundary Tribunal, Convened at London . . . under the Treaty Concluded at Washington, January 24, 1903*, 2: 264–65.

CHAPTER 5

1. Edward Smith to George Simpson, September 8, 1825, D. 5/1 fos. 161, Hudson's Bay Company Archives, Winnipeg, Manitoba. Hereafter this repository will be referred to as HBCA. Spelling errors have not been corrected.
2. Ibid., fos. 162.
3. Edward Smith to Governor George Simpson and the Council of the Northern Department, November 28, 1828, D. 5/3 fos. 274d, HBCA.
4. Emile Petitot, *The Amerindians of the Canadian North-West in the 19th Century, as seen by Émile Petitot*, ed. Donat Savoie, vol. 2, *The Loucheux Indians*, p. 33.
5. Edward Smith to Governor George Simpson and the Council of the Northern Department, November 28, 1828, D. 5/3 fos. 274d, HBCA.
6. R. Harvey Fleming, ed., *Minutes of Council, Northern Department of Rupert's Land, 1821–1831*, p. 235.

7. "The Character Book of George Simpson, 1832," in Williams, ed., *Hudson's Bay Miscellany*, p. 213.

8. Ibid.

9. Fleming, ed., *Minutes of Council, Northern Department*, p. 235.

10. R. M. Patterson, *The Dangerous River*, p. 92.

11. Ibid., p. 94.

12. Pierre Duchaussois, *Mid Snow and Ice: The Apostles of the North-West*, p. 285.

13. Fort Halkett Journal, B. 85/a/1 fos. 1, HBCA.

14. John Halkett was one of the more active directors of the Hudson's Bay Company. He was the executor of Lord Selkirk's will and a trustee for the Red River Colony. In 1821 he journeyed to Rupert's Land and in 1822 aided Governor Simpson in the reorganization of the Hudson's Bay Company. E. E. Rich, *The History of the Hudson's Bay Company, 1670–1870*, p. 423.

15. Edward Smith to Governor George Simpson and Northern Department Council, July 28, 1830, D. 5/3 fos. 475d, HBCA.

16. Edward Smith to Governor George Simpson and Northern Department Council, November 28, 1830, D. 5/3 fos. 481d–482, HBCA.

17. Edward Smith to Governor George Simpson and Council of the Northern Department, November 29, 1829, D. 5/3 fos. 420d, HBCA.

18. G. P. DeT. Glazebrook, ed., *The Hargrave Correspondence, 1821–1843*, p. 38.

19. Ibid.

20. Edward Smith to Governor George Simpson and Council of the Northern Department, November 28, 1830, D. 5/3 fos. 481d–482, HBCA.

21. Governor Simpson to Edward Smith, June 16, 1830, D. 4/17 fos. 15d–16d, HBCA.

22. Glazebrook, ed., *Hargrave Correspondence, 1821–1843*, p. 38.

23. Governor Simpson to Edward Smith, June 16, 1830, D. 4/17 fos. 15d–16d, HBCA.

24. Governor Simpson to Edward Smith, December 5, 1830, D. 4/18 fos. 6d–7, HBCA.

25. Glazebrook, ed., *Hargrave Correspondence, 1821–1843*, p. 75.

26. Governor Simpson to Edward Smith, June 1, 1831, D. 4/18 fos. 47–47d, HBCA.

27. Glazebrook, ed., *Hargrave Correspondence, 1821–1843*, p. 75.

28. Ibid., p. 76.

29. Ibid.

30. Fort Simpson Journal, 1831, B. 200/a/14 fos. 3, HBCA.

31. Ibid.

32. Ibid.

33. Ibid.

34. Warburton Pike, *Through the Sub-Arctic Forest: A Record of a Canoe Journey from Fort Wrangel to the Pelly Lakes and down the Yukon River to the Behring Sea*, p. 69.

35. Ferdi Wenger, "Canoeing the Wild Liard River Canyon," *Canadian Geographical Journal*, Winter, 1976, p. 3.

36. Eric W. Morse, *Fur Trade Canoe Routes of Canada: Then and Now*, p. 112.

37. R. G. McConnell, *Report on an Exploration in the Yukon and*

Mackenzie Basins, N.W.T., in *Geological and Natural History Survey of Canada Reports for the Year 1887*, Part D, p. 34.

38. Fort Simpson Journal, 1831, B. 200/a/14 fos. 3d, HBCA.

39. Ibid.

40. Fort Simpson Journal, 1831, B. 200/a/14 fos. 4, HBCA.

41. Ibid.

42. Ibid.

43. Fort Simpson Journal, 1831, B. 200/a/14 fos. 4d, HBCA.

44. McConnell, "Report on the Yukon and Mackenzie Basins," *Geological Survey of Canada, 1891*, p. 50.

45. Fort Simpson Journal, 1831, B. 200/a/14 fos. 4d, HBCA.

46. R. M. Patterson, "Liard River Voyage," *The Beaver*, Spring, 1955, p. 23.

47. Fort Simpson Journal, 1831, B. 200/a/14 fos. 4d, HBCA.

48. McConnell, "Report on the Yukon and Mackenzie Basins," *Geological Survey of Canada, 1891*, p. 480.

49. Fort Simpson Journal, 1831, B. 200/a/14 fos. 5, HBCA.

50. Ibid.

51. Ibid.

52. Ibid.

53. Ibid.

54. Fort Simpson Journal, 1824, B. 200/a/14 fos. 6, HBCA.

55. Ibid.

56. Ibid.

57. Fort Simpson Journal, 1824, B. 200/a/14 fos. 7, HBCA.

58. McConnell, "Report on the Yukon and Mackenzie Basins," *Geological Survey of Canada, 1891*, p. 470.

59. Ibid.

60. Ibid.

61. Fort Simpson Journal, 1831, B. 200/a/14 fos. 7d, HBCA.

62. Fort Simpson Journal, 1831, B. 200/a/14 fos. 8, HBCA.

63. Ibid.

64. Fort Simpson Journal, 1831, B. 200/a/14 fos. 9, HBCA.

65. Ibid.

66. McConnell, "Report on the Yukon and Mackenzie Basins," *Geological Survey of Canada, 1891*, p. 410.

67. Fort Simpson Journal, 1831, B. 200/a/14 fos. 9, HBCA.

68. Ibid.

69. The modern name for this river is the Kechika.

70. Fort Simpson Journal, 1831, B. 200/a/14 fos. 9d, HBCA.

71. Ibid.

72. Fort Simpson Journal, 1831, B. 200/a/14 fos. 10, HBCA.

73. Richard Finne, *The Headless Valley*, p. 111.

74. Fort Simpson Journal, 1831, B. 200/a/14 fos. 10d, HBCA.

75. Fort Simpson Journal, 1831, B. 200/a/14 fos. 11d, HBCA.

76. Fort Simpson Journal, 1831, B. 200/a/14 fos. 12d, HBCA.

77. Ibid.

78. Fort Simpson Journal, 1831, B. 200/a/14 fos. 13, HBCA.

79. Fort Simpson Journal, 1831, B. 200/a/14 fos. 13d, HBCA. McLeod named the mountains after Nicholas Garry, deputy governor of the company, and John George McTavish, chief factor.

80. Ibid.

81. Ibid.

82. Ibid.

83. Fort Simpson Journal, 1831, B. 200/a/14 fos. 13d–14, HBCA.

84. Ibid.

85. Ibid.

86. Ibid.

87. Fort Simpson Journal, 1831, B. 200/a/14 fos. 14d, HBCA.

88. Ibid.

89. Ibid.

90. G. P. DeT. Glazebrook, ed., *The Hargrave Correspondence, 1821–1843*, p. 84.

91. Ibid.

92. "The Character Book of George Simpson, 1832," in Williams, ed., *Hudson's Bay Miscellany*, p. 93.

93. Baron von Wrangel to the Board of Directors, Russian American Company, April 28, 1834, *Proceedings of the Alaskan Boundary Tribunal, Convened at London . . . under the Treaty Concluded at Washington, January 24, 1903*, 2: 266–67. Hereafter the proceedings will be referred to as *ABT*.

94. Anglo-Russian Convention of 1825, *ABT*, 2: 15.

95. Gloria Griffen Cline, *Peter Skene Ogden and the Hudson's Bay Company*, p. 113.

96. Ibid., p. 114.

97. Report of Chief Trader Peter Skene Ogden of Transactions at Stikine, 1834, *ABT*, 2: 266.

98. Cline, *Peter Skene Ogden*, p. 115.

99. Baron von Wrangel to the Board of Directors, Russian American Company, April 30, 1835, *ABT*, 2: 276.

100. "The Character Book of George Simpson, 1832," in Williams, ed., *Hudson's Bay Miscellany*, p. 193.

101. Cline, *Peter Skene Ogden*, p. 115.

102. Ibid.

103. Baron von Wrangel to the Board of Directors, Russian American Company, April 30, 1835, *ABT*, 2: 275–77.

104. Lord Durham to Count Nesselrode, November 29, 1835, *ABT*, 2: 287.

105. Count Nesselrode to Lord Durham, December 21, 1835, *ABT*, 2: 288.

106. Board of Directors of the Russian American Company to the Department of Trade and Manufacturers, January 3, 1836, *ABT*, 2: 289–90.

107. "The Character Book of George Simpson, 1832," in Williams, ed., *Hudson's Bay Miscellany*, p. 176.

108. Ibid., p. 175.

109. Ibid., p. 174.

110. Ibid., p. 175. Stuart would have done better minding his own domestic front. Shortly after reaching Fort Simpson, his country wife began an affair with a young postmaster. Although the marriage was eventually patched up, Stuart would later abandon the wife when he returned to Great Britain. For more details on the problems of fur-trade women see Sylvia Van Kirk, *Many Tender Ties: Women in Fur Trade Society, 1670–1870* (Winnipeg: Watson & Dwyer, 1981).

111. E. H. Oliver, ed., *The Canadian North-West: Its Early Development and Legislative Records*, 2: 692.

112. Governor Simpson to Edward Smith, July 5, 1834, D. 4/20 fos. 16d, HBCA.

113. Fort Halkett Journal, 1834, B. 85/a/6 fos. 1, HBCA.

114. Ibid.

115. Morse, *Fur Trade Canoe Routes of Canada*, p. 5.

116. Fort Halkett Journal, B. 85/a/6 fos. 1d, HBCA.

117. Robert Campbell later named the stream the Caribou River. Modern maps refer to it as the Blue River.

118. Fort Halkett Journal, 1834, B. 85/a/6 fos. 2d, HBCA.

119. Fort Halkett Journal, 1834, B. 85/a/6 fos. 3, HBCA.

120. Ibid.

121. Ibid.

122. Fort Halkett Journal, 1834, B. 85/a/6 fos. 3d, HBCA.

123. Ibid.

124. Fort Halkett Journal, 1834, B. 85/a/6 fos. 4, HBCA.

125. Ibid.

126. Fort Halkett Journal, 1834, B. 85/a/6 fos. 3d, HBCA.

127. Fort Halkett Journal, 1834, B. 85/a/6 fos. 4, HBCA.

128. Fort Halkett Journal, B. 85/a/6 fos. 4d, HBCA.

129. Ibid.

130. Ibid. John Norquoy, a longtime servant of the company, was the father of the first premier of Manitoba. Clifford Wilson, *Campbell of the Yukon*, p. 12.

131. Fort Halkett Journal, 1834, B. 85/a/6 fos. 5, HBCA.

132. Fort Halkett Journal, 1834, B. 85/a/6 fos. 5d, HBCA.

133. R. M. Patterson, *Trail to the Interior*, p. 54.

134. Fort Halkett Journal, 1834, B. 85/a/6 fos. 5, HBCA.

135. Ibid.

136. Ibid.

137. Fort Halkett Journal, 1834, B. 85/a/6 fos. 5d, HBCA.

138. Ibid.

139. Ibid.

140. Ibid.

141. Governor Simpson to John McLeod and Murdock McPherson, July 4, 1834, D. 4/20 fos. 15, HBCA.

142. Edward Smith to Governor Simpson and Council of Northern Department, B. 200/b/7 fos. 49, HBCA.

CHAPTER 6

1. Robert Campbell, *Two Journals of Robert Campbell (Chief Factor, Hudson's Bay Company), 1808 to 1853: Autobiographical Journal—1808 to 1851, Later Journal—1850 to Feb. 1853*, ed. John W. Todd, Jr., p. 1.

2. Robert M. Ballantyne, *Hudson's Bay, or Everyday Life in the Wilds of North America, During Six Years' Residence in the Territories of the Honourable Hudson's Bay Company*, p. xii.

3. Campbell, *Two Campbell Journals*, p. 3.

4. Ballantyne, *Hudson's Bay*, pp. 72–73.

5. Ibid.

6. Campbell, *Two Campbell Journals*, pp. 10–11.

7. Ibid., p. 27.

8. Ibid., p. 29.

9. Ibid., p. 30.

10. E. H. Oliver, ed., *The Canadian North-West: Its Early Development and Legislative Records*, vol. 2, *Minutes of the Northern Department Council*, p. 712.

11. G. P. De T. Glazebrook, ed., *Hargrave Correspondence, 1821–1843*, p. 233.

12. Fort Simpson Post Journal, March 20, 1836, MG. 19D6, Public Archives of Canada, Ottawa, Ontario. Hereafter this repository is referred to as PAC.

13. Fort Simpson Post Journal, April 9, 1836, MG. 19D6, PAC.

14. Glazebrook, ed., *Hargrave Correspondence, 1821–1843*, p. 243.

15. Ibid., p. 254.

16. Oliver, ed., *Canadian North-West*, p. 728. The council made this resolution as if it were a matter of convenience; servants going out of the Mackenzie District to Europe via York Factory would have an easier journey than those trying to reach Canada.

17. Governor Simpson to Murdock McPherson, June 30, 1836, D. 4/22 fos. 42, Hudson's Bay Company Archives, Winnipeg, Manitoba. Hereafter this repository will be referred to as HBCA. Spelling errors are not corrected.

18. Fort Simpson Journal, 1836, B. 200/c/1 fos. 2d, HBCA.

19. Murdock McPherson to Governor Simpson and Northern Department Council, November 30, 1836, D. 5/4 fos. 211d, HBCA.

20. Ibid.

21. "The Character Book of George Simpson, 1832," in Glyndwr Williams, ed., *Hudson's Bay Miscellany, 1670–1870*, p. 213.

22. Governor Simpson to Murdock McPherson, June 30, 1837, D. 4/23 fos. 49d–50, HBCA.

23. Glazebrook, ed., *Hargrave Correspondence, 1821–1843*, p. 272.

24. Campbell, *Two Campbell Journals*, p. 32.

25. Ibid.

26. Ibid.

27. Ibid.

28. Ibid., p. 34.

29. Ibid., p. 35.

30. Ibid., p. 36.

31. Jennifer Brown, "Ultimate Respectability: Fur Trade Children in the Civilized World," *The Beaver*, Spring, 1978, p. 51.

32. Campbell, *Two Campbell Journals*, p. 38.

33. Ibid., p. 39.

34. Ibid., pp. 39–40.

35. Ibid., p. 40.

36. For a colorful account of a legendary battle between the Tlingits and the Tahltans, see Anton Money, *This Was the North*, pp. 27–32.

37. Catharine McClellan, *My Old People Say: An Ethnographic Survey of the Southern Yukon Territory*, 2: 510–11.

38. G. T. Emmons, "The Tahltan Indians," *University of Pennsylvania Museum Publications in Anthropology* 4 (January, 1911): 5–6.

39. McClellan, *My Old People Say*, pp. 511–14.

40. Campbell, *Two Campbell Journals*, p. 41.

41. Ibid., p. 42.

42. Ibid.

43. Glazebrook, ed., *Hargrave Correspondence, 1821–1843*, p. 271. Campbell does not mention the presence of the Russians in his autobiographical journal. Our source is a letter from Murdock McPherson to James Hargrave of November 24, 1838. McPherson interviewed Campbell about the incident only a few weeks after it occurred, and in other respects McPherson's brief account agrees with Campbell's detailed story.

44. Campbell, *Two Campbell Journals*, p. 43.

45. Ibid.

46. Ibid., p. 44.

47. Ibid.

48. Ibid., p. 43.

49. Ibid., p. 45.

50. Ibid., p. 46.

51. Glazebrook, ed., *Hargrave Correspondence, 1821–1843*, p. 271.

52. Campbell, *Two Campbell Journals*, p. 47.

53. Ibid.

54. Ibid., p. 49.

55. Ibid., p. 40.

56. Ibid., pp. 51–52.

57. Ibid., p. 51.

58. Ibid., p. 53.

59. Ibid., p. 55.

60. Ibid., p. 56.

61. John S. Galbraith, *The Hudson's Bay Company as an Imperial Factor*, p. 151.

62. E. E. Rich, *History of the Hudson's Bay Company, 1670–1870*, pp. 653–54.

63. Galbraith, *Hudson's Bay Company as an Imperial Factor*, p. 10.

64. John Franklin, *Narrative of a Second Expedition to the Shores of the Polar Sea in the Years 1825, 1826, and 1827*, p. 2.

65. Ibid., p. 180.

66. Ibid., p. 182.

67. R. Harvey Fleming, ed., *Minutes of Council, Northern Department of Rupert's Land, 1821–31*, p. 179.

68. Ethel G. Stewart, "Fort McPherson and the Peel River Area" (M.A. thesis, Queen's University, Kingston, Ontario, 1955), p. 339.

69. Fleming, ed., *Minutes of Council, Northern Department*, p. 235.

70. Peter Warren Dease to Governor Simpson, September 5, 1837, D. 5/4 fos. 327–327d, HBCA. On modern maps the Colville River is spelled with two *l*s, unlike the name Colvile.

CHAPTER 7

1. G. P. De T. Glazebrook, ed., *The Hargrave Correspondence, 1821–1843*, pp. 253–54.

2. "The Character Book of George Simpson, 1832," in Glyndwr Williams, ed., *Hudson's Bay Miscellany, 1670–1870*, p. 213.

3. John Richardson, *Arctic Searching Expedition: A Journal of a Boat-Voyage in Search of the Discovery Ships Under the Command of Sir John Franklin Through Rupert's Land and the Arctic Sea*, p. 74.

4. Ibid., p. 79.

5. Glazebrook, ed., *Hargrave Correspondence, 1821–1843*, p. 223.

6. Governor Simpson to Murdock McPherson, May 31, 1838, D. 4/23 fos. 160–160d, Hudson's Bay Company Archives, Winnipeg, Manitoba. Hereafter this repository will be referred to as HBCA. Grammatical and spelling errors are reproduced verbatim.

7. Ethel G. Stewart, "Fort McPherson and the Peel River Area" (Master's thesis, Queen's University, Kingston, Ontario, 1955), p. 343.

8. R. G. McConnell, "Report on an Exploration in the Yukon and Mackenzie Basins, N.W.T.," *Geological and Natural History Survey of Canada Reports for the Year 1887*, Part D, p. 115.

9. Alexander Kennedy Isbister, "Some Account of the Peel River, N. America," *Journal of the Royal Geographic Society* 15 (1845): 336.

10. John Bell to Murdock McPherson, August 11, 1839, B. 200/b/12 fos. 2d, HBCA.

11. Ibid.

12. Isbister, "Some Account of Peel River, N. America," *Journal of the Royal Society* 15 (1845): 337.

13. Ibid., p. 338.

14. John Bell to Murdock McPherson, August 11, 1839, B. 200/b/12 fos. 3, HBCA.

15. Richardson, *Arctic Searching Expedition*, p. 378.

16. Isbister, "Some Account of Peel River, N. America," *Journal of the Royal Geographic Society* 15 (1845): 338.

17. John Bell to Murdock McPherson, August 11, 1839, B. 200/b/12 fos. 2d, HBCA.

18. Governor Simpson to Murdock McPherson, February 28, 1838, D. 4/24, fos. 5, HBCA.

19. Glazebrook, ed., *Hargrave Correspondence, 1821–1843*, p. 294.

20. Isbister, "Some Account of Peel River, N. America," *Journal of the Royal Geographic Society* 15 (1845): 335.

21. Peel River Post Journal, B. 157/a/1 fos. 1, HBCA.

22. Isbister fared well in his studies, eventually becoming a barrister in London. He also became an influential advisor to the British government on North American affairs, opposing the Hudson's Bay Company. He was a powerful ally of the expansionist party in Canada, which eventually succeeded in taking control of Rupert's Land and forming Canada as the continental nation that it is today. W. L. Morton, *The Critical Years: The Union of British North America, 1857–1873*, pp. 29 and 81.

23. Peel River Post Journal, B. 157/a/1 fos. 10, HBCA.

24. Isbister, "Some Account of Peel River, N. America," *Journal of the Royal Geographic Society* 15 (1845): 339.

25. Glazebrook, ed., *Hargrave Correspondence, 1821–1843*, pp. 359–60.

26. Stewart, "Fort McPherson and the Peel River Area," p. 346.

27. E. H. Oliver, ed., *The Canadian North-West: Its Early Development and Legislative Records*, vol. 2, *Minutes of Northern Department Council*, p. 776.

28. Murdock McPherson to Robert Campbell, March 29, 1840, B. 200/b/12 fos. 7d, HBCA.

29. Ibid.

30. George M. Dawson, "Report on an Exploration in the Yukon District, N.W.T. and Adjacent Northern Portion of British Columbia," *Geological Survey of Canada Report, 1889*, p. 103.

31. Fenley Hunter, *Frances Lake, Yukon*, pp. 37–41.

32. Anton Money, with Ben East, *This Was the North*, p. 93.

33. Robert Campbell, *Two Journals of Robert Campbell (Chief Factor, Hudson's Bay Company), 1808 to 1853: Autobiographical Journal— 1808 to 1851, Later Journal—1850 to 1853*, ed. John W. Todd, Jr., p. 58.

34. Ibid.

35. Dawson, "Report on an Exploration in the Yukon District," *Geological Survey of Canada Report, 1889*, p. 115.

36. Campbell, *Two Campbell Journals*, p. 59.

37. Ibid.

38. Ibid.

39. Ibid.

40. Ibid., p. 60.

41. "The Character Book of George Simpson, 1832," in Glyndwr Williams, ed., *Hudson's Bay Miscellany, 1670–1870*, p. 185.

42. Glazebrook, ed., *Hargrave Correspondence, 1821–1843*, p. 329.

43. Governor Simpson to John Lee Lewes, December 1, 1842, D. 4/28 fos. 3, HBCA.

44. Clifford Wilson, *Campbell of the Yukon*, p. 43, quoting a letter from Robert Campbell to John Lee Lewes.

45. Ibid.

46. Glazebrook, ed., *Hargrave Correspondence, 1821–1843*, p. 319.

47. Ibid.

48. Ibid.

49. Campbell, *Two Campbell Journals*, p. 60.

50. John Lewes to Governor Simpson, November 20, 1840, D. 5/5 fos. 371, HBCA.

51. Campbell, *Two Campbell Journals*, pp. 60–61.

52. John Lee Lewes to Governor Simpson, November 20, 1841, D. 5/5 fos. 371–371d, HBCA.

53. Jennifer Brown, "Ultimate Respectability: Fur Trade Children in the Civilized World," *The Beaver*, Spring, 1978, p. 52.

54. Campbell, *Two Campbell Journals*, p. 61.

55. Frances Lake Post Journal, B. 73/a/1 fos. 6, HBCA.

56. John A. Hussey, "Unpretending but not Indecent: Living Quarters at Mid-19th-Century H.B.C. Posts," *The Beaver*, Spring, 1975, p. 15.

57. Frances Lake Journal, B. 73/a/1 fos. 9d, HBCA.

58. Campbell, *Two Campbell Journals*, p. 64.

59. Ibid., pp. 61–62.

60. Robert Campbell to Sir George Simpson, May 26, 1843, D. 5/8 fos. 269–269d, HBCA.

61. Ibid.

62. Ibid.

63. Ibid.

64. James W. Vanstone, *Athapascan Adaptations: Hunters and Fishermen of the Subarctic Forests*, p. 68.

65. Campbell, *Two Campbell Journals*, pp. 65–66.

66. Ibid.

67. Dawson, "Report on an Exploration in the Yukon District," *Geological Survey of Canada Report, 1889*, pp. 120–23.

68. Ibid.

69. Campbell, *Two Campbell Journals*, p. 67.

70. Catharine McClellan, *My Old People Say: An Ethnographic Survey of the Southern Yukon Territory*, 1: 22.

71. Campbell, *Two Campbell Journals*, p. 68.

72. Ibid.

73. Robert Campbell to Governor George Simpson, May 26, 1843, D. 5/8 fos. 268d, HBCA.

74. Campbell, *Two Campbell Journals*, p. 69.

75. Ibid.

76. Ibid.

77. The tent was a luxury usually reserved for company officers. The voyageurs normally slept under the stars or, when it rained, huddled under the canoe.

78. Hervey's *Meditations Among the Tombs* were originally published in London in 1746. A second edition in two volumes was published in London in 1748 with the title *Meditations and Contemplations*. The description of the camp and subsequent events is in Campbell, *Two Campbell Journals*, p. 70.

79. Campbell, *Two Campbell Journals*, p. 70.

80. Ibid.

81. Sir George Simpson to John Lee Lewes, June 5, 1843, D. 4/28 fos. 50d, HBCA.

82. Sir George Simpson to Robert Campbell, June 3, 1844, D. 4/31 fos. 49, HBCA.

83. Glazebrook, ed., *Hargrave Correspondence, 1821–1843*, p. 378.

84. Ibid., p. 379.

85. Ibid., p. 378.

86. Ibid., p. 402.

87. Sir George Simpson to John Lee Lewes, June 5, 1843, D. 4/28 fos. 50d–51, HBCA.

88. Oliver, ed., *Canadian North-West*, 2: 692.

89. Richardson, *Arctic Search Expedition*, pp. 165 and 170.

90. Fort Simpson Post Journal, October 28, 1834, MG 19D6, Public Archives of Canada, Ottawa, Ontario. Hereafter this repository will be referred to as PAC.

91. Fort Simpson Journal, December, 1826–February, 1827, PAC.

92. John Henry Lefroy, *In Search of the Magnetic North: John Henry Lefroy, A Soldier Surveyor's Letters from the North-West 1843–1844*, ed. George F. G. Stanley, p. 114.

93. Captain Robert F. Scott's two Antarctic expeditions between 1901 and 1904 and 1910 and 1912 both suffered from scurvy. Scott believed that the disease was caused by tainted canned and preserved foods rather than by a lack of fresh food.

94. Campbell, *Two Campbell Journals*, p. 46.

95. Dawson, "Report on an Exploration in the Yukon District," *Geological Survey of Canada Report, 1889*, p. 140.

96. Glazebrook, ed., *Hargrave Correspondence, 1821–1843*, p. 323.

97. Ibid., p. 324.

98. Ibid., pp. 377 and 327.
99. Ibid., p. 323.
100. Ibid., p. 325.
101. Ibid., p. 322.

CHAPTER 8

1. Peel River Post Journal, 1842, B. 157/a/2 fos. 3, Hudson's Bay Company Archives, Winnipeg, Manitoba. Hereafter this collection will be referred to as HBCA. Grammatical and spelling errors are reproduced verbatim.
2. Ibid.
3. G. P. de T. Glazebrook, ed., *The Hargrave Correspondence, 1821–1843*, p. 407.
4. Alexander Hunter Murray, *Journal of the Yukon, 1847–1848, by Alexander Hunter Murray*, ed. Lawrence J. Burpee, Publications of the Canadian Archives, no. 4, pp. 35–36.
5. Shepard Krech, III, "On the Aboriginal Population of the Kutchin," *Arctic Anthropology* 15 (1978) : 97.
6. Glazebrook, ed., *Hargrave Correspondence, 1821–1843*, p. 360.
7. Peel River Post Journal, 1842, B. 157/a/2 fos. 7, HBCA.
8. Sir George Simpson to John Lee Lewes, December 1, 1842, D. 4/28 fos. 3, HBCA.
9. Sir George Simpson to John Lee Lewes, June 5, 1843, D. 4/28 fos. 52, HBCA.
10. Peel River Post Journal, 1842, B. 157/a/2 fos. 6d, HBCA.
11. John Bell to John Lee Lewes, November 17, 1843, B. 157/a/2 fos. 6d, HBCA.
12. R. G. McConnell, "Report on an Exploration in the Yukon and Mackenzie Basins, N.W.T." *Geological and Natural History Survey of Canada Reports for the Year 1887*, p. 116.
13. Ibid., p. 117.
14. Peel River Post Journal, B. 157/a/2 fos. 7d, HBCA.
15. McConnell, "Report on the Yukon and Mackenzie Basins," *Geological Survey of Canada*, p. 118.
16. Peel River Post Journal, B. 157/a/2 fos. 7d, HBCA. In a letter to James Hargrave, dated August 22, 1842, Bell says that he took five days to cross the mountains (Glazebrook, ed., *Hargrave Correspondence. 1821–1843*, p. 382) , but he mentions only a four-day journey in a November 17, 1842, letter to Chief Factor Lewes (Peel River Post Journal B. 200/b/15 fos. 5, HBCA) . I have used the four-day figure because the Peel River Post Journal account of the trip, written the day after Bell returned, mentions four days.
17. John Bell to John Lee Lewes, November 17, 1842, B. 200/b/15 fos. 5, HBCA.
18. McConnell, "Report on the Yukon and Mackenzie Basins," *Geological Survey of Canada*, p. 121.
19. John Bell to John Lee Lewes, November 17, 1842, B. 200/b/15 fos. 5, HBCA.

20. Peel River Post Journal, 1842, B. 157/a/2 fos. 7d, HBCA.

21. John Bell to John Lee Lewes, November 17, 1842, B. 200/b/15 fos. 5d, HBCA.

22. Ibid.

23. Peel River Post Journal, 1842, B. 157/a/2 fos. 7d, HBCA.

24. Glazebrook, ed., *Hargrave Correspondence, 1821–1843*, p. 408.

25. Ibid.

26. Ibid.

27. William C. Wonders, "Athabasca Pass: Gateway to the Pacific," *Canadian Geological Journal*, December, 1974, p. 26.

28. Peel River Post Journal, 1843, B. 157/a/3 fos. 7d, HBCA.

29. For the early explorers there were two Rat Rivers. One was west of the mountains and is today known as the Bell River, while the eastern river is now properly known as the Rat River.

30. Peel River Post Journal, 1843, B. 157/a/3 fos. 7–7d, HBCA.

31. Ibid.

32. Richard Slobodin, "Eastern Kutchin Warfare," *Anthropologica* 2, no. 1 (1960) : 90–92.

33. Murdock McPherson to Sir George Simpson, November 18, 1845, D. 5/15 fos. 464d, HBCA.

34. John Rae, *John Rae's Correspondence with the Hudson's Bay Company on Arctic Exploration, 1844–1855*, ed. E. E. Rich, p. 130.

35. E. H. Oliver, ed., *The Canadian North-West: Its Early Development and Legislative Records*, vol. 2, *Minutes of the Northern Department Council*, p. 727.

36. Adam McBeath to John Lee Lewes, August 1, 1843, B. 200/b/18 fos. 1, HBCA.

37. Journal of an Attempt to Ascend the Gravel River by A. M. McBeath, 1843, B. 200/b/18 fos. 32, HBCA.

38. Gravel River Journal, 1843, B. 200/b/18 fos. 32d, HBCA.

39. Ibid.

40. Gravel River Journal, 1843, B. 200/b/18 fos. 33, HBCA.

41. Ibid.

42. Ibid.

43. Ibid.

44. Ibid.

45. Gravel River Journal, 1843, B. 200/b/18 fos. 34, HBCA.

46. Ibid.

47. Ibid.

48. Ibid.

49. Governor Simpson to John Lee Lewes, December 14, 1843, D. 4/30 fos. 23d, HBCA.

50. William Lucas Hardisty, "The Loucheux Indians," *Annual Report of the Smithsonian Institution for 1866*, pp. 311–20.

51. Robert Campbell, *Two Journals of Robert Campbell (Chief Factor, Hudson's Bay Company), 1808 to 1853: Autobiographical Journal—1808 to 1851, Later Journal—1850 to Feb. 1853*, ed. John W. Todd, Jr., p. 73.

52. Ibid.

53. Robert Campbell to Sir George Simpson, October 23, 1843, D. 5/9 fos. 13, HBCA.

55. Catharine McClellan, *My Old People Say: An Ethnographic Survey of Southern Yukon Territory*, pp. 501–509.

56. Robert Campbell to Sir George Simpson, May 16, 1844, D. 5/11 fos. 226, HBCA.

57. Campbell, *Two Campbell Journals*, p. 73.

58. Anton Money with Ben East, *This Was the North*, p. 140.

59. Campbell, *Two Campbell Journals*, p. 73.

60. John Henry Lefroy, *In Search of the Magnetic North: A Soldier-Surveyor's Letters from the North-West, 1843–1844*, ed. George F. G. Stanley, p. 98.

61. Campbell, *Two Campbell Journals*, p. 73.

62. Ibid.

63. "The Character Book of George Simpson, 1832," in Glyndwr Williams, ed., *Hudson's Bay Miscellany, 1670–1870*, p. 223.

64. Campbell, *Two Campbell Journals*, p. 74.

65. Ibid.

66. Robert Campbell to Sir George Simpson, October 31, 1844, D. 5/12 fos. 428, HBCA.

67. Lefroy, *In Search of the Magnetic North*, p. 154.

68. John McLean, *Notes of a Twenty-five Years' Service in the Hudson's Bay Territories*, ed. Wallace W. Stewart, p. 344.

69. Ibid., p. 332.

70. Glazebrook, ed., *Hargrave Correspondence, 1821–1843*, p. 375.

71. Campbell, *Two Campbell Journals*, p. 76.

72. McLean, *Notes on a Twenty-five Years' Service in the Hudson's Bay Territories*, p. 346.

73. Ibid., p. 308.

74. John Bell to Murdock McPherson, December 31, 1844, B. 200/b/15 fos. 25.

75. John Bell to Murdock McPherson, April 9, 1845, B. 200/b/15 fos. 27.

76. Murdock McPherson to Sir George Simpson, November 18, 1845, D. 5/15 fos. 464, HBCA.

77. McConnell, "Report on the Yukon and Mackenzie Basins," *Geological Survey of Canada, 1891*, p. 129.

78. Murdock McPherson to Sir George Simpson, November 18, 1845, D. 5/15 fos. 464, HBCA.

79. Ibid.

80. Ibid.

81. Ibid.

82. Ibid.

83. Murdock McPherson to Sir George Simpson, November 28, 1845, D. 5/15 fos. 466, HBCA.

84. Ibid.

85. Governor Simpson to Robert Campbell, June 1, 1845, D. 4/32 fos. 94d, HBCA.

86. Pierre Berton, *The Klondike Fever: The Life and Times of the Last Great Gold Rush*, p. 7.

87. Lavrentiy Alekseyevich Zagoskin, *Lieutenant Zagoskin's Travels in Russian America, 1842–1844*, ed. Henry N. Michael, p. 10.

88. James Vanstone, ed., "Russian Explorations in Interior Alaska: An

Extract from the Journal of Andrei Glazunov," *Pacific Northwest Quarterly*, April, 1959, p. 37.

89. Zagoskin, *Travels in Russian America*, p. 10.

90. Ibid., p. 15.

91. Ibid., p. 159.

92. Ibid., p. 162.

93. Ibid.

94. Ibid., p. 16.

95. Ibid., p. 173.

96. Ibid., p. 162.

97. Ibid., pp. 169–71.

98. Ibid., p. 174.

99. Ibid., p. 175.

100. Ibid., p. 183.

101. Governor Simpson to Robert Campbell, June 3, 1844, D. 4/31 fos. 49, HBCA.

102. Sir George Simpson, *Fur Trade and Empire: George Simpson's Journal, 1824–1825*, ed. Frederick Merk, p. xxvi.

103. Glazebrook, ed., *Hargrave Correspondence, 1821–1843*, p. 321.

104. Ibid.

CHAPTER 9

1. Robert Campbell to Sir George Simpson, September 12, 1845, D. 5/15 fos. 69d–70, Hudson's Bay Company Archives, Winnipeg, Canada. Hereafter this repository will be referred to as HBCA. Grammatical and spelling errors are reproduced verbatim.

2. Robert Campbell, *Two Journals of Robert Campbell (Chief Factor, Hudson's Bay Company), 1808 to 1853: Autobiographical Journal— 1808 to 1852, Later Journal—1850 to Feb. 1853*, ed. J. W. Todd, Jr., p. 77.

3. Ibid.

4. Robert Campbell to Sir George Simpson, March 29, 1846, D. 5/17 fos. 235, HBCA.

5. Clifford Wilson, *Campbell of the Yukon*, p. 86.

6. Governor Simpson to Murdock McPherson, June 3, 1845, D. 4/32 fos. 114d, HBCA.

7. Governor Simpson to Robert Campbell, June 3, 1846, D. 4/34 fos. 93d, HBCA.

8. Robert Campbell to Sir George Simpson, August 23, 1847, D. 5/20 fos. 134, HBCA.

9. Campbell, *Two Campbell Journals*, p. 78.

10. Robert Campbell to Sir George Simpson, August 23, 1847, D. 5/20 fos. 133–34, HBCA.

11. Robert Campbell to Sir George Simpson, March 28, 1848, D. 5/24 fos. 506d, HBCA.

12. Campbell, *Two Campbell Journals*, pp. 79–80.

13. Ibid.

14. Ibid.

15. John Rae, *John Rae's Correspondence with the Hudson's Bay Company on Arctic Exploration, 1844–1855*, ed. E. E. Rich, p. 170.

16. Campbell, *Two Campbell Journals*, p. 80.

17. Ibid., p. 81.

18. Ibid., pp. 81–82.

19. Ibid., p. 82.

20. Ibid.

21. Ibid., p. 83.

22. Ibid.

23. Robert Campbell to Sir George Simpson, September 14, 1848, D. 5/22 fos. 665, HBCA.

24. Alexander Hunter Murray, *Journal of the Yukon, 1847–1848, by Alexander Hunter Murray*, ed. Lawrence J. Burpee, Publications of the Canadian Archives, no. 4, p. 1.

25. Ibid., pp. 9–10.

26. Rae, *Arctic Correspondence*, p. 141.

27. Alexander Hunter Murray to Sir George Simpson, November 25, 1845, D. 5/15 fos. 446, HBCA.

28. Bernard Rogan Ross, "Fur Trade Gossip Sheet," *The Beaver*, Spring, 1955, pp. 17–18.

29. Alexander Hunter Murray to Sir George Simpson, November 25, 1845, D. 5/15 fos. 445, HBCA.

30. Ibid.

31. Murdock McPherson to Governor Simpson, July 7, 1846, B. 200/b/21 fos. 2d, HBCA.

32. Robert Kennicott, "The Journal of Robert Kennicott, May 19, 1859–January 20, 1862," in A. J. James, ed., *The First Scientific Exploration of Russian America, and the Purchase of Alaska*, p. 28.

33. Hunter, *Journal of the Yukon*, pp. 21–22.

34. Ibid., p. 25.

35. Ibid., p. 26.

36. Ibid., p. 27.

37. Ibid., pp. 30–31.

38. Ibid., p. 35.

39. Ibid., p. 43.

40. Ibid., pp. 42–43.

41. Ibid., p. 49.

42. Ibid., p. 45.

43. Ibid., p. 52.

44. Ibid., p. 61.

45. Ibid. It is doubtful that the Han Indians ever participated in a skirmish with the Russians. The Hans were probably referring to the Tlingit Indians, who often fought with the Russians in the first decades of the nineteenth century.

46. Ibid.

47. Ibid.

48. Ibid., pp. 66–67.

49. Ibid., p. 78.

50. Ibid., pp. 75–76. In his journal Murray confuses the Pelly with the Lewes River. When he describes one, he means the other.

51. Sir John Richardson, *Arctic Searching Expedition, A Journal of a*

Boat-Voyage Through Rupert's Land and the Arctic Sea in Search of the Discovery Ships Under the Command of Sir John Franklin (London: Longman, Brown, Green, and Longmans, 1851), map.

52. For a good general account of the Franklin search expeditions, see Leslie H. Neatby, *The Search for Franklin* (Edmonton, Alta: M. G. Hurtig, 1970).

53. Richardson, *Arctic Searching Expedition*, pp. 143–44.

54. Rae, *Arctic Correspondence*, p. liv.

55. W. J. S. Pullen, "Pullen in the Search for Franklin," *The Beaver*, June, 1947, p. 22.

56. Rae, *Arctic Correspondence*, p. 174.

57. Ibid., pp. 175–76.

58. Ibid., p. 119.

59. Ibid., pp. 130–31.

60. Neatby, *The Search for Franklin*, pp. 220–21.

61. Robert Campbell to Sir George Simpson, March 28, 1849, D. 5/24 fos. 506d, HBCA.

62. Rae, *Arctic Correspondence*, p. 87.

63. Campbell, *Two Campbell Journals*, p. 84.

64. Ibid., p. 85.

65. Ibid., p. 86.

66. Ibid., p. 87.

67. Rae, *Arctic Correspondence*, p. 131.

68. Lieutenant W. H. Hooper, R.N., *Ten Months Among the Tents of the Tuski, With Incidents of a Arctic Boat Expedition in Search of Sir John Franklin*, pp. 330–33.

69. Campbell, *Two Campbell Journals*, p. 88.

70. Ibid.

71. Rae, *Arctic Correspondence*, p. 131.

72. Campbell, *Two Campbell Journals*, p. 88.

73. Ibid., p. 89.

74. Ibid.

75. Ibid., p. 27.

76. Catharine McClellan, "Indian Stories about the First Whites in Northwestern America," in *Ethnohistory in Southwestern Alaska and the Southern Yukon: Method and Content*, ed. Margaret Lantis, p. 111.

77. "The Character Book of George Simpson, 1832," in Glyndwr Williams, ed., *Hudson's Bay Miscellany, 1670–1870*, p. 158.

78. Campbell, *Two Campbell Journals*, pp. 94–95.

79. Robert Campbell to George Simpson, May 26, 1843, D. 5/8 fos. 286d, HBCA.

80. Campbell, *Two Campbell Journals*, p. 93.

81. Ibid., p. 97.

82. Ibid., p. 98.

83. Ibid., pp. 115–17.

84. Ibid., p. 123.

85. Robert Campbell to Donald Ross, August 30, 1851, quoted in J. R. Kirk and C. Parnell, "Campbell of the Yukon," *The Beaver*, December, 1942, p. 24.

86. Eden Colvile was made governor of Rupert's Land in 1849. Sir George Simpson was the governor-in-chief.

87. James Anderson to Eden Colvile, November 22, 1851, MG 19 A 29, James Anderson Papers, Public Archives of Canada, Ottawa, Ontario. Hereafter this repository is referred to as PAC.

88. Harold A. Innis, *The Fur Trade in Canada*, rev. ed., p. 324.

89. Ibid.

90. James Anderson to Sir George Simpson, November 30, 1852, MG 19 A 29, James Anderson Papers, PAC.

91. Campbell, *Two Campbell Journals*, p. 109.

92. Ibid., p. 109.

93. Ibid., p. 126.

94. Ibid., p. 133.

95. Ibid.

96. Ibid., pp. 133–34.

97. Ibid.

98. Ibid.

99. Ibid., p. 135.

100. Ibid., p. 136.

101. Ibid.

102. Ibid., p. 137.

103. Report, Robert Campbell to James Anderson, November 4, 1852, quoted in Clifford Wilson, *Campbell of the Yukon*, p. 126.

104. James Anderson to Sir George Simpson, November 20, 1852, MG 19 A 29, James Anderson Papers, PAC.

105. Campbell, *Two Campbell Journals*, p. 146. This remarkable journey caused J. W. Waddy, the husband of Campbell's granddaughter, to note in the margin of the explorer's journal, "My God, what a man."

CHAPTER 10

1. Adrian Tanner, *Trappers, Hunters, and Fishermen: Wildlife Utilization in the Yukon Territory*, Yukon Research Projects Series no. 5, p. 11.

2. James Anderson to Sir George Simpson, November 20, 1852, MG 19 A 29, James Anderson Papers, Public Archives of Canada.

3. Sir George Simpson, *Fur Trade and Empire: Sir George Simpson's Journal, 1824–1825*, ed. Frederick Merk, rev. ed., p. 96 n.

4. James Anderson to John Ballenden, November 30, 1851, B. 200/b/ 26 fos. 11, Hudson's Bay Company Archives, Winnipeg, Manitoba. Hereafter this repository will be referred to as HBCA.

5. Catharine McClellan, *My Old People Say: An Ethnographic Survey of the Southern Yukon Territory*, 1: 317–18.

6. Alexander Hunter Murray, *Journal of the Yukon, 1847–1848*, ed. Lawrence H. Burpee, Publications of the Canadian Archives, no. 4, pp. 72, 67.

7. Ibid., p. 94.

8. McClellan, *My Old People Say*, pp. 506–507.

9. John Wilson to William Tolmie, August 27, 1869, A 1/85 fos. 21–22, HBCA.

10. B. D. Lain, "The Fort Yukon Affair, 1869," *The Alaska Journal* 7 (Winter, 1977) : 15–16.

11. G. P. De T. Glazebrook, ed., *The Hargrave Correspondence, 1821–1843*, p. 253.

12. John S. Galbraith, "The Enigma of Sir George Simpson," *The Beaver*, Spring, 1976, p. 9.

Bibliography

PRIMARY SOURCES

Unpublished

Winnipeg, Man. Hudson's Bay Company Archives, Provincial Archives of Manitoba. Sir George Simpson's Outward Correspondence, 1822–52, D. 4/2–D. 4/45; Sir George Simpson's Inward Correspondence, 1825–51, D. 5/1–D. 5/3; Northern Department General Accounts, 1825–26, B. 200/b/12–B. 200/a/26; Mackenzie District Report, 1822, B. 200/e/1; Fort Simpson Journal, 1822–31, B. 200/a/1–B. 200/a/14. Fort Halkett Journal, 1830–34, B. 85/a/1–B. 85/a/6; Peel River Post Journal, 1840–44, B. 157/a/1–B. 157/a/4; Frances Lake Post Journal, 1842–45, B. 73/a/1–B. 73/a/3; Fort Good Hope Journal, 1838–40, B. 80/a/14–B. 80/a/16; Fort Yukon Journal, 1847–52, B. 240/a/1–B. 240/a/5; Fort Selkirk Journal, 1848–52, B. 196/a/1–B. 196/a/3.
Chicago, Ill. Newberry Library. Ayer Collection, Laut Transcripts; Fort Simpson Post Journal, 1834; Peel River Post Journal, 1840; Journal of the Simpson's River Expedition, 1833.
Ottawa, Ont. Public Archives of Canada. Peel's River House Journals, 1847–53, MC 19D12; Fort Simpson Post Journals, 1826–27, vol. 1, MG 19D6; Fort Simpson Post Journals, 1834–37, vol. 2, MG 19D6; James Anderson Papers, 1808–1894, MG 19A25; Account of Mackenzie River, by Williard Ferdinand Wentzel, 1821, MC19A1.

Published

Alaskan Boundary Tribunal. *Proceedings of the Alaskan Bound-*

ary Tribunal, Convened at London Under the Treaty Concluded at Washington, January 24, 1903. Vols. 1–8. Washington, D.C.: Government Printing Office, 1903.

Back, George. *Narrative of the Arctic Land Expedition to the Mouth of the Great Fish River, and Along the Shores of the Arctic Ocean, in the Years 1833, 1834, and 1835.* Reprint. Edmonton: M. G. Hurtig, 1970.

Black, Samuel. *Black's Rocky Mountain Journal, 1824.* Edited by E. E. Rich. Introduction by R. M. Patterson. London: Hudson's Bay Record Society, 1955.

Campbell, Robert. *Two Journals of Robert Campbell (Chief Factor, Hudson's Bay Company), 1808 to 1853.* Edited by John W. Todd, Jr. Seattle: Shorey Books, 1958.

Canada, *Certain Correspondence of the Foreign Office and the Hudson's Bay Company.* Ottawa: Queen's Printer, 1899.

Cook, James, and James King. *A Voyage to the Pacific Ocean.* 3 vols. London: G. Nicol and T. Cadell, 1784.

Davies, K. G., ed. *Northern Quebec and Labrador Journals and Correspondence 1819–1825.* Introduction by Glyndwr Williams. London: Hudson's Bay Record Society, 1963.

Fleming, Harvey, ed. *Minutes of Council, Northern Department of Rupert's Land, 1821–31.* Introduction by H. A. Innis. London: Hudson's Bay Record Society, 1940.

Franklin, John. *Narrative of a Journey to the Shores of the Polar Sea in the Years 1819, 20, 21, and 22.* 1824 Reprint. Rutland, Vt.: Charles E. Tuttle, 1970.

———. *Narrative of a Second Expedition to the Shores of the Polar Sea in the Years 1825, 1826, and 1827.* 1828 Reprint. Edmonton: M. G. Hurtig, 1971.

Gates, Charles M., ed. *Five Fur Traders of the Northwest, Being the Narrative of Peter Pond, and the Diaries of John MacDonell, Archibald N. McLeod, Hugh Faries and Thomas Connor.* Saint Paul: Minnesota Historical Society, 1965.

Glazebrook, G. P. de T., ed. *The Hargrave Correspondence, 1821–1843.* Toronto: Champlain Society, 1938.

Hooper, W. H. *Ten Months Among the Tents of the Tuski, With Incidents of a Arctic Boat Expedition in Search of Sir John Franklin.* London: John Murray, 1853.

Houston, C. Stuart, ed. *To the Arctic by Canoe: The Journal and Paintings of Robert Hood, Midshipman with Franklin.* Montreal: Aeon Institute of North America and McGill-Queen's University Press, 1974.

Innis, Harold A., ed. "Rupert's Land in 1825." Minutes of the Hudson's Bay Company's Council of the Northern Department. *Canadian Historical Review* 7 (1926) : 303–320.

Isbister, Alexander Kennedy. "Some Account of the Peel River, N.

America." *Journal of the Royal Geographic Society* 15 (1845) : 335–41.

Lamb, W. Kaye, ed. *Sixteen Years in the Indian Country: The Journals of Daniel William Harmon.* Toronto: Macmillan of Canada, 1958.

Lefroy, John Henry. *In Search of the Magnetic North: John Henry Lefroy, A Soldier-Surveyor's Letters from the North-West, 1843–1844.* Edited by George F. G. Stanley. Toronto: Macmillan of Canada, 1955.

McDonald, Archibald. *Peace River, A Canoe Voyage From Hudson's Bay to the Pacific; by the Late Sir George Simpson; in 1828. Journal of the Chief Factor, Archibald McDonald, Who Accompanied Him.* Edited by Malcolm McLeod. Reprint. Edmonton, Alta.: M. G. Hurtig, 1971.

Mackenzie, Alexander. *Voyages from Montreal, on the River St. Lawrence, through the Continent of North America, to the Frozen and Pacific Oceans; in the Years 1789 and 1793. With a Preliminary Account of the Rise, Progress, and Present State of the Fur Trade of the Country.* London: R. Noble, 1801.

McLean, John. *Notes of a Twenty-five Years' Service in the Hudson's Bay Territories by John McLean.* Editted by Wallace W. Stewart. Toronto: Champlain Society, 1932.

McLeod, Margaret Arnett, ed. *The Letters of Letitia Hargrave.* Toronto: Champlain Society, 1947.

——— and Richard Glover, eds. "Franklin's First Expedititon as Seen by the Fur Traders." *Polar Record* 15 (1971) : 669–82.

Masson, L. R., ed. *Les bourgeois de la Compagnie du Nord-Ouest, récits de voyages, lettres et rapports inédits relatifs au nord-ouest Canadien.* 1889–90. Reprint. New York: Antiquarian Press, 1960.

Murray, Alexander Hunter. *Journal of the Yukon, 1847–1848, by Alexander Hunter Murray.* Edited by Lawrence J. Burpee. Publication of the Canadian Archives, no. 4. Ottawa: Government Printing Bureau, 1910.

Oliver, E. H., ed. *The Canadian North-West: Its Early Development and Legislative Records.* Ottawa: Government Printing Bureau, 1915. Vol. 2, *Minutes of the Northern Department Council.*

Pullen, W. J. S. "Pullen in the Search for Franklin." *Beaver,* June, 1947, pp. 22–25.

Rae, John. *John Rae's Correspondence with the Hudson's Bay Company on Arctic Exploration, 1844–1855.* Edited by E. E. Rich. Introduction by J. M. Wordie and R. J. Cyriax. London: Hudson's Bay Record Society, 1953.

Rezanov, Nikolai Petrovich. *The Rezanov Voyage to Nueva Cali-*

fornia in 1896. Edited by T. C. Russell. San Francisco: privately printed by T. C. Russell, 1926.

Rich, E. E., ed. *McLoughlin's Fort Vancouver Letters, 1825–38*. Introduction by W. Kaye Lamb. London: Hudson's Bay Record Society, 1944.

———. *McLoughlin's Fort Vancouver Letters, 1839–44*. Introduction by W. Kaye Lamb. London: Hudson's Bay Record Society, 1943.

———. *McLoughlin's Fort Vancouver Letters, 1844–46*. Introduction by W. Kaye Lamb. London: Hudson's Bay Record Society, 1944.

———. *Eden Colvile's Letters, 1849–52*. Introduction by W. L. Morton. London: Hudson's Bay Record Society, 1956.

———. *Colin Robertson's Correspondence Book, September 1817 to September 1822*. Introduction by E. E. Rich. London: Hudson's Bay Record Society, 1939.

———. *Simpson's 1828 Journey to the Columbia*. Introduction by W. Stewart Wallace. London: Hudson's Bay Record Society, 1947.

Richardson, John. *Arctic Searching Expedition: A Journal of a Boat-Voyage Through Rupert's Land the Arctic Sea in Search of the Discovery Ships under the Command of Sir John Franklin*. London: Longman, Brown, Green, and Longmans, 1851.

Rickman, John. *Journal of Captain Cook's Last Voyage to the Pacific Ocean*. Amsterdam: N. Israel, 1967.

Ross, Bernard Rogan. "Fur Trade Gossip Sheet." *Beaver*, Spring, 1955, pp. 17–18.

Simpson, Alexander. *The Life and Travels of Thomas Simpson, the Arctic Discover*. London: Edward Arnold, 1845.

Simpson, George. *Simpson's Athabaska Journal and Report, 1821–1822*. Edited by E. E. Rich. Introduction by Chester Martin. London: Hudson's Bay Record Society, 1938.

———. *Fur Trade and Empire: George Simpson's Journal, 1824–1825*. Edited by Frederick Merk. Revised edition. Cambridge, Mass.: Harvard University Press, 1968.

———. *Narrative of a Journey Round the World During the Years 1841–1842*. London: Henry Colburn, 1847.

———. "The Character Book of George Simpson, 1832." In *Hudson's Bay Miscellany, 1670–1870*, ed. Glyndwr Williams. Winnipeg: Hudson's Bay Record Society, 1975.

Simpson, Thomas. *Narrative of the Discoveries on the North Coast of America; Effected by the Officers of the Hudson's Bay Company During the Years 1836–39*. London: Richard Bentley, 1843.

Tolmie, William Fraser. *Journals of William Fraser Tolmie, Physician and Fur Trader*. Vancouver: Mitchell Press, 1963.

Vanstone, James W., ed. "V. S. Kromchenko's Coastal Explorations in Southwestern Alaska, 1822." *Fieldiana: Anthropology* 64 (1973).

———. "A. F. Kashevarov's Coastal Explorations in Northwest Alaska, 1838." *Fieldiana: Anthropology* 69 (1977).

———. "Russian Explorations in Interior Alaska: An Extract from the Journal of Andrei Glazunov." *Pacific Northwest Quarterly*, April, 1959, pp. 37-40.

Wallace, W. Stewart, ed. *Documents Relating to the North West Company.* Toronto: Champlain Society, 1934.

———. "Sir Henry Lefroy's Journey to the North-West in 1843-1844." *Transactions of the Royal Society of Canada*, Sect. II (1938), pp. 67-117.

Wentzel, W. F. "Notice Regarding the Map of Mackenzie's River by Mr. W. F. Wentzel of the Northwest Fur Company." *Memoirs of the Wernerian Natural History Society of Edinburgh* 4 (1822) :562-63, map.

———. "Notice of the Attempts to Reach the Sea by Mackenzie's River, Since the Expedition of Sir Alexander Mackenzie." *Edinburgh Philosophical Journal* 8 (1823) :78-79.

Williams, Glyndwr, ed. *Hudson's Bay Miscellany, 1670-1870.* Introduction by Glyndwyr Williams. Winnipeg: Hudson's Bay Record Society, 1975.

———. *Simpson's Letters to London, 1841-42.* Introduction by John S. Galbraith. London: Hudson's Bay Record Society, 1973.

Zagoskin, Lavrentiy Alekseyevich. *Lieutenant Zagoskin's Travels in Russian America, 1842-1844.* Edited by Henry N. Michael. Toronto: Arctic Institute of North America and University of Toronto Press, 1967.

SECONDARY SOURCES

Bancroft, H. H. *History of Alaska, 1730-1855.* San Francisco: History Company, 1886.

Bemis, Samuel F. *John Quincy Adams and the Foundations of American Foreign Policy.* New York: Alfred A. Knopf, 1950.

Berton, Pierre. *The Mysterious North.* New York: Alfred A. Knopf, 1956.

———. *The Klondike Fever: The Life and Times of the Last Great Gold Rush.* New York: Alfred A. Knopf, 1958.

Brown, Jennifer. "Ultimate Respectability: Fur Trade Children in the Civilized World." *Beaver*, Winter, 1944, pp. 4-10, and Spring, 1978, pp. 48-55.

Cameron, Alan E. "South Nahanni River." *Canadian Geographic Journal*, May, 1930.

Campbell, Marjorie Wilkins. *The North West Company.* Toronto: Macmillan of Canada, 1957.

Camsell, Charles. *Son of the North.* Toronto: Ryerson Press, 1954.

Caruthers, Wade C. "The Sea-Borne Frontier on the Northwest Coast." *Journal of the West* 10, no. 2 (April, 1971) : 211–57.

Chevigny, Hector. *Lord of Alaska: Baranov and the Russian Adventure.* New York: Viking Press, 1943.

———. *Lost Empire: The Life and Adventures of Nikolai Rezanov.* New York: Viking Press, 1943.

———. *Russian America, the Great Alaskan Venture, 1741–1867.* New York: Viking Press, 1965.

Cline, Gloria Griffen. *Peter Skene Ogden and the Hudson's Bay Company.* Norman: University of Oklahoma Press, 1974.

Cooke, Alan, and Clive Holland. "Chronological List of Expeditions and Historical Events in Northern Canada." *Polar Record,* nos. 24–30 (1968–71).

Crowe, Keith J. *A History of the Original Peoples of Northern Canada.* Montreal: Arctic Institute of North America and McGill-Queen's University Press, 1974.

Davidson, Donald Curtis. "Relations of the Hudson's Bay Company with the Russian American Company on the Northwest Coast, 1829–1867." *British Columbia Historical Quarterly* 5 (January, 1941) : 92–107.

Davidson, Gordon Charles. *The North West Company.* Berkeley: University of California Press, 1918.

Dawson, George M. *Report on an Exploration in the Yukon District, N.W.T. and Adjacent Northern Portion of British Columbia.* Geological Survey of Canada Report, 1889. Reprint. Ottawa: Queen's Printer, 1898.

DeVoto, Bernard. *Across the Wide Missouri.* Boston: Houghton Mifflin, 1947.

———. *The Course of Empire.* Boston: Houghton Mifflin, 1952.

Dillon, Richard. *Siskiyou Trail: The Hudson's Bay Fur Company Route to California.* New York: McGraw-Hill, 1975.

Duchaussois, Pierre. *Mid Snow and Ice: The Apostles of the North-West.* Buffalo, N.Y.: Missionary Oblates of Mary Immaculate, 1937.

Drury, Clifford M. *Marcus and Narcissa Whitman and the Opening of Old Oregon.* Glendale, Calif.: Arthur Clark Co., 1973.

Emmons, G. T. "The Tahltan Indians." *University of Pennsylvania Museum Publicatitons in Anthropology,* January, 1911.

Farrar, Victor J. "The Reopening of the Russian-American Convention of 1824." *Washington Historical Quarterly* 11, no. 2 (April, 1920) : 83–88.

Fyodorva, S. F. *The Russian Population of Alaska and California.* Kingston, Ont.: Limestone Press, 1973.

Finne, Richard. *The Headless Valley*. New York: Macmillan, 1967.

Florinsky, Michael T. *Russia: A History and Interpretation*. New York: Macmillan, 1947.

Footner, Herbert. *New Rivers of the North*. New York: George H. Duran Company, 1912.

Fraser, Esther. *The Canadian Rockies: Early Travels and Explorations*. Edmonton: M. G. Hurtig, 1969.

Galbraith, John S. *The Hudson's Bay Company as an Imperial Factor, 1821–1869*. Berkeley: University of California Press, 1957.

Gibson, James R. *Imperial Russia in Frontier America*. New York: Oxford University Press, 1976.

———. *Feeding the Russian Fur Trade: Provisionment of the Okhotsk Seaboard and the Kamchatka Peninsula, 1639–1856*. Madison: University of Wisconsin, 1969.

Glazebrook, G. P. De T. *A History of Transportation in Canada*. 2 vols. Toronto: McClelland and Stewart, 1964.

Goetzmann, William H. *Exploration and Empire: The Explorer and the Scientist in the Winning of the American West*. New York: Random House, 1966.

Gough, Barry M. *The Royal Navy and the Northwest Coast of North America, 1810–1914*. New York: Oxford University Press, 1971.

———. "The 1813 Expedition to Astoria." *Beaver*, Autumn, 1973, pp. 44–51.

Hall, Edwin S. "Speculations on the Late Prehistory of the Kutchin Athapaskans." *Ethnohistory* 16, no. 4 (Fall, 1969): 317–33.

Hardisty, William Lucas. "The Loucheux Indians." In *Annual Report of the Smithsonian Institution for 1866*, pp. 311–30. Washington, D.C.: Government Printing Office, 1872.

Helm, June, ed. *Subarctic*. Handbook of North American Indians Series, vol. 6. Washington, D.C.: Smithsonian Institution, 1982.

Hoagland, Edward. *Notes From the Century Before: A Journal of British Columbia*. New York: Random House, 1969.

Honigman, John J. "Ethnography and Acculturation of the Fort Nelson Slave." *Yale University Publications in Anthropology, no. 33*. New Haven, Conn.: Yale University Press, 1946.

———. "Culture and Ethos of Kaska Society." *Yale University Publications in Anthropology, no. 40*. New Haven, Conn.: Yale University Press, 1949.

———. "The Kaska Indians: An Ethnographic Reconstruction." *Yale University Publications in Anthropology, no. 51*. New Haven, Conn.: Yale University Press, 1954.

————. "Are There Nahanni Indians?" *Anthropologica* 3 (1956) : 35–37.

Hunter, Fenley. *Frances Lake, Yukon.* New York: privately printed, 1924.

Hussey, John A. "Unpretending but not Indecent: Living Quarters at Mid-19th Century H.B.C. Posts." *Beaver*, Spring, 1975, pp. 12–17.

Innis, Harold A. *The Fur Trade in Canada.* Revised edition. Toronto: University of Toronto Press, 1970.

Irving, Washington. *Astoria: or Anecdotes of an Enterprise Beyond the Rocky Mountains.* Norman: University of Oklahoma Press, 1964.

James, Robert R. *The Archaeology of Fort Alexander, N.W.T.: Report of Investigations of the 1974 Mackenzie River Archaeological Project.* Ottawa: Environmental-Social Committee, Northern Pipelines Task Force on Northern Oil Development, 1974.

Johnson, Stephen Marshall. "Russia on the Pacific Northwest Coast in the 1830s: Baron Wrangel vs. the Government of Russian Colonial Policy." *Muskox* 17 (1975) : 14–21.

Jones, Strachan. "The Kutchin Tribes." In *Annual Report of the Smithsonian Institution for 1866*, pp. 320–27. Washington, D.C.: Government Printing Office, 1872.

Karamanski, Theodore J. "Life in the Service of the Hudson's Bay Company: The Mackenzie District." *Alaska Journal* 7, no. 3 (Summer, 1977) : 166–73.

————. "Westward to the Mountains: Preliminary Hudson's Bay Company Exploration of the Northern Rocky Mountains, 1789–1824." Master's thesis, Loyola University of Chicago, 1978.

Kindle, E. D. *Geological Reconnaissance Along Fort Nelson, Liard, and Beaver Rivers, Northeastern British Columbia, and Southwestern Yukon.* Canadian Geological Survey Paper no. 44–16. Ottawa: Department of Mines and Resources, Mines and Geology Branch, 1944.

Krech, Shepard. "On the Aboriginal Population of the Kutchin." *Arctic Anthropology* no. 15, 1 (1978) : 89–104.

Kushner, Howard I. *Conflict on the Northwest Coast, American-Russian Rivalry in the Pacific Northwest, 1790–1867.* Westport, Conn.: Greenwood Press, 1975.

Lain, B. D. "The Fort Yukon Affair, 1869." *Alaska Journal* 7, no. 1 (Winter, 1977) : 12–17.

McClellan, Catharine. *My Old People Say: An Ethnographic Survey of the Southern Yukon Territory.* 2 vols. Ottawa: National Museum of Canada, 1975.

————. "Indian Stories about the First Whites in Northwestern America." In *Ethnohistory in Southwestern Alaska and the*

Southern Yukon: Method and Content, edited by Margaret Lantis. Lexington: University of Kentucky Press, 1970.

McConnell, R. G. "Report on an Exploration in the Yukon and Mackenzie Basins, N.W.T." In *Geological and Natural History Survey of Canada Reports for the Year 1887.* Montreal: William Foster Brown, 1891.

MacGregor, J. G. *Peter Fidler: Canada's Forgotten Surveyor, 1769–1822.* Toronto: McClelland and Stewart, 1966.

MacKay, Corday. "Pacific Coast Fur Trade." *Beaver,* Summer, 1955, 38–42.

MacKay, Douglas. *The Honourable Company.* Toronto: McClelland and Stewart, 1966.

Mason, Michael. *The Arctic Forests.* London: Hodder and Stoughton, 1924.

Millar, James F. V., and Gloria J. Fedirchuk. *Report on Investigations: Mackenzie River Archaeological Survey.* Ottawa: Environmental-Social Committee, Northern Pipelines Task Force on Northern Oil Development, 1975.

Milne, Jack. *Trading for Milady's Furs: In the Service of the Hudson's Bay Co. 1923–1943.* Saskatoon, Sask.: Western Producer Prairie Books, 1975.

Mirsky, Jeannette. *To the Arctic: The Story of Northern Exploration from the Earliest Times to the Present.* Chicago: University of Chicago Press, 1948.

Money, Anton, with Ben East. *This Was the North.* New York: Crown Publishers, 1975.

Moodie, D. W., and Barry Kaye. "Taming and Domesticating the Native Animals of Rupert's Land." *Beaver,* Winter, 1976, pp. 10–19.

Morice, A. G. *The History of the Northern Interior of British Columbia, 1660–1880.* London: Arthur Briggs, 1906.

Morison, Samuel Eliot. *The Maritime History of Massachusetts, 1783–1860.* Boston: Houghton Mifflin, 1941.

Morse, Eric W. *Fur Trade Canoe Routes of Canada: Then and Now.* Ottawa: National and Historic Parks Branch of Ministry of Indian Affairs and Northern Development, 1969.

Morton, Arthur S. *A History of the Canadian West to 1870–71.* Second edition. Edited by L. G. Thomas. Toronto: University of Toronto Press, 1973.

Morton, W. L. *The Critical Years: The Union of British North America, 1857–1873.* Toronto: McClelland and Stewart, 1964.

Nanton, Paul. *Arctic Breakthrough: Franklin's Explorations, 1819–1847.* Toronto: Clarke, Irwin, 1970.

Neatby, Leslie H. *The Search for Franklin.* Edmonton: M. G. Hurtig, 1970.

————. *In Quest of the North West Passage*. Toronto: Longman's, Green, 1958.

Nichols, Irby C. "The Russian Ukase and the Monroe Doctrine: A Re-evaluation." *Pacific Historical Review* 36 (February, 1967) : 18–24.

Nute, Grace Lee. "A Peter Pond Map." *Minnesota History* 16 (1933) : 81–84.

————. *The Voyageur*. Reprint. Saint Paul: Minnesota Historical Society, 1955.

Patterson, R. M. *Trail to the Interior*. Toronto: Macmillan of Canada, 1966.

————. *The Dangerous River*. Sidney, B.C.: Greys Publishing Co., 1966.

————. *Finlay's River*. New York: William Morrow, 1968.

————. "The Nahanny Lands." *Beaver*, Summer, 1961, pp. 40–47.

————. "Liard River Voyage." *Beaver*, Spring, 1955, pp. 18–25.

Petitot, Émile. *The Amerindians of the Canadian North-West in the 19th Century, as seen by Émile Petitot*. Edited by Donat Savoie. Ottawa: Northern Science Research Group, Department of Indian Affairs and Northern Development, 1970. Vol. 1, *The Tchigit Eskimo*. Vol. 2, *The Loucheux Indians*.

Phillips, Paul Chrisler. *The Fur Trade*. Concluding chapters by J. W. Smurr. Norman: University of Oklahoma Press, 1961.

Pierce, W. H. *Thirteen Years of Travel and Exploration in Alaska, 1877–1889*. Edited and updated by R. N. De Armond. Anchorage: Alaska Northwest Publishing Company, 1977.

Pike, Warburton. *Journeys to the Barren Ground of Northern Canada, 1889–1891 in Search of Musk-Ox*. London: Macmillan, 1892.

————. *Through the SubArctic Forest: A Record of a Canoe Journey From Fort Wrangel to the Pelly Lakes and down the Yukon River to the Behring Sea*. London: Edward Arnold, 1896.

Ray, Arthur J. *Indians in the Fur Trade: Their Role as Hunters, Trappers, and Middlemen in the Lands Southwest of Hudson Bay, 1660–1870*. Toronto: University of Toronto Press, 1974.

————. "Some Conservation Schemes of the Hudson's Bay Company, 1821–1850: An Examination of the Problems of Resource Management in the Fur Trade." *Journal of Historical Geography* 1, no. 1 (1975) : 42–59.

Rich, E. E. *The Fur Trade and the Northwest to 1857*. Toronto: McClelland and Stewart, 1967.

————. *History of the Hudson's Bay Company, 1670–1870*. London: Hudson's Bay Record Society, 1958.

————. "The Fur Traders: Their Diet and Drugs." *Beaver* (Summer, 1975) : 42–53.

Robinson, H. M. *The Great Fur Land or Sketches of Life in the*

Hudson's Bay Territory. New York: G. P. Putnam's Sons, 1879.

Ross, Eric. *Beyond the River and the Bay.* Toronto: University of Toronto Press, 1970.

Royal Canadian Mounted Police. "The Valley of No Return." Unpublished report. N.d.

Saum, Lewis. *The Fur Trader and the Indian.* Seattle: University of Washington Press, 1965.

Saw, Reginald. "Treaty with the Russians." *Beaver,* December, 1948, pp. 30–33.

Schlesser, Norman Dennis. *Fort Umpqua: Bastion of Empire.* Oakland, Ore.: privately printed, 1973.

Seton, Ernst Thompson. *The Arctic Prairies: A Canoe Journey of 2,000 Miles in Search of the Caribou.* New York: Charles Scribner's Sons, 1917.

Simmons, Norman M., and George W. Scotter. "Nahanni: Wilderness Revealed, Legend Preserved." *Canadian Geographical Journal,* June, 1971, pp. 4–9.

Slobodin, Richard. "Eastern Kutchin Warfare." *Anthropologica* 2, no. 1 (1962) : 76–94.

Stager, John K. "Fur Trading Posts in the Mackenzie Region up to 1850." Occasional Paper no. 3. Vancouver, B.C. Canadian Association of Geographers, B. C. Division, 1962.

Stefansson, Vilhjalmur. *Unsolved Mysteries of the Arctic.* New York: Collier Books, 1962.

———. *Northwest to Fortune: The Search of Western Man for a Commercially Practical Route to the Far East.* New York: Duell, Sloan, and Pearce, 1958.

Stewart, Ethel G. "Fort McPherson and the Peel River Area." Master's thesis, Queen's University, Kingston, Ontario, 1955.

Tanner, Adrian. *Trappers, Hunters, and Fishermen: Wildlife Utilization in the Yukon Territory,* Yukon Research Projects Series, no. 5. Ottawa: Northern Co-ordination and Research Centre, Department of Northern Affairs and National Resources, 1966.

Tikhmener, P. A. *A History of the Russian-American Company.* Translated and edited by Richard A. Pierce and Alton Donnelly. Seattle: University of Washington Press, 1978.

Turner, Dick. *Nahanni.* Saanichton, B.C.: Hancock House, 1975.

Usher, Peter J. *Fur Trade Posts of the Northwest Territories, 1870–1970.* Ottawa: Northern Science Research Group, Department of Indian Affairs and Northern Development, 1971.

Van Alstyne, Richard. "International Rivalries in Pacific Northwest." *Oregon Historical Quarterly* 46, no. 3 (September, 1945): 185–213.

Van Kirk, Sylvia. *Many Tender Ties: Women in Fur Trade Society, 1670–1870.* Winnipeg, Man.: Watson & Dwyer Publishing, Ltd., 1982.

Vanstone, James W. *Athapaskan Adaptations: Hunters and Fishermen of the Subarctic Forests.* Chicago: Aldine Publishing Co., 1974.

Wallace, J. N. *The Wintering Partners on Peace River From the Earliest Records to the Union in 1821, with a Summary of the Dunvegan Journal.* Ottawa: Thornburn and Abbott, 1929.

Warkentin, John, ed. *The Western Interior of Canada: Record of Geographic Discovery, 1612-1917.* Toronto: McClelland and Stewart, 1964.

Wenger, Ferdi. "Canoeing with Wild Liard River Canyon." *Canadian Geographic Journal,* Winter, 1976, pp. 4-13.

Whymper, Frederick. *Travel and Adventure in the Territory of Alaska, Formerly Russian America—Now Ceded to the United States—and in Various Other Parts of the North Pacific.* 1868. Reprint. New York: Readex Books, 1966.

William, Glyndwr. *The British Search for the Northwest Passage in the Eighteenth Century.* London: Longmans, Greenard Co., 1962.

Wilson, Clifford. *Campbell of the Yukon.* Toronto: Macmillan of Canada, 1970.

Wolforth, J. R. *The Mackenzie Delta . . . Its Economic Base and Development, A Preliminary Study.* Ottawa: Department of Indian Affairs and Northern Department, 1967.

Wonders, William. "Athabasca Pass: Gateway to the Pacific." *Canadian Geographical Journal,* December, 1974, p. 26.

Wright, Allen A. *Prelude to Bonanza: The Discovery and Exploration of the Yukon.* Sidney, B.C.: Gray's Publishing Ltd., 1976.

Index